The Travel Map 2

First Edition

Published by

    www.TheTravelMap.com

Printed by

    www.lulu.com

This Edition

    July 2009

Although the author and publisher have tried to make the information as accurate as possible, they accept no responsibility for any loss, injury or inconvenience sustained by any person using this book.

ISBN 978-0-9561586-0-4

Text and Photographs © Marko Anton Tusar 2009

www.TheTravelMap.com

All rights reserved. No part of this publication may be reproduced, stored in a retrieval system or transmitted in any form by any means electronic, mechanical, photocopying, recording or otherwise, except brief extracts for the purpose of review, without the written permission of the publisher and copyright owner.

The Travel Map 2

Introduction

This book is a journal of my one year travel break in 2006-2007 and a 2009 trip. I decided to take time off and my employer was kind enough to give me the option of an unpaid year with a job to go back to. How lucky I am to be in such a position! A year sounds like a long time but after looking at all the round-the-world ticket options and trying to visit the places I have not visited before I had to be careful with my choices. Obtaining visas in a short time was part of the challenge.

The first trip was Central America (Guatemala, Mexico, Belize and Honduras) then Shanghai, finishing with Asia (Thailand, Cambodia, Laos, Vietnam) and back home. Fitting in West Africa on a round-the-world ticket is not practical so the next trip was to Africa and back, covering Mali, Ghana, Kenya, Tanzania, and Madagascar. The third trip included Jordan, UAE (Dubai), Nepal, Tibet, India, Malaysia (Borneo), Fiji and a stop off in New York on the return. A final Canada, USA, Brazil, Bolivia, New Zealand, Australia, Egypt trip at the end completed a busy year.

It was an interesting and exciting time. You know it is not going to happen unless you schedule it! I am now lucky enough to be able to read a journal entry for almost every day of a full year. In the planning process I still had to reject places due to cost, captive markets, luxury non-backpacker locations, wrong time of year (climate) and culturally or geographically too similar to places already visited or too local to London. Places like Alaska, Nunavut (Eskimos in northern Canada), Greenland, most of Europe including Scandinavia (Norwegian Spitsbergen), some easy places which can always be done later in life, Galapagos Islands, Senegal, Japan, Indonesia and Tasmania (there was just not enough time). Sudden political destabilisation rules out parts of the Middle East at short notice (Lebanon, Syria) and potentially countries like Iran. How could governments and diplomats spoil my travel plans! Columbia and Pakistan remain a challenge. I have become choosy in my destinations. Those mysterious regions along the Silk Road in Central Asia are still secretive and enticing.

The first Travel Map book describing trips spread over a number of years gave me the basis and curiosity to discover more. This book appears to show that I am now an experienced traveller. The Internet has become more important. As I progressed I blogged at my website www.TheTravelMap.com which felt like an electronic home and uploaded videos to YouTube.

The total cost was about £13,000 (US $26,000) for the year for all food, travel and accommodation – cheaper than living at home in London! I noticed my fitness and well-being improved after only two months of travel. There were no disasters. Rather than one big trip I split the year into smaller circuits which allowed me to recharge my energies in a familiar home environment – and made some administrative tasks easier. A full year away would necessitate some planned down time from hectic adventurous backpacking.

Please enjoy the trip!

The Author

Marko Anton Tusar

Marko began world travel quite late in life at the age of 29. Born in London, of Slovenian parentage, he graduated in electronic engineering and later studied music technology at York. He has worked in technical support for the BBC for many years, helping to look after the World Service and the BBC News Website. From a Highgate base, travel continues to be an important part of his life adding much greater meaning and significance to the large world map hanging on his living room wall.

Completed Trips during the Year 2006-2007 and 2009

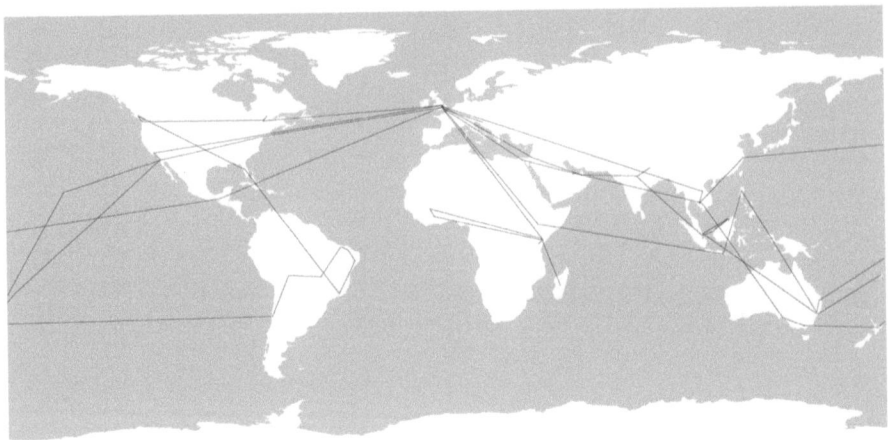

1. London – Guatemala – Mexico – Belize – Honduras – China – Thailand – Cambodia – Laos – Vietnam.

   ...page 7

2. London – (Paris) – Mali – Ghana – Kenya –Tanzania – Madagascar.

   ...page 89

3. London – Jordan – UAE – Nepal – China (Tibet) – India – Malaysia – Singapore – Fiji – USA.

   ...page 161

4. London – (Slovenia) - Canada – USA – Brazil – Bolivia – New Zealand – Australia – Thailand – Bahrain – Egypt.

   ...page 285

5. London – Uganda – Indonesia – Philippines – Australia – Fiji – Tonga – USA.

   ...page 387

START

1. London (England) to LA (USA) to Guatemala City (Guatemala), Monday 30th October 2006

I am trying to write through what feels like a night shift haze at gate 75B at Los Angeles Airport under a dome-like area. Looking back at previous trips I feel more self-conscious to avoid being banal and naïve in my descriptions, although doing this may filter out some spontaneity which can sometimes be entertaining.

After taking three days to clear my room and squirrel away all my junk, I have saved my pennies, let out my flat and am ready for a whole year of wandering about. What a chance of complete freedom with no worries! I have enough cash to survive and enjoy myself.

It was great having dad escort me to Heathrow, although his coughing fit did not sound too healthy before boarding the bus. I tried to identify what makes a long haul flight mildly uncomfortable. It may not be just the dry atmosphere and cramped seat but the reduced pressure that causes a slight headache. After a long 11 hours with fancy on-demand video and the latest navigational graphics I had a secondary search on arrival and it seems to be a requirement to remove shoes. The plane was continuing to New Zealand where a Kiwi teacher sitting one row behind was returning home and commenting on the unruly behaviour of English kids compared to sensible, calm New Zealand ones. After taking the loop bus to terminal six (it would have been quicker to walk) I am sitting here listening to the occasional airport announcement. The annoying restriction on liquids is still in force both here in LA and London so I could not take my aftershave, shampoo, toothpaste and insect repellent. My only remaining tasks are to choose a place to stay in Antigua (Guatemala, not the Caribbean island!) and decide how to navigate there from Guatemala City. I arrive very early at around 6.00am.

Guatemala City to Antigua (Guatemala), Tuesday 31st October

The plane had to abort landing once due to poor misty visibility at the last minute. The shuttle trip from the airport was relatively painless and friendly, along steep valley roads past a goat standing on the bonnet of an old car wreck. I was dropped off at the backpackers place called "Mochilero" (backpacker) above a supermarket. I was relaxed and happy to stay at any place I could recognize the name of but had to wait twenty minutes for the room to be cleaned before my body dictated that my priority was sleep – I slept until noon and began an exploratory stroll for lunch. Everything is super cheap.

Accommodation is less than $10 and "menu del dia" only $2 at a courtyard restaurant. I should be able to survive a long time at these prices. I became used to touristy approaches as I strolled through a monastery-like hotel and tourist sites in the Main Square watching French skipping, shoeshine boys and kids posing for photos. I have booked my volcano walk and bus departure heading north on Saturday. It is early days and I feel a lesser voracious need for "culture vulture" activities and am satisfied just to stumble across and experience ordinary life in an extraordinary country. I write this in a plain room with energy saving light bulbs and a dark panelled ceiling. Weather is not quite warm enough for sandals. The priority is still to sleep more and engage with this time zone – a large negative shift of 6 hours.

Antigua (Guatemala), Wednesday 1st November

I have set myself a slow pace as I sit here waiting for food (forget the description and assume it is delicious and cheap). I suppose what I am doing can be accurately described as living as others do rather than travelling in the sense that I am subjecting myself to similar local experiences. It is a fascinating process. Whether I am watching uncoordinated football with shoes flying off when the ball is kicked or a field full of kite flyers, it is difficult to beat. Some people do crosswords; I have navigational, physical and linguistic puzzles during my travel break. Most of the sites are ruined churches and cathedrals. I imagine an earthquake creates the initial ruin and the following years are spent rebuilding and renovating until the next one happens. An internet session briefly transported me back home for an hour. I followed a route around the grid-like town, past the church with a giant rosary hanging on the front. I startled a dove, walked past armed guards at shop entrances and past friendly people - I get the impression most of the other tourists are American. I filled the time between breakfast, lunch and dinner successfully, stopping at the main square when required. I had an ordinary walking day in extraordinary surroundings. I hope the volcano does not erupt tomorrow when we are walking on it. Compared to past trips, I have planned this one in less detail, which means a less focussed more flexible approach depending on how I feel at the time. I will try and make observations that are strikingly different or exceptional compared to past trip observations, which is quite a challenge. I still cannot believe I am only a few days into a whole year of travel! I am quite a naughty boy doing this for such a long time. It feels quite comfortable and natural for me to be travelling – it may not suit everyone in not having a social support structure or not being able to cope with the degree of constant cultural shock. In summary: I love it. I have only just less than twelve months to go. I have no time to improve my hotel Spanish by doing a course here as there is too much to see in the rest of Central America.

Antigua (Guatemala), Thursday 2nd November

I visited the active Pacaya volcano. After pressing the buzzer to wake the owner to unlock the door of my hotel, I waited outside the tour place (a block and a half away) with a French-Canadian couple. It is quite dramatic being three metres away from a flow of lava. After a steep bus ride through poverty characterised by breeze-block and corrugated dwellings, the hour climb exposed my lack of fitness which can only get better. A couple of small hungry dogs followed the group, led by tour leader Rodolfo in an orange cap. It is quite unstable walking on recently solidified lava and standing close to the flow which extended down from the ridge – I felt the heat through my walking boots. The heat haze obscured the clearing landscape. We were dropped somewhere in town and I soon found the centre and my usual "menu del dia". After just a little exercise the food tasted heavenly. Apart from snoozing, doing a shop for liquids (and factor 15 suntan lotion) from the supermarket directly below the hotel, sitting in the square watching people go by there is nothing else to talk about. I have a minor personal ailment – the dry skin on my foot has split slightly but not to worry. I might search for more food; that taco place that many of the locals frequent looks ok and maybe I will try the café at the edge of the square. Earlier the frozen yoghurt with mixed fruit was exceptional, chosen after I spotted a gang of boys all eating one sitting on the kerb outside the shop. The hotel is friendly but not very conducive to meeting other international travellers.

Antigua (Guatemala), Friday 3rd November

So in the absence of work or monetary pressure, would I spend the day as I did today? I filled my time strolling about, eating at restaurants and drinking coffee, reading and amusing myself with local points of interest. During a day like this all I can really do is talk about my personal philosophies. Even just walking about you can observe things that are hopefully culturally significant to a wider audience. I am already arrogantly assuming that I am talking to a wider audience. Some observations: a musical DJ inside the supermarket entrance to attract more customers; local kids playing networked Counterstrike (a combat computer game) in the internet café; the ringing of a metallic customer bell on leaving the Taco fast food place to signal that you are satisfied with the service and people playing cards on a doorstep. The level of development of this country can be taken as a default reference point that does not need to be mentioned all the time (for example cheap accommodation for $15). The National Museum occupied my time for ten minutes. As a general comment about the museums I have visited on my travels, military hardware is such a common theme. I was in no mood to see more ruined churches and the café

Chichicastenango Market, Guatemala

Carvings for sale and Shoeshine, Chichicastenango Market, Guatemala

with the hidden courtyard beckoned. What else did I do? Well not much. I could have accepted an offer of Spanish tuition from an affable teacher who gets to talk to an international group of people, probably dominated by Americans – even retirees come here to learn the language. I lay on the sofa in reception listening to an American film dubbed in Spanish. In my working life I am exposed to a source of international news all the time and it takes a while for the addiction to subside – it is a comfort available everywhere. I continue my loop north tomorrow with an early bus to Panajachel, which is a small town next to a lake. In total contrast to my working life, my body is now dictating my needs, snoozing when I want to. I am really enjoying my generous sleep. I was just thinking about the comment Anne made before I left: Although she worked for an International NGO, she saw so little of the countries because the work usually involved flying in, having a meeting and then flying back out.

Antigua (Guatemala) to Panajachel, Saturday 4th November

I felt the need for my journal to have a dramatic event and it came in the form of a dog nipping the back of my leg just above the ankle when I was visiting one of the lakeside towns. The morning minibus journey was misty and rainy with a lively European Spanish group. I was dropped off at the "Real Santander" and needed to walk the short distance down an alley to another cheaper place called "Rooms Santander" with rooms surrounded and covered by trees and green foliage – I have to stoop to enter. I ventured to the lakeside along a route lined with handicraft stalls. I had no intention of going by boat anywhere until tomorrow but after persuasion and negotiation secured a boat stopping for thirty minutes at the two most eastern lakeside towns. The frequency of hawkers has increased. I walked up and down the streets just interested in taking photographs.

A change of scenery with nachos at the sunset café: watching the sunset and the twinkling lights in the distance across the lake (the other restaurant was booked for a function). I am surrounded by laughing chatting groups including Italians and flickering candles. I will make an effort tonight and see if the live piano place is active or have an alcoholic drink at the bar outside my accommodation – but I am not really a bar person. I think I will just pretend to be a travel writer! Socially it is a bit quiet but on past experience I meet people mainly on excursions so I am trying to amuse myself here in the restaurant. Just relax and enjoy the atmosphere. I have a boat trip around the lake to look forward to tomorrow.

Chichicastenango, Sunday 5th November

I spontaneously reassessed my travel plans last night walking past an agency and discovered it was market day on Sunday (today) and I decided to visit the six-syllable Chi-Chi-Cas-Ten-Nan-Go. Booking the direct shuttle to San Cristobal in Mexico also made good sense for Tuesday. Well Chi-Chi is a very busy market, geared for both tourists and locals – a change from Camden Town. There were some people sitting on the church steps swinging incense. The primitive restaurant stalls serving lunch appeared intensely cultural and while strolling, interruptions were plentiful but not annoying - you just have to accept it is part of life here. I temporarily donated my waist to some French ladies who were buying a belt and were unsure and needed a model of about my size. This middle-aged backpacking is not a bad activity. Most tourists bought colourful cloth items. I just bought some fresh pineapple and melon and continued strolling past the indoor vegetable market and butchery section, until a needed rest at a table outside a café – I spilt the sugar shooing away another seller. There was some fuss with a squealing pig that refused to go in his sack while we were waiting for the minibus to depart among other chaotically parked minibuses. Along the steep winding route we passed a group of mainly men jogging, connected with rope - I believe I correctly spotted that they were volunteer firemen. It only takes a minute to become used to a cold shower. I enjoyed a super steak and pleasurable glass of Chilean red wine at a table previously occupied by an elderly backpacker. Another thought about travel routing; it is sometimes a bit like air travel: A geographically logical route is not necessarily a sensible or practical route. Travel hubs develop where it makes sense to regard as a base to explore places in the surrounding region.

Panajachel (lakeside San Pedro, Santiago, San Antonio), Monday 6th November

I have come back from the lakeside after attempting to take night photos of the distant lightning – an excuse to play with the camera's manual mode. Today I was visiting simple lakeside villages and towns. There is nothing much to see and do apart from be absorbed by normal happenings of people in a village – although there seemed to be lots of building work. The number of passengers booked on the tour determines the boat size – a small group today. In each place I followed the steep climbing cobbled path to the centre, trying to search out striking things to photograph. A cinnamon bun bought from a seller with a bowl sitting on the pavement was delicious. The lake sky was clear and sun strong. There were nets full of avocados, crowds of locals around a new batch of fish, street football, drying of coffee beans, kite flying even in the middle of town with many stuck in the telegraph wires, chicken soup, begging old ladies and washing of clothes. I cannot believe I am going to eat in restaurants for a year! The Greek group were making full face video commentaries about the tourist sights. I accepted an offer of coconut juice and at the moment feel no need to buy any local handicrafts or souvenirs – it is not a shopping trip. My priorities are photos and food – quite a simple life. I was woken by someone spending about thirty minutes noisily sticky taping some parcels outside their room.

Panajachel (Guatemala) to San Cristobal de Las Casas (Mexico), Tuesday 7th November

Today was essentially a 10-hour bus journey (the extra time due to road works) crossing into Mexico. We descended through deep valleys and bushy pines to a warmer flatter country. Despite usual border chaos I concluded that taking a shuttle really does save time even if it is more sterile and expensive. Technical IT travel tip I discovered: The "@" sign is marked on Spanish keyboards but does not seem accessible directly. As it is necessary for email, use ALT 64 instead. I was content to listen to conversations: some complaints, some philosophical. Plantain crisps provided breakfast and lunch. My mp3 player is a great gadget for instant familiarity and those radio stations with sonorous voices enunciating each Spanish syllable. Hotel entry was through a gate, leading to my orange room. I found a cafeteria near the square where an American girl was teaching the owner's kids English – today's lesson was past tense verbs. A quick photo of the church in the dying daylight, booking the Mayan trip and internetting when I found out the gorilla trip may need rethinking as they are now asking for a single supplement. Oh, and some little kids playfully put a newspaper on my head as I was sitting in the square. The evening was cold enough for my compact fleecy sweatshirt. After a week of walking outdoors, great food and not sitting in front of a computer too much, I already feel healthier.

San Cristobal (Mexico), Wednesday 8th November

After watching some breakfast news in the café just south of the square I toured the surrounding Mayan Village. This is a cultural rather than architectural delight. The houses (or "places for sleeping") are simple and contain an altar (with incense burner) made up of a mixture of Christian and animalistic symbols. Activities: some potent alcohol, dressing up in traditional Mayan clothes and eating home made tacos with ground pumpkin seeds, black beans, cheese or tomato made from corn ground manually before our eyes. The group comprised of an Irish couple, a South African and a Mexican girl. I just transferred to a cosier candle-at-the-table restaurant – the traditional food was fine (the sauce was a bit like Peking duck sauce) but the live Marimba was not very impressive and it was a bit presumptuous filling in the tip part of the bill – it shows that here they cater mainly to tourists. The Mayan church was strange with many small candles everywhere and pine needles as a carpet. A deaf and dumb Mayan old lady with a very happy smile hugged the tour guide. The conversation turned philosophical at times. My circuitous walk back in town covered the northern church (the fancy wall was being renovated) and market, making a wide loop past a pack of wild dogs, a colonial house, amber museum, a video presentation in the square about indigenous repression (San Cristobal is in the Chiapas state, home of the Zapatista rebellion) and back to base for a quick rest. I eventually ended up at this high ceiling restaurant with soothing jazzy Mexican piano, throaty vocals and a group of Italians to my left. Tomorrow will be an administrative day: book the bus to Palenque, sort out Africa, pay the departure tax at a bank and target a tourist site, send postcards and anything else I can think of. I love just walking around interesting places.

San Cristobal, Thursday 9th November

All chores were completed efficiently and early. I walked about one kilometre north to the Mayan medicine museum with a video at the end about how the women give birth on their knees in the arms of the father. I exited via the herb garden. Then across town up the many steps to the San Cristobal church for a vista. Lunch: a visit to the bakery and sitting in the square opposite - a simple but pleasurable activity. A sudden downpour and I had to take shelter in the arches on one side of the square. Another thing I noticed was the noise pollution coming from speakers mounted on cars usually advertising some product. It may be more annoying because I cannot fluently understand it. Health is one reason for this trip. I need a step change in physical activity, quality of life and diet. Laziness triumphs when I am back home and comfortable. I need to remind myself when reading this that it does not take much effort to eat less processed food and do a few miles of walking and exercising my spine. In the wet afternoon I watched Cyrano on my mp3 player but it had encoded incompletely without the important ending. Oh what to write! It is more interesting eating rather than listing the items on the menu. I am actually sitting at a restaurant table by a window and can see the same square where earlier I had lunch on a bench. Music has switched from African to slow Indian in style. The street environment no longer feels foreign. I am in Mexico barely a week in total but it is enough time to explore my choice of sites. I like the smell of candles in the evening. Because I am not a conventional creative writer, I will merely try to reflect reality – but you may need to wait for the daily entry containing the single sentence "Nothing of any significance happened today".

Restaurant and fresh produce, Chichicastenango Market, Guatemala

Street Football in San Pedro, spices in Santiago Atitlan, Guatemala

Santiago Street Life, Lake Atitlan, Guatemala

Avocados in Santiago Atitlan and distant lightning, Panajachel, Guatemala

San Cristobal to Palenque, Friday 10th November

The day of bus travel was an almost continuous forest descent and a jump in temperature of 10°C to a hot and humid 31°C. The journey was more than 5 hours of rapid bends and I felt slight motion sickness as I kept an eye on the loud, overdubbed Jodie Foster film. The rotating fan on maximum above me now is hardly evaporating my sweat. The journey was interrupted by some kind of political group (Zapatistas?) stopping the traffic and asking for monetary support to allow the bus to pass: Some passengers contributed to a kitty an amount equivalent to a driver's tip, which it probably was. The jump in temperature also adds to the unfamiliarity of this small untidy town with a square bursting with birdsong louder than the traffic. A large bottle of water was my constant support as I explored with my unadventurous choice of restaurant determined by the presence of air-conditioning. The other hotel had closed down and I paid for two nights in advance with discount. It looks like I will be forced to cancel my African gorilla trip in March but I have plenty of time to think of alternatives.

Palenque, Saturday 11th November

After an essential breakfast I boarded the collectivo (shared minivan) to the "Ruinas". After entering the site of the Aztec ruins it was fun exploring in a DIY style – I will have to read up later about the historical details. The basic procedure was an excuse for exercise; walk up the pyramid then walk down. I caught snippets of historical description from the guides here and there but it was fun just walking around the place, following the path through the forest, swinging bridge and past streams. The giant fan on the museum counter was welcome. The return collectivo was packed full of passengers with the sliding door left open. A large group of Dutch entered the restaurant and the waitress dropped a full tray of drinks. I bought my ticket to Chetumal which leaves late tomorrow at 21:00. Swimming near waterfalls may be an appropriate option to fill the day. The noisy starlings were active again at the park square. I am watching adverts and football on TV (Showbol, 5-a-side with past famous players). A short haircut really makes a difference in these temperatures.

Palenque, Misol-ha and Agua Azul waterfalls, Sunday 12th November

I needed my fancy waterproof camera bag when I decided to go behind a waterfall – the soft spray is ultimately refreshing and as I was warned my rain cape made no difference to keeping me dry. I was enjoyably soaked immediately. I only paddled but none of the group swam - they had previously

Mayan Village Cooking and children, near San Cristobal, Mexico

Cobbled San Cristobal Street and Colonial House Mural, Mexico

visited the ruins. Ok, as far as waterfalls go, nothing touches Foz in Brazil but they are in general fun to explore. The Azul was larger and had a path to the top. It was amazing to watch the banana seller approach tourists: a fantastic smile and after they had refused to buy anything, a normal expression returned to her face, almost a scowl that the passing tourist never saw. I sat in the straw covered restaurant next to the minibus. After a short walk I had to shelter from a sudden downpour. It was a good choice of trip as I believe I would have run out of options in town - natural waterfalls in jungle are nice! People eating pizza in front, a taco trolley on my left, a TV with dancing behind and maybe I have enough Pesos for a dessert somewhere else. I have an overnight bus journey and when I arrive at Chetumal at 4.30am I need to taxi to the other terminal for an early bus straight to Belize City. Well that is the plan. If not, then I will do something different.

Palenque to Chetumal (Mexico) to Belize City (Belize), Monday 13th November

I actually managed to sleep a little on the night coach journey, mainly because it was almost empty and I stretched across to the opposite seats, resting my head on the day pack. All I could see on the journey were misty trees close to the roadside. I found out at Chetumal that the Belize bus conveniently leaves directly from the same bus station. I was twenty Pesos short for the ticket so had to withdraw a tiny amount from the ATM – food was a priority too. It was so surprising to use English with the relaxed driver (Belize is English speaking, UK ex-colony). Between the two immigration posts there was a flashing lights casino. The border process was a blur as we boarded the old fashioned bus with destination plate "Foxy Traveller" through the mist. The journey into Belize City provided a small snapshot of everyday life: commuters joined filling the bus, a news discussion and phone-in radio programme and kids going to school. The accent has a lilt, what I perceive as slight Jamaican. I felt some freedom in that I could now converse beyond the hotel basics and understand background chatter. I am writing this on the following morning from the river terrace at the back of the hotel next to my room. Every so often the lapping noise increases from the wake of a passing speed boat. I tried the local recommended Tamale from an unsigned restaurant – a corn based pasta wrapping meat with a lime juice drink seemed appropriate. Because the Belcove Hotel was fully booked for Wednesday, I reserved at another place (called Seaside) which looks more like an ordinary house – the owner threw down the keys from the upper balcony so that I could unlock the front door and enter. After the museum, a walk along the coastal road and eating a traditional and staple "rice and beans", I crashed out catching up on lost sleep.

Belize City, Tuesday 14th November

I just finished writing my journal for yesterday and I am continuing to sit on the back terrace with boats going by, near the swing bridge. I understand the need to be wary on the streets with lots of people just hanging about - I cannot see myself walking about much at night. Planning is on a single step-by-step basis. My first step is breakfast. I walked to the south "Bird Island" and sat on the basketball stalls, watching some blokes transport a couple of planks of wood in the heat. The side streets are deserted. Stopping for refreshment on the way with some friendly comments about my size, I finally made it back for an afternoon snooze. I cannot think of much else to do in this heat. I hear conversations outside on the porch about crocodiles. I still feel the need to keep up with editorial issues at the BBC Editors Blog, although they seem quite distant issues and of course catch up with emails. After my bread pudding I braved the dark streets with confidence. I expect more inactivity tomorrow and diving in a few days time.

Belize City, Wednesday 15th November

There is absolutely nothing to do in Belize City. I transferred to the friendly Seaside Guesthouse, with the dog greeting me on the stairs. I accepted the suggestion to go to the zoo, a short 45-minute bus ride away. The animals were fine, including spider monkeys and a jaguar - another excuse to have a wander. The elderly tourists could not see the monkeys for the trees. I received an offer of a lift back from another tour guide but decided to wait in the shelter for the bus which soon came. Apart from keeping myself fed and watered, all I did was experience things as a local. A simple bus ride but it was interesting to see how people related to each other – all very friendly and happy. I am swinging on a hammock on the breezy back balcony. I have no worries and am ahead of schedule, which was a very rough plan anyway. All the windows in the city seem to have metal outer security frames or shutters to counter theft. I have total freedom.

Belize City to the island of Caye Caulker, Thursday 16th November

From the slightly edgy atmosphere of the city to the completely relaxed atmosphere of Caye Caulker with the fastest and noisiest vehicle on the road being the taxi "golf trolley". My predicted diarrhoea is quite expressive but manageable! For the first time I experienced poor circulation in my legs while sleeping (I think due to the cooling night). I waited for the 10.30am speedboat in the nearby pastry shop and the bumpy 40-minute journey was soon over. I

City Shop and Bakery, Belize

quickly secured Albert's, above the supermarket and wandered up and down the front street in a slow manner looking at dive options for the coming week – all sorted and I am settled on this small narrow island. I strolled from the northern tip near the split to the airstrip in the south as a plane came into land. I chose an empty pier to listen to music and I was soon joined by some swimmers. I moved to another and a boat full of noisy tourists landed but it was fine to finally experience the pleasure of Tito Puente (Latin Jazz) music sitting on a wooden pier propped up by a mooring post. Again I am doing a hotel transfer to the better recommended Tropic – if you are busy all day the room essentially functions as a large locker. It is possible to buy an island here for $2.9 million from realestateofbelize.com opposite. I am doing a couple of days diving to become comfortable again before tackling the famous Blue Hole. I am going to be spending most of the day diving with few opportunities for photos unless I hire a dive camera or go out specifically to do a photo study of the island. I am curious to find out from the local people what the main source of stress is in everyday life. It is certainly more comfortable here and I am looking forward to a relaxing evening stroll. From what I can remember about my recent dreams, they are either about lack of revision for a coming unexpected exam or about luxurious homes. It is remarkable how easily one accommodates a certain cost of living as a normal reference. I see coloured lights spiralled around columns in front of me. The breeze through the palms is slightly louder than the folksy accordion music. So after recently seeing various states of development in three different countries, is the USA the most refined?

Caye Caulker (Dive: Holchan Marine Reserve), Friday 17th November

I am not really a hardcore diver, two dives and the afternoon free suits me fine. I have just come back from a splurge at the Rasta Pasta with sand on the floor and by splurge I mean paying as much as I would in a restaurant in London. For the first time I was actually cold on the boat trip to the dive site. I just need to note for future reference my belt weight needs to be 8 kilograms. A friendly mixed group included Londoner Claire my dive buddy. Apart from having the mask on too tightly the first dive was comfortable with good conservation of air. All the normal chores of diving were taken care of by our instructors. The feeling of pleasant tiredness was complemented by a banana, honey and peanut butter sandwich on the beach side of a restaurant. The Tropics hotel room is far more comfortable as I lie here on a bed writing and watching the fan set to slow. There are some British squaddies on exercise in town. The atmosphere continues to be friendly. Even the dogs and restaurant cats (who only have one priority) are friendly. According to the restaurant names, the lobsters and iguanas are happy too. People driving golf taxis are happy. I am happy. The odd insect bite on my feet seems a minor irritation. I dumped my passport bum-bag in the dive centre safe (Velcro pockets are perfect for the hotel key).

Sergeant Caye Wall, Saturday 18th November

I forgot to mention swimming through the tunnel during yesterday's dive. Normally light enters each side but this one was long enough and appeared completely dark – I could just make out fluorescent fins ahead. Today was a similar reef diving day but warmer. The drift current was very strong and visibility quite poor. There was pleasant comfortable conversation on the boat with the Dutch couple, Axel and Mascha. Part of the trip back crossed an island through a mangrove channel and there were stops for dolphin which promptly disappeared. I am sitting with rum on the balcony of a restaurant, again approaching cheap European prices – this backpacker island is developing towards a resort. On my evening stroll back I watched football being played on the pitch behind the hotel and used my journal as a seat on the fence for extra support. My remaining task for the day: kill the single mosquito in my room with my old t-shirt and set my alarm for tomorrow's early dive start.

Caye Caulker, Sunday 19th November

I knew it was going to be a slow day given that I had my first beer at 11.00am. I got up for the 5.45am arrangement to the Blue Hole but due to high wind the dive was cancelled – it was cold even without the expected breeze caused by the speed of the boat. A warm bed for another few hours sleep was an attractive alternative. I had a full English breakfast with some expatriates in the restaurant with the low ceiling I am sitting at now. Again I wandered up and down the main street, looking for things to photograph, a bit of sunbathing with a cat for company, pharmacy, watched the basketball where the single tall European was two foot above the rest and playful dogs (one much larger than the other). In addition to relaxation, one serious purpose of all this travel is to challenge my assumptions, which I believe is called learning. It is good to see people being civil to each other. A break in the diving relaxes my schedule even more. The food here is reasonable so I am going to have another dinner. The background of CNN seems so irrelevant on the island. Bob, who does the breakfasts really enjoys and seems to win on the slot machines. I am pleasantly full now so am forced to go for another slow walk soon, as slow as possible. I am having all these weird ideas about building balconies at home, buying commercial property, and looking at why restaurants or places here survive. The Tropic where I am staying appears to be a visual clone of the previously popular Tropical Hotel. The sick snapper fish unable to sustain swimming was eventually partially eaten by the lobster in the restaurant display tank.

Caye Caulker Main Coastal Road, Belize

Beach Restaurant and Back Street, Caye Caulker, Belize

Caye Caulker, Monday 20th November

I was so cold on the boat. The first boat had an engine problem so we swapped to a second. The planned dive site was too rough – the captain could not see the bottom so visibility was too poor and declared it unsafe. The water was pleasantly warm compared to the chilly outside atmospheric temperature. Lunch was welcome as a means to warm up. The Blue Hole was cancelled again due to rough weather. My normal working environment makes the body lazy – a few changes are needed to stimulate internal change. An important part of living is being in a changing environment. It was a physical strain climbing the ladder after the second dive. The fish and lobster are now segregated in the restaurant tank by a wall made of blocks. An exceptional lobster kebab completes the day. The fan is motionless and so am I.

Caye Caulker, Tuesday 21st November

I cancelled diving for today, picked up my free t-shirt and spent a lazy day ambling about. It was essentially a repeat of Sunday with nothing of any significance, with ordinary everyday things taking an elevated event status. I ended up on my feet for a couple of hours exploring almost every road and track, through the trails, giving me a good idea about the natural undeveloped state of the island, a repeat bakery stop, a girl who kept missing basketball shots with a short arc that was far too low, buying a boat ticket, a melon juice stop on the first floor open-air restaurant and little concern for urgency or priority. I begin my route west back towards Guatemala tomorrow, remaining within Belize at a place called San Ignacio. I believe it is time to step up sightseeing activity. Some people feel you have to be rich to take a year off (well it does help) but their conception of a holiday is spending a couple of grand for two weeks away, on expensive activities and luxury accommodation. This is a world away from a target average of less than $30 a day, easily achievable in Central and Southern America, even with double dinners. Just by being outside London I am saving so much money on living expenses. At the risk of stating the obvious, knowledge of the language gives a far more intimate experience of the richness of the local culture (sometimes the obvious needs to be stated). Then you have a choice to become involved or steer your own path.

Caye Caulker to San Ignacio (Belize), Wednesday 22nd November

On the smooth crossing on a full boat back to the mainland, I was sitting right at the back next to the engines but sheltered from the wind by the drivers seat support – headphones and earplugs were useful. I believe bread pudding (or the love of pudding of all kinds) is everywhere in this country. A few swampy areas, lots of Roman Catholic schools and higher ground characterised the bus journey to San Ignacio - the Jesuits must have arrived a long time ago. I was expecting a bus station but the large welcome letters was just about a big enough prompt for me to get off the bus. The Tropicool Hotel looked as if it was being built but it was actually expanding and fully open. I have committed to a full day tour to visit some caves tomorrow – Actun Tunichil Muknal (A.T.M). The café near the hotel, a gathering place for expatriates and travellers, was a mixture between a restaurant, bar, tour shop, internet café and an art gallery. I am beginning to develop a taste for lime juice. I do not use my body when I am at home (apart from playing football and squash). After just three weeks, my back and leg muscles have strengthened.

San Ignacio (caves), Thursday 23rd November

The cave tour is quite an experience. After a 40-minute hike through the forest, crossing a shin-high river three times, you arrive at the A.T.M. cave. Entry requires swimming and the water level varies from ankle height, with sections that have to be climbed via perhaps four or so well defined foot holes. There are narrow sections where you have to carefully lower yourself and turn around to enter the next section. The American bloke was bigger than me so I was ok. Our helmet torches provided enough light but you had to be sure of your footing, with extra support and balance from arms pushing against overhanging rock formations. Some structures were extremely sharp so care and caution was a top priority. This is my first wet cave. I must admit cave diving does not appeal to me but this was fun and manageable. As well as the geology the cave was a living museum, with calcified Mayan pottery scattered all over the place with various old bones and skeletons of sacrifice victims which we were careful to avoid stepping on. My hiking boots saturated with clear water but they were suited to stepping on the eroded and slippery rock. Combined with an expert historical commentary and lunch sitting on a log, this was a professional and enjoyable trip. Complete darkness is a great sensation for short periods. I found the cave was not too cold, presumably because we were following a shallow passage. There was a sink hole close to the entrance we used where alternatively you can be lowered into the cave. After the wet sections there was a clearly defined dry chamber where we could take photos and continue to listen to Mayan history from the guide. And do not forget the catfish, spiders and bats to add to the mix. I do not know how this compares with caving experiences on a global scale but I was impressed. You do feel that you are exploring parts of the earth that should remain hidden and begin to understand the mystical associations of such a dark place.

San Ignacio (Belize) to Tikal (Guatemala), Friday 24th November

If I am paying for a fancy red-seat reception I might as well sit in it and write my journal. I decided on the early shuttle direct to Tikal, knowing that I would pay a relative premium to stay within the Mayan park. The border crossing was painless and I sat in the front seat, listening to the staccato conversation from the driver about everything on the route. He had great skill at bird spotting. Some people feel that ultimate freedom would be driving your own vehicle but you are paying for the local knowledge of the driver who knows where the uneven surfaces are, when to veer off the road or in the opposite lane for the smoothest path and the location of the unmarked speed bumps. What makes a ruin special (oh no, not another pile of old stones) is that it is something to climb and walk around, surrounded by spider monkeys and deep forest canopy. In error I followed a path deep into the forest for 20 minutes and had to eventually retrace my steps. This is your bona fide proper forest – noisy, with movements and rich smells. Climbing the steep steps or ladder to the top reveals a spectacular view of the monuments rising above the forest canopy extending to the far distance. It is almost like a climbing frame for adults and slightly too big and challenging for small children. If the lodge is three times the price of a normal Guatemalan hotel I expect the service to be perfect. I demand my towel! I had dinner at the restaurant a bit further down the dark road and when invited to the primitive camp-style kitchen to pay the bill, I felt the friendliness of the family as grandma handed money to the waitress who then handed the change back to me. There must be something that is free in this hotel. I was exhausted by all the walking but at the moment feel I will make an effort to do it again early tomorrow to catch more atmospheric wildlife and the morning photographic light.

Tikal to Flores (Guatemala), Saturday 25th November

Flores is a transitional destination, a transport hub to go further south. I woke 30 minutes after my alarm went off (6.30am) looked at the overcast sky and was persuaded to remain where I was and rest. There is an enormous dripped wax candle on the restaurant counter here at the Luna. I was sure I could hear a woodpecker while my clothes were drying on the wooden rail. Securing a minivan to Flores was easy and more passengers were picked up on the way. Flores is a little island connected by road that juts out into a lake, around 15 minutes of exploration by foot. I withdrew into my own world – mp3 player (I am listening to much more music on this trip, lots of jazz piano), internet and a phone call home. I like the style of the hotel on multiple levels, essentially a closed courtyard, rooms with windows all inward facing, a large roof terrace and colourful decoration. I believe the menu of the day was pig's trotters which I left on the plate. Last night in Tikal the auto-scan found no fm radio stations to listen to and here I have ten. I am struggling to fill the rest of the evening – maybe I will do nothing. As an alternative to work, travel is a great option. A small glass of potent liquor on the house is a great distraction while paying the bill. I walked and watched the mad football scrum and kids driving around the square in an electrically driven pink toy jeep.

Flores to Livingston (Guatemala), Sunday 26th November

There were noises from 6.00am with a large group filling the restaurant for breakfast before my turn. A German tourist asked about the bus to Guatemala City (same direction as me to Rio Dulce) and in fact it left earlier than I had been told at 9.45am – lucky I too was early. Some houses along the route which was lined with rocks painted white were even less developed wooden structures with thatched roofs. There was non-stop German conversation en route. I was shepherded onto the boat to Livingston. A jungle route but misty and raining, past yachts overtaken by a long line of birds just skimming the surface of the water, steep rocky faces covered with trees and vegetation. The dock had the feeling of another world. It took me time to adjust to the variation in activity, faces, noise and music of the people. Both first choice hotels were full because there was some kind of Garifuna (black Caribbean) cultural festival – a gathering with food stalls. I just sat and watched people milling past. Again a basketball and football area is a focus of activity just near the dock. The Punta music (African and Latin American with calls and answers) with commentary continues to boom and play as I write this back in the Hotel California, a simple and adequate hotel that looks a bit derelict from the outside and is reached down a dark road directly from the main centre. I sense great opportunities for photos in this lively and peculiar town.

Livingston, Monday 27th November

The festival disappears and the town returns to its sleepy state where the restaurants and streets are almost empty under a light sprinkling of rain. Ruben (the hotel owner) repaired the toilet and I was ready for the all day hike in the surrounding areas. The rain was ok and did not affect my mood that much walking through Garifuna settlements, graveyard, jungle, along the narrow beach, with a short section in an unstable canoe (water entered at maximum swing), a plunge in the dry waterfall (pool), a sandwich and more hiking back along the beach avoiding rubbish washed up along the way. A Catalonian biologist with umbrella and an English group were humorous company. Russell took a great photo of a spider's web with suspended droplets of water. The jungle trek took all day. The seafood coconut soup was hard work but I got to the food in the end. If you sit outside a restaurant people do talk to you and sit at your table and strike up conversations, some weird and normal people commenting on my watch or just asking for a beer.

Livingston (Guatemala) to Tela (Honduras), Tuesday 28th November

In summary it was a full day of travel to cross the border between Guatemala and Honduras, involving a boat and four separate local buses. The captain of the boat from Livingston gave the passengers a thick plastic sheet as a shelter from the rain. I did not even have to reach the market area to catch the first minibus as it found me on its way to the border. Bananas lined the route for many miles, protected by plastic bags while still hanging in bunches on the trees. A couple of souvenir passport stamps and I changed a modest amount of money just for the next bus to another port called Cortez. The ATM did not accept my card so I thought I would double check inside the bank. Security is tight and literally you cannot enter the internal door of the bank with any metallic objects. The metal detector will only successfully open the door when it has detected no metal (which you leave in small lockers just inside the entrance). I was directed to another bank which worked ok. It must be a well trodden route as the San Pedro collectivo driver quickly recognised me as a potential passenger. At the end of the journey, he kindly pointed out the bus terminal for the next leg to El Progresso and I caught the bus just as it was leaving and the conductor was shouting the destination. Local buses are quite an event. At one point in time six sellers in a row entered the bus offering refreshment. The sliding glass windows had to be shut during the rain. The bus connected with the Tela bus and I finally arrived at my destination at around 4.00pm (after an early 7.00am start!). There is so much space in the hotel room – the ceiling height is almost double my height. The dogs quickly disposed of the chicken bones from my dinner on the beach. The tour guide was humorous but there is little hope of a tour to the national park without more people turning up.

Tela, Wednesday 29th November

It is such a luxury to sleep when you want to sleep. I had no plan for today. It took me a while to find a place for breakfast and I must admit this was because I found many places too dark and dingy before I found a small ok place. I sat and let everyday life wash around me. I looked at what others ordered and if it looked good, ordered the same. The locals try out their English in a genuine attempt to engage with me. I notice more recognisable brand names here compared to Guatemala. I had a "Bajito" (very short) at the barbers as the day turned out clear and hot. It is much easier taking unposed pictures of local life if there is some kind of event happening that acts as a distraction – I felt and was quite conspicuous near the main park square. The day disappeared with juices, gazing at the shore and walking up and down busy streets. The Hondurans seem to stare more than the Guatemalans, but not too much.

Tela to the island of Roatan, Thursday 30th November

I do like contrasts: an increase in temperature, bugs and prices. Again the La Ceiba bus was leaving the terminal just as I had arrived. The windows slid open and the speed breeze was intense on my left. The terminal was not near the central square I had planned to visit for lunch, so I took a taxi directly to the port but a ridiculous 4 hours before the departure of the ferry. There was food, an air-conditioned waiting room but the internet place was closed. It is at a time like this that you need your mp3 player. "People watching" was the main entertainment. It was dark when the ferry arrived and I shared a taxi with a Swiss-Spanish couple. The island is in its own economic bubble with prices suddenly approaching shocking European levels. It is not surprising really as I would not be shocked if I had arrived here immediately from the UK. The Milka place was the cheapest place to stay much better than the warren of a dump shack from the book recommendation. I feel a strong need not to pay such inflated prices, by Honduran standards. I picked out the least developed restaurant. Even the Indian restaurant was more expensive than Highgate's best! The Norwegians were playing cards under candle light. There is a strong smell of wood and the high-speed fan is a real necessity in this humidity and heat. I will try out the diving place on the corner in the morning.

Roatan (West End), Friday 1st December

It has been raining most of the day. I managed to sleep with the fan directed towards my body. It always seems less comfortable if you arrive somewhere by night and settle, without any real knowledge of your immediate surroundings. The Pura Vida diving place seems fine. One American bloke's large family had all recently qualified – the young son corrected me on the initial position of the regulator. I saw a couple of turtles on the second dive but there was driving rain on the way back to the dock. After drying off I walked up and down the sandy strip, avoiding the large and deep puddles and drinking coffee. The half-a-chicken was a necessity in a reasonable restaurant. Incidentally the diving instructor looks like Bill Bailey. Another aspect of travelling is that you are forced to read signs and pay more attention to your surroundings. Back home it is easy to be stuck in a routine with little navigational stimulation and just

Helpful Tourist Information and Garifuna Food, Livingston, Guatemala

cursory glances at signage. After a month my body has noticeably recovered from my normal work routine. My eyesight is better. Everything is better. I bruised the back of my knee slightly with the backward entry into the water – I need to be more positive with the rotational leg entry. Diving means that I take very few photos. The problem with light-weight porous combat trousers is that determined mosquitoes, whipped up into frenzy by a sudden downpour manage to sting through the material!

Roatan, French Harbour (Caye), Saturday 2nd December

The sky is clear now but not this morning so I decided it would be an Iguana day. The double bus journey via Coxen Hole was bearable – they carry many people and all sorts of cargo. A mentally retarded girl punched the side of the bus and enjoyed being chased by the conductor. I was dropped off by the main road sign and it was still a significant number of signs before I eventually got to the farm. In fact it does not farm Iguanas for food but for conservation. Iguanas littered the pathway, a real spectacle of clambering during feeding with leaves. Some appeared to pose for photos. From a human point of view they seemed happy. They had some parrots, monkeys and fish but the sheer number of Iguanas formed the main event. I met the owner. I was the recipient of a random act of kindness when he gave me a lift all the way back to West End with a pizza stop on the way – your friendly authentic genuine helpful local. He was impressed that someone was prepared to walk from the main road to visit his pets. The room back at the hotel was stiflingly hot and the Norwegians had been replaced by Swedes who also liked playing cards. I lay on one of the piers listening to music as the sun went down before another treat at the Lighthouse restaurant. As everywhere in the world, people here are fascinated with mobile phones. I hope the weather remains clear for tomorrow's diving.

Roatan, Sunday 3rd December

With clear skies the diving was great. Last night I tried Swedish Snuss (tobacco in a small bag that you put under your lip, neither good nor bad), rum and coke and found out that a traditional Swedish Christmas involves watching a Donald Duck story, Ivanhoe and ski jumping from Garmisch. I dived with the huge American family whose youngest diver is only ten years old – just imagine scaling up the weight and size of the tank. The father had eight children (taught at home) was involved in health work and had been living in the capital of Honduras (Tegucigalpa) for many years. The second dive was through canyons, quite narrow tunnels of coral and a challenge of control for a large diver. Dolphins were spotted at the end of the dive but they soon disappeared. Natalie

Mobile Refreshment in Tela and Posing Iguana in Roatan, Honduras

my dive buddy seemed very comfortable in the water and my launch off the side was much better this time. I managed to lose one cap of my headphones a minor disaster in the scheme of things. To quote a comedian, here we might actually be "human slaves in an insect nation".

Roatan, Monday 4th December

The theme for this trip could be a world tour of ruins. A wreck dive and normal coral dive filled the morning – the large blue Parrot fish look comical with a "smiling" face. I sorted my photo backups using the dive centre laptops as always there are problems with computers and the cheap USB memory corrupted photo files after the 300th file – do not ask me how but I backed up to the LG USB memory and mp3 player ok and have left the original memory card intact. I may still burn to CD and post it home. I looked around the fancy mansion for sale for the price of my flat just near the beach with the playful dogs, one four times the size of the other, chasing and darting along the sand. I am leaving early tomorrow morning for the other island called Utila. It is a full moon and I am wearing my yellow Roatan Marine Park wristband. You always learn something with diving – optimum positioning of the mask, coping with a BCD that does not seem to expel all the air, better buoyancy and so on. I do not feel it is possible to live through a day here without at least one mosquito bite from their apparent random encrypted flight patterns. I am jotting notes in my schedule to remind me to do certain tasks in advance and also sketching ideas for life back home in the back of the journal. Where to next in the world of work? Something more engineering oriented? Or just any revenue stream, from merchant banking to a stress free revenue stream or some amazing clever idea with the internet or working for LP? Or music related? I have asked the same questions before and never answered them.

Roatan to Utila, Tuesday 5th December

An early start and they had flattened the bumps on the road during the night. I sprayed pineapple air freshener in the car ventilation system, as instructed by the taxi driver. The size of the island is related to the size of the ferry that supplies it. The wide white soft seats at the back were comfortable and most stable but sunny. An elderly gentleman was videoing all the backpackers at the stern. After cheeky negotiation including another couple, I secured a room at Rubi's on the end of a pier in plenty of fresh air. To reach the diving school which seems well organised you walk through the diving research area the people of whom appear to study whale sharks – sounds like a holiday and apparently they saw one yesterday so there is hope out-of-season. I was caught in torrential rain which

Roatan Sunset and Cat in Utila, Honduras

appeared minutes after super hot sunshine and after 5 minutes or so, normal sunny weather resumed. I walked past wooden house construction, electric scooters, a bakery (and entered), swinging hammocks, small cinemas, realty (estate agents), dirt tracks running parallel to the main and single lane road, cows, a brightly coloured house, great walls hiding large mansions on stilts and muddy puddles. The high quality and low price of restaurant food has returned at the porch that overlooks the street. The cats sleeping on the wooden walkways seem happy and relaxed. I must try making a large batch of real coffee and storing it in the fridge ready for microwaving. I sit waiting for dessert after another noisy few minutes downpour.

Utila, Wednesday 6th December

The diving was quite relaxed and professional with the dive leader wearing a colourful headscarf in the style of a pirate. The regulator would not seal so it was replaced. There was a lot of waiting around, waiting for the rain to stop but there were dive books on the table to remind me of some of the basics. Two hour-long but shallow dives were probably my most relaxed yet. Afterwards there was enough time to get changed out of the wet shorts and visit the bakery with the heavenly cinnamon rolls and great coffee. One American customer taught his daughter to order another roll in Spanish. I enjoy my afternoon snooze and later a dinner with the talkative owner who showed me her photos of Copan Ruinas. Add some internetting and that was almost all there was to my day. Of course I was thinking about travel plans for the immediate future. Dreams tend to be about family and physical challenges. I just hear the sound of the oscillating fan, the odd boat horn and the lapping of waves against rocks.

Utila, Thursday 7th December

What can I say, more of the same. The first dive was aborted after 15 minutes because we had moored at the wrong buoy, revealing just sharp rock and no reef – the boat moved along the coast for a minute and we soon found the expected dive site. The buoys are to be labelled in the near future. The small group (Joe and Sue) makes a relaxed diving experience and again the second dive was for a full hour. A research diver accompanied the group and was tasked with counting species of fish. Diving affects the teeth – a slight ache – or any part of the body that may have trapped air. I spent some time at the intersection thinking slowly about budgeting for the last couple of days in Honduras. The only ATM on the island does not accept my cards so I have to enter the bank with my passport for a visa withdrawal. The Bundu Café had an arty backpacker atmosphere and I enjoyed just listening to all the conversations and accents from the centre of the room. Internetting is a useful activity in rainy weather. I watched a crab step along the gutter while I was sheltering from the rain.

Utila, Friday 8th December

I thought the rain had subsided allowing me to have an evening wander but the roar of intense seasonal rain has returned and keeps recurring. I feel entrenched in my position in room eleven. The rough waters this morning meant a change in dive site but this one involved a very strong current where I used significant energy just to remain stationary – keeping streamlined or close to the coral are the instructions that are meant to help in these situations. I joined the open water boat with many new divers and was reminded of the chaos of a group of fledgling divers, all pointing in different directions at different heights and expending much wasted flapping energy to maintain buoyancy. I completed my bank chore, bakery visit and relaxed on the cushioned seats at the Bundu Café where the music was drowned out by the droplets hitting the metal corrugated roof. The adjacent group were playing the board game Risk and others were reading. As I navigated the unavoidable deep puddles there were friendly hellos. I am hoping that tomorrow is clear so that I have a chance to explore the island. It was appropriate to jettison (unzip) the soaking lower half of my trousers and walk around in shorts. The wind chimes mounted low on the long balcony hallway continues to act as a tall people warning signal. I had an interesting chat at the bar with someone who teaches diving here in the summer for six months and snowboarding in Canada in the winter for six months. Maybe that divemaster qualification is looking more attractive? Apparently it takes six weeks to two months to complete (although you can do it in three weeks) but it is better to extend the time and accumulate lots of free dives.

Utila, Saturday 9th December

Snoozing, eating and walking filled the day. My optimism for clear weather proved false. I walked quite far west of town, burnt my photos to CD, internetted and read American business and current affairs magazines in the café. It is the rainy season on the Caribbean side of Honduras so I should not really be surprised but it does limit my activities and opportunities for good photographic light – it was not worth hiring transport for the day. A few stepping stones were placed at the entrance to the Inn so that you could enter and exit without soaking your feet. Remember if you are patient enough in the shower, hot water may eventually come. I watched a scary caving film at the cinema next door where there were technical problems at the beginning so we watched a few more minutes of Bugs Bunny than planned. An early start tomorrow with the ferry at 06.00 and I expect to be on buses all day.

Utila to Copan Ruinas, Sunday 10th December

This was written retrospectively (written late on a following day rather than the same evening) as I was exhausted by being on the bus all day. I managed to buy some bread rolls for the early 6.20am ferry to the mainland. The sky was beginning to clear and the sea will always be calmer than the Southern Ocean. I took a taxi to a feature that seems common to all Central American towns, the central park square and asked about a direct bus to Copan. The terminal was situated next to a supermarket. The Executive bus company treats the bus service as an airline so you are paying to remove the chaos and detours of the normal local services. There was a long transit in the San Pedro waiting lounge and we did not arrive in Copan until it was just becoming dark. I walked to the Iguana Azul with American Kim and quickly secured a room. The bending road made the second half of the journey tiring, partially compensated by the American films. As I had snacked most of the day I did not feel hungry and I just crashed out. I just remembered what the taxi driver said a couple of days ago when he found out that I was English. Sometimes they respond with the name of a footballer but immediately he repeated the name "Camilla Parker-Bowles". So England does seem to be represented by royalty - anyway, moving on to today.

Copan Ruinas, Monday 11th December

I bought my first souvenir – a small Mayan stone mask that can hold a candle. After a large breakfast and securing the Antigua shuttle for tomorrow I walked to the ruins and this time concentrated on taking close-up photos of the stone carvings. The tunnels available for high extra admission were actually those built by the excavators for access. I walked to the domestic dwelling site a few kilometres in the same direction but it was not as impressive as the elite temple site. I sent my photos on CD, visited the small museum just off the main square and drank so much water. I was trying to find the word for bubble wrap by acting out popping the bubbles which I needed to wrap my parcel. The sun suddenly appeared in the late afternoon and I quickly took photos of street scenes but the bank security guard with the big gun was shy and hid behind the pillar while I was framing the shot. I fully paid for the room so that I could budget accurately for my last day. I did make multiple trips and haggle at the souvenir place. The coffee at the "house for everything" was strong – I lost count of the different tourist services this place provides, from laundry to internet to souvenirs. Everyone in Central America seems to own a large pickup truck to drive along the uneven streets. Many of the older blokes in the square wear cowboy hats. If I had started my journey at Copan I would be moderately culturally shocked. The surprising benefit of spending the last five weeks in Central America is that the environment seems so normal. There are lots of kids playing with fireworks in the streets. The small size of the town makes the atmosphere friendly. I still find travelling quite an amazing activity. Marimba music can be heard in the distance.

Copan Ruinas (Honduras) to Antigua (Guatemala), Tuesday 12th December

I have completed my loop of Central America by returning to Antigua. Five weeks is enough to become emotionally attached to an area and I do feel attached. I have listened to enough Spanish and met entertaining friendly people. I managed a slow breakfast in Copan, some sitting around in the square and it was soon time for the midday shuttle to Antigua. An interesting international group (Australian Canadian, Irish, German, Spanish and unusually no Americans) on board and the 6-hour journey flew by with talk of travel adventures. I was a beginner compared to some of the people, even the young Australian (lawyer and history of art) seemed to have travelled everywhere, in a life of leisure, meeting up with family and friends and earning money from tips working in a ski resort night club. The Irish boys had entertained the older woman. Tactile Suzie and the others were dropped off in Guatemala City. There was traffic and fumes entering the city and it grew dark before we reached Antigua. The Christmas lights on the trees brightened up the square. I lead the lads to the hostel and later really treated myself to a double strudel. I think one of the Norwegians I met in Roatan recognised me and said hello. It makes a change to actually live my life.

Antigua (Guatemala) to LA (USA), Wednesday 13th December

An overnight stop is useful when jumping many time zones. So overly casual, I forgot that I was staying rather than only transiting in LA. Some of the people on the early morning shuttle were grumpy about paying extra for the luggage. At 5.00am thought processes are slow and of course you need your boarding pass before you queue up for departure tax! I was worried about the short transit time when the Singapore Airline check-in repeated that my reservation was for the following day and I suddenly understood and remembered. I took a free shuttle to the Adventurers (also known as the "Backpacker's Paradise" with fancy large hotel room with settee and all mod cons for $45) a hostel near the

Sculpture in Copan Ruinas, Honduras and Misty Shanghai, China

airport on the flight path; in fact I can hear a plane coming in to land now. I took a city tour stopping at Venice Beach, Farmers Market, that place they have premieres (Mann's Chinese Theatre) and through all the posh and varied urban areas, contextualised by referencing film stars, with simultaneous translation immediately struck by the total dominance of the car and isolation of people with little unfocussed random interaction or encounters, except when carrying out a transaction. Is it the inevitable advanced vision of what London will be like in the future? I am not sure how I would survive here as the skill to earn money seems to involve advanced and subtle marketing with large investments of money. I managed to pick up a Shanghai guide so I will be ok for the next few days. Weather: a warm and hazy day in LA.

LA (USA) to Tokyo to Shanghai (China), a lost day crossing the Date Line, Thursday 14th and Friday 15th December

It is time to catch up on my journal. As I was waiting for the airport shuttle the receptionist in the Adventurer was joking that one of the boys had asked her to his room. The style of this old hotel is firmly stuck in the 80s with mirrors and patterns everywhere. Queuing with Japanese school kids I was soon on my way across the Pacific to Tokyo with the sunset through my left window. As there was little time for the connection to Shanghai, I was instructed to contact ground staff and escorted to the correct gate – you still have to go through security screening, taking off shoes and so on. I was upgraded to Premium Economy which is a different world with more space and fully adjustable seat from Upright to Relax to Bed mode. It really makes a difference to the normal cramped seat where the person reclines in front impacting your knees. I took the bus through misty Shanghai roads and was dropped off at People's Square. It was dark and I could not make out anything, not even the adjacent park. If I had not had my trusty guidebook I would have been completely lost. My written tube instructions were useless as it was already 11.00pm and closed for the night. With no language skills in Mandarin (I had trouble with the word "yes") I was reduced to pointing to place names printed in Chinese characters in the book. The first taxi driver gave up. It was a challenge to get enough light to read the book and the headlight of the taxi was the best reading lamp to light up the small print. The second taxi driver managed to transport me to the nearest underground station where I again sought light this time from a shop to read the guidebook. A local girl gave spontaneous help and confirmed my orientation. I arrived at the hostel at midnight and secured a dorm bed as no rooms were available. The place was full of drinking gap year people and most of the toilets were blocked. I entered the top bunk of an empty four-bed dorm, thinking I was lucky but it filled by 1.00am. Someone was talking in their sleep: "Is this an Australian test!" but I managed to sleep until 7.00am.

Shanghai, Saturday 16th December

I had enough sleep and was not keen to hang about in the hostel so ventured to the nearby "more Chinese" hotel and secured a room – you pay such a premium for the hostel facilities and all I really need is a secure quiet room after an exhausting day of sightseeing. The pancake egg trolley just outside the hostel provided a welcome warming breakfast. My long-sleeved t-shirt makes a great improvised scarf. I strolled along admiring the misty modern skyline of the Bund and the older backstreets with large bicycle-driven loads and ringing bells. The Chinese tea from the vacuum flask in the new hotel was also very welcome. I walked into town along the main busy pedestrianised shopping street and was approached by many pretty young girls who offered massages and said I was strong and looked like a boxer. The buildings are impressive and you have the impression that the planners looked around the world for inspiration, especially at Hong Kong. I reached the 38th floor of a hotel via express elevator from which the view of the People's Square was spectacular. At the food mall I had sweet beans on a mound of soft ice for dessert! The place was packed. You pay for your meal from all the food outlets using a charge card you collect at the entrance to the food mall. Some have steaming cooking pots at the table itself. I wandered back to the Bund and admired the view at night with icy cold wind. The pace of development of Shanghai is astonishing.

Shanghai, Sunday 17th December

A crystal clear morning and I had to wait a few minutes by the fountain before the Shanghai Museum opened – ceramics, sculpture, calligraphy, art and bronze. I found out that if you press an area on the screen marked "English" the ticket machine for the metro system is much easier to use. There was lots of queuing for lifts at the tripod tower and at the very top the windows were murky so I could not take a perfect shot – the levels below were better, the lower level being open and having wire barriers. The architectural views are impressive. Even the partially built skyscrapers are interesting. It is often not worth having food at tourist sites. My next stop was the Maglev train that goes to the airport so I went for a ride at 431 km per hour (270 mph), doing the 30 km journey in about 8 minutes. Most of the journey is spent accelerating and then decelerating; remaining at top speed for less than a minute and it is quite impressive and reminiscent of a plane during take-off. There were offers of Rolex watches, massage, art from students and lady bars while walking down the main shopping street. The lights are impressive but the crowds were tiring and I wanted to eat something familiar – pizza. I am happy to be back in the warm hotel room. Chinese tea is the colour of white wine.

Cheap Breakfast and Haulage, Shanghai, China

Shanghai, Monday 18th December

I headed towards the French area early in the morning with people rushing to work. The pavements have a knobbled lined section and I am not sure if this is to guide the blind or try to separate people walking in different directions into lanes. The underground train was incredibly packed for the People's Square where everyone exited – far more packed than the tube in London. There was nothing much to photograph, just a pleasant walk past addresses that were important in communist history and a ride up a lift. Instead of feral teenagers, the parks are full of older and retired people dancing, doing graceful movements to music, writing Chinese characters on the paths or just chatting. I walked all morning and had to stop for a posh coffee. I then explored the old area of town with compact houses and narrow alleys with washing strung across them, contrasting with the skyscrapers in the distance. The blokes gather round live crickets (removed from cylindrical containers) and watch them crawl about and gamble on the outcome. It is not my bad breath, pronunciation or charisma that deters taxi drivers – a driver refused to take me as a passenger even though I pointed to a photo of a famous landmark building. A taxi sped me to the Jinmao tower, the better tower that I thought I visited yesterday (which was in fact the TV tower) – I automatically assumed it was the tower closest to the metro station of the same name. There were spectacular views at dusk and a great view internally, looking down the cylindrical structure to the lobby below. Again I was seated at the front of the restaurant, a westerner prominently on display presumably seen as attractive marketing. I love food courts and after a previous visit ordering was casual and relaxed. Even though I set a blistering pace along the pedestrianized road, I was approached twelve times for various financial transactions – a normal pace would have attracted more unwanted attention. The friendly receptionist assures me that trains begin at 5.30am, which I need to get to the airport on time.

Shanghai (China) to Phuket (Thailand), Tuesday 19th December

I received a helpful wakeup call and was lucky that the metro started early. I had to wait a little for the first Maglev so had a meat dumpling breakfast on the ground floor, in one of those circular steaming dishes that are stacked in a column. I am not sure why the train ran only at a maximum of 300 km per hour – perhaps because it was the first run of the morning? I chatted to a Canadian most of the way to Bangkok. Unlike in some countries, there is a domestic transfer so I entered the country (and went through an immigration procedure)

Shanghai Skyscrapers and the Bund at Night, China

The Bund Promenade and Rapid Development, Shanghai, China

Looking down from the TV Tower and the Shining Jinmao, Shanghai, China

Old Town and Smoggy Views, Shanghai, China

Jinmao Views, Shanghai, China

after the domestic leg to Phuket. After some self grooming (haircut, shave, massage) I feel great. I adored the spicy Thai food in a restaurant where the locals go – cheap and tasty. There was no room at my first choice hostel but their recommendation a short walk away seems ok with rooms down a long corridor.

Phuket (Patong Beach), Wednesday 20th December

A simple breakfast is actually included in the hotel price with blaring morning traffic accelerating past the front entrance. I spontaneously decided to use a moped taxi to reach Patong Beach. The traffic lights here in Phuket have large coloured digit countdowns indicating when they are going to change. Patong beach is a monstrous centre of hedonism with lots of old men accompanied by young Thai girls. I heard some Irish accents. My task was to organise diving for the next few days and a bookshop with guides helped point the way. After a long discussion I booked different sites with different boats over the next four days. I cannot believe staying in the middle of the madness of Patong constitutes a relaxing holiday but it can be described as an experience. There were lots of package tourists paying inflated prices, so many watch shops, reflected heat from the pavement and a beach full of sun loungers and umbrellas. The "No 6" restaurant supplied food at the authentic Thai level of spice. I watched football on the sand pitch and relaxed listening to music on the beach, leaning against a rock as the sun set. All the dodgy bars and discos were empty as it was still early. I took another taxi moped back to Phuket town, firmly holding on to the back bar. Enough of the Benidorm-like cultural experience and on to the diving which is the reason I came to Thailand.

Phuket, Thursday 21st December

I let myself out of the locked hostel and found the same moped taxi to take me to Chalong Pier. The pier is long enough to need special bus transport to reach the end where maybe about twenty different dive boats are moored. I decided to risk breakfast as the dive site was almost 2 hours away. I was mildly shocked on entry to the first dive, a wreck dive where the water appeared to be filled with jellyfish, long metre chains of transparent box-like cells which were in fact eggs. The water maximum temperature was 30°C with many transitions from hot to cold and back again during the dive. The sea was rough with a

The TV Tower, Shanghai, China to Chaotic Phuket, Thailand

difficult entry back on to the fluctuating boat. On the second dive a leopard shark was "sleeping" on the sea bed. The final dive was to an island, well more of a rock with a wall of coral and so many schools of different fish. It still feels cold when you exit from the water. My regulator was stuck on free flow for a short time. There was a 1.5 metre long swordfish lying on the dock pavement. Dinner with loud video was acceptable and the landmark fountain remained colourful. I have a slight cold. I had some dilemma about what to take with me to the dive and what to leave in the hostel room which I resolved.

Phuket, Friday 22nd December

I feel complete exhaustion returning to the room in the late evening. The exhaustion originates from the diving and coping with the cold after the dives. My body craves the warmth (no need for the fan), sugary drink and caffeine. The last dive site at Phi Phi is about 2 hours away from the dock. I had to wait about 45 minutes before the Dive Asia group arrived and we were soon on our way – a friendly international crowd including Thai dive masters. Jane looked after us experienced divers and all the three dives were pleasurable, particularly the last with a very playful attitude and threats to stamp out and kill the Nudibranch (sea slug) because they are just too small to be interesting. My body puts aside any worries about a sore throat or sea sickness if the food provided is primarily required to generate heat. The chill factor on the boat was immense and it was a moderately serious priority to eat the pasta quickly with lots of hot tea. Lying here is such a joy. Strangely I received a mobile phone call on the boat rearranging my dive trip for tomorrow morning but initially the reception was so poor that I had to wait until we were closer to shore before the line was intelligible. I may just have enough energy to brush my teeth.

Phuket, Saturday 23rd December

Drinking a small can of sweet ice coffee should give me some energy to write something coherent. It was an unconventional diving day. The reason for all the last minute changes was because the original dive boat had been stolen so the company chartered another boat. The taxi man who picked me up at Tesco Lotus, an out-of-town shopping centre, did not even have my correct name. I ended up with a different speed boat with a different company from a different pier and going to different dive sites. As there was only one other customer, a Russian, the trip did feel like a private charter. The visibility during the first dive was very poor, like a snow storm and my fellow diver was a novice so used up far too much air forcing a short dive time. I remained on my own near the sea bed for a further 15 minutes. This marked my one-hundredth dive. Lunch was at the resort island where pots of water with coconut cups are used to wash sand off your feet.

Phuket, Sunday 24th December

Diving is a pleasant way to spend Christmas Eve. It was the usual routine of moped taxi to the dock, waiting around and meeting up with varied people. I used up too much energy trying to swim to the buoy on the second dive, which probably reduced my air by 15 minutes. Another diver had a free-flowing regulator which meant almost an empty tank on entry. Hopefully I will be sent a photo record of the dives from a Hong Kong diver. I find the Moray Eels have more character than the Leopard Sharks. I have no diving tomorrow and plan to relax which will probably involve a quick inspection of another beach. I craved some familiar food which in my case usually means pizza. My ankles do not feel very robust.

Phuket, Monday 25th December

I received someone's spare bananas at breakfast so that makes a change from normal Christmas presents. My plan was to spend time in town doing ordinary things: find post office, send postcards, walk around shops, eat satay, drink coffee, eat cakes and watch a film in very cold air-conditioning (a light version of Lord of the Rings). If I have not mentioned this already there are so many watch shops here in Phuket. Well it is Christmas, a rest day before entering a new country. I have been trying to phone home but I cannot believe my parent's phone has been engaged for so long so it may be that the international lines are engaged at this peak time. Anyway, I will try a little later. In fact I did get through once but they could not hear me although I could hear them. This morning I walked around the market area but had no urge to take photos. The spicy soup made me use up so many tissues. There is a beach up in the north of Phuket near the airport that has nesting turtles which may be interesting to look at before my flight in the afternoon. I could feel the heat from the Christmas lights draped over the hotel wall.

Phuket to Bangkok (Thailand) to Phnom Penh (Cambodia), Tuesday 26th December

A day of travel: Two short flights and a long transit soon fill a day. There was drama late last night with a French family desperately trying to get into the hotel and the owners had gone for the night. I let them in. I waited in the bus station

Loading the Dive Boat, Phuket, Thailand and Phnom Penh Puppy, Cambodia

for the airport bus near the display of a painting of the King. There was more minor drama at the burger place at the airport with only one till of the three working. I did the usual people watching on the flight and amused myself with food at the new cylindrical Bangkok airport, where an exotic dish like duck is regarded as an ordinary meal. The infrastructure in Phnom Penh is a step down compared to Thailand: fewer lights, cars, signs and roads. Everything seems to cost one or two dollars. I changed $120 which was equivalent to half-a-million of the local currency! Obtaining a visa at the airport was reasonably quick and I was soon on my way into town on the back of a moped taxi. Similar to the long deep corridor of the hotel in Phuket, I secured a room at the "Sister No 9". The room however was not secure so I have to be careful. I managed to find the usual facilities in this backpacker's ghetto. A puppy was chewing the top edge of a pool table.

Phnom Penh, Wednesday 27th December

Mosquito repellent was essential to get a good night's sleep. I decided to walk. The streets of Phnom Penh are not really designed for pedestrians. The scale is too large and pavements are not continuous and often contain obstacles and other vehicles. I managed to find the pagoda on a hill near the US embassy, near an elephant being washed. There was just nothing to see on the riverside road. I explored the National Museum with lily pond courtyard. By the riverbank they were offering to free caged birds - I really do not understand the logic. I had a quick zip around the market and CD media stalls and a coffee shop rest. The adoption of this western style café must seem alien to Cambodians. I had enough time to see the Royal Palace. A super cheap set curry back at the lakeside, a bottle of beer and I am ready to rest. There is something comforting but unauthentic about a backpacker ghetto.

Phnom Penh, Thursday 28th December

The lakeside tourist enclave is popular because there is no traffic on one side. I had breakfast and listened to a couple learning the Khmer alphabet. An aggressive fight broke out between two young boy street booksellers, both about ten years old. The Killing Fields memorial was a long moped-ride along dirt roads. I was curious to see (but not participate in) the shooting range close by where they present you with a munitions menu (small pistols to automatic weapons) and where the going rate for an AK47 with a magazine of 25 bullets is $30. I found the memorial with stacked and graded skulls less moving than the old school that was used as a prison where torture and many killings took place, filled with black-and-white photos of all those young and old that passed

Royal Palace and Killing Fields Memorial, Phnom Penh, Cambodia

through the "mound of guilt". You can buy crickets at the market and again there is a disproportionate number (compared to the UK) of watch and optical shops. I suppose the UK has a large number of estate agents. A cool corner café was a refuge from the noise, fumes, humidity and heat of the streets. I forget that even London is unpleasant from a pedestrian perspective during a heat wave. I have booked my Siem Reap bus for Saturday. Another curry finished the day with chat from the Gujarati owners – a relative splurge of $6! My laundry finally arrived.

Phnom Penh, Friday 29th December

I began with a slow breakfast and shopping at the Russian market. The Psar Tuol Tom Pong market is quite dark with narrow paths between goods. I was exhausted looking at the CDs and again needed refuge in a café, upstairs where incidentally I did not get served. Reading the local and national English speaking newspapers was interesting. I was back early to buy some travel guides and pay for the room. Nothing culturally extraordinary happened today. As you walk the streets so many moped taxis (motos) offer their services and children carry trays of books. In this area I estimate more than half the restaurants are Indian. It is time to move on and see some ruins. The only reason to change currency in Cambodia is to have amounts smaller than one US$.

Phnom Penh to Siem Reap, Saturday 30th December

I had hoped that I would be in Siem around midday seeing as I got up around 5.45am. The factors that contributed to the unpleasantness of the bus journey were: I was told to meet up at 6.30am outside the agency which meant wait around until 7.00am to be taken a short distance by moto to the bus; multiple exchanges of receipts; lots of mosquitoes buzzing around while waiting in the bus; no clear unambiguous declaration of destination as the bus also seems to act as an intermediary transport to the station for other routes; it arrives at the bus station and just waits; persistent sellers arrive on board; the bus does a slow circuit around the pagoda and then stops; it starts moving again and an older tourist gets on in panic because his bus to Bangkok with his luggage left him behind as he bought some food for the journey; the bus chases the Bangkok bus in a larger circuit but fails, pulls into an alley and stops; There is chatter on mobiles; I escape with my mp3 player for a minute and then get interrupted because apparently my seat is reserved but no other seats on the bus are reserved; I stay put; the air-conditioning does not work; We finally start the journey 2 hours later with a fully packed bus including the aisle area; There are two long food stops and many beeps at two-wheeled vehicles on the way;

Market Traffic in Phnom Penh and Angkor Wat Reflections, Cambodia

At the destination the taxis initially ignore you if you are not going to specific hotels; I finally arrived at 4.00pm! The hotel was a step up in luxury to $12 a night (three times yesterday's hotel rate) and it certainly shows. I had enough time to walk around the market and enjoy traditional Khmer food in a recommended restaurant which I initially thought was a spoof twin but had expanded so much that it appears across the alleyway through to the next street.

Siem Reap, Sunday 31st December

I got up super early at 5.00am and managed to attract a moto to take me to Angkor Wat for sunrise. Unfortunately I paid the rider at the ticket booth and still had a brisk unplanned 30-minute walk to the temple in the dark as tuk-tuks, bicycles, tour minibuses and coaches sped past. Angkor is more a city than a site. Many had gathered by the lily pool as the sun came up behind the spires. A quick breakfast at the stalls and I had enough energy to begin walking – I was already tall Mayan ruin trained and so was fit enough for all the climbing. The scale is impressive. I did the first half of the small walking circuit. Although the distances between temples is large and walking exhausting, it does provide a less touristy experience, bumping into more locals. The trees strangling the stones were overrun by posing tourists. Some sellers showed great charisma in persuading you to enter their restaurant or buy their goods – thousands pass through so they must have many opportunities to test what does and does not work. I soon gave up on all the walking and took two trips with a moto. Just walking the length of a temple is a significant trek. I have booked an all day tuk-tuk for tomorrow to reach the places further out, around 40 km away. I might check out Bar Street around midnight seeing as it is New Years Eve (for tourists not Cambodians) - it depends how I feel; anyway anything better than last year when I was actually working at midnight.

Siem Reap, Monday 1st January 2007

I am not sure I have the energy to explore more temples. I heard the countdown to New Year last night and got up early at 6.00am for my second day of Angkor exploration. I visited a far away waterfall with river rock carvings. The route through dirt roads, poverty and friendly waves took over an hour. People seemed to be just living simply as opposed to sipping lattes and surfing the net. Ironically, many people in wealthy Europe aspire to a more rural, self-reliant, self-sufficient lifestyle without all the mod-cons. I saw more temples, some with elaborate carvings and others with strangling trees (surrounding the stones) and of course many people. I believe two long days starting from sunrise is enough for me. I caught fragments of guides' explanations of the symbolism and background stories about the wall carvings. It was a luxury covering all those kilometres on a tuk-tuk. The constant offers of services and food and drink are an indication of the wealth inequality and tendency of tourists to increase inflation. The secondary tourist attractions seem insignificant compared to the Angkor temple complex so I will probably just hang about in the town for the next two days.

Siem Reap, Tuesday 2nd January

Unusually I am writing this in an Indian restaurant (on the edge of the market) as recently I was too lazy to carry my journal with me! Transferring photos and burning CDs takes a while with old fashioned computers (USB 1) and all was accomplished and dispatched in the post. Two young kids are now staring at me through the wire partition saying "one dollar, please sir" – a spontaneous description. I had two full-on days at Angkor and it was the last day of the pass. I arranged a token look at the sunset at an obviously popular viewing spot but quite far from the main temple. After an interesting moon and colourful sunset I negotiated the busy night traffic back to town. My plan for tomorrow is just to read some fiction and something about my next destination of northern Laos. I am still toying with whether I should sacrifice my mobility now and start shopping here - a decision that I will make tomorrow. An overheard comment from a large tour group that thankfully does not apply to me: "What time do we *have to* go out to dinner?"

Siem Reap, Wednesday 3rd January

How can I make shopping sound exciting? I do not want to exaggerate my description of the day by saying something dramatic almost happened – nothing did. The traveller's staple breakfast of banana pancake was fitting. I dithered and finally came to the conclusion that I needed more dollars (a currency accepted in my next two countries) which I could obtain directly from the ATM. After a tired haggle I bought a small backpack but could not face buying more DVDs – although I did later visit a café download place and some of the slow tempo audio CDs sparked my interest. I can hear the traditional music (sounds Chinese in style) played by the victims of landmines, earning a living by busking. Just as I am becoming used to my transitory environment it is time to move on. Transit is becoming my home.

Angkor Wat, Siem Reap, Cambodia

Strangling Trees and Buddha Statue, Angkor Wat, Cambodia

Angkor Wat, Cambodia

Siem Reap (Cambodia) to Luang Prabang (Laos), Thursday 4th January

My domestic boiler cannot live without me as I received an email from Ruth saying that it had gone wrong again and the callout charge and cost of repair was significant – astronomical compared to my current Asian money values. All should be sorted out soon. With an afternoon flight I lazed with a late breakfast and coffee. I had a seat next to the propeller and admired the mountainous scenery and shadow of the plane on the clouds. I noticed some specks of forest fires. Covering the distance by road would have been exhausting. After a refuelling stop the visa-on-arrival process was quick and I soon corralled some friendly people to share a taxi downtown in an open vehicle with parallel benches. The guesthouse felt like stepping into someone's home and walking through the living room. It is about 10°C cooler here and Luang Prabang strikes me as a calmer place and certainly my first impression is a further drop in the level of infrastructure. I followed the long line of market sellers and obtained my 9000 Kip to one US dollar currency (!). It seems polite to use local currency rather than always expecting the locals to accept dollars.

Luang Prabang, Friday 5th January

My adventurousness is sinking to zero. I am struggling for unique experiences when considering the adventure hiking, boating, caving, hill tribes and elephants offered here at the tour shops. I am content just walking, looking and stopping for refreshment. I completed a circuit including one of the temples with ornate mosaics on the walls. I sat sipping my mixed fruit shake at an outdoor riverside restaurant. A quick hike up the central hill past Buddha's footprint and I watched the sunset as others gathered. This morning I was forced to leave last night's guest house because they had other reservations. This had only happened to me once or twice before so you can not always assume that if you have a room you can effectively choose how long you would like to stay - a little annoying but bearable. I moved to another guesthouse two roads down with bathroom. Originally when I chose this town I was considering a long scenic boat trip excursion but it now seems less logical to do it, just for the sake of the journey rather than choosing a destination in the right general direction. I need to read up a little about the history of Laos (a job for the reader).

Luang Prabang, Saturday 6th January

Reading was my only productive act today. I was woken by love-making at about 5.00am – someone else's. I quickly visited the National Museum and followed the arrows to the photographic exhibition. I bought my VIP bus ticket

Angkor Wat, Cambodia and Decorative Temple, Luang Prabang, Laos

to the capital and my morning was over. I had no real intention of exploring the cutting edge of tourism today. After a couple of postcards it was time for my siesta. An email informed me that my gorilla tour had been cancelled for the second time so I need to think about alternatives, essentially Ethiopia, re-visiting Kenya and Tanzania or even going further south to Vic falls - something to think about over the next few days. My whole trip is like a long museum visit, reading a little history and description of each country as I go along.

Luang Prabang, Sunday 7th January

The thin cats here behave like scavengers, very different to the lazy comfortable cats back home. As you can guess it was a time out day. I was preoccupied with deciding what to do with the cancelled gorilla trip. After internet research I decided to choose the Serengeti trip mainly for the animals which are never the same twice. My choice was restricted as I was limited to that area of Africa within a certain time frame. I replied to the email and we will see what happens. The bakery coffee shop provided some familiar comfortable surroundings. I managed to walk up and down a few times but had no enthusiasm for the handicrafts. Hopefully I have not turned into a jaded traveller but Laos is basically on the way to Vietnam, a young country struggling to stand up as a tourist destination among colourful neighbouring countries on a competitive global stage. Footsteps from above can be heard through the wooden floor.

Luang Prabang to Vientiane, Monday 8th January

A 9-hour VIP coach journey filled the day. "VIP" means slightly quicker, snacks, freshen-up towel, simple lunch and Lao karaoke on the TV – and a guard with a machine gun for part of the way. The air-conditioning was cold so I had to retrieve my sweatshirt from the luggage compartment at the last minute. Lao was mountainous most of the way with deciduous forests and simple wooden huts with woven basket parquet-style walls, some with large satellite dishes. There were many goats, cows and dogs in the path of the coach. The first place was surprisingly full but I soon found a recommended place with the entrance to the room via the side garage. I walked to the river where they were doing keep fit aerobics and had my fill of Thai food. Maybe I will brave some traditional Lao food tomorrow.

Vientiane, Tuesday 9th January

As a legacy of the French colonial past, Boule is a popular public pastime in Laos. I took a tuk-tuk to the "L'arc de Triomphe" style arch for a hazy view of the city. I walked through the market with below head-height shade, past wats (Buddhist temples) and eventually for a posh but cheap French set lunch. Vientiane has city dimensions but a small town level of activity. I was curious about the shooting range and just watched the professional club members shoot pistols at targets. One of the pleasures of a trip like this is to read regional newspapers or magazines that one would not normally read. The digital BBC world channel regularly faded out in the bakery. I am currently sitting in my plain white room with secondary netted mosquito door and occasional washing machine noises from just outside. I believe I only took one photo today (of the landmark arch) – I am struggling to capture something specifically Lao as I walk the dusty streets. The clapping catch method with slightly splayed fingers is proving effective against lone mosquitoes. Incidentally there is a device here that looks like a tennis racquet that is battery powered and actually electrocutes mosquitoes. I have no idea what to do tomorrow. I am not too impressed with Laos mainly because I have experienced many things the country has to offer in other countries.

Vientiane, Wednesday 10th January

I decided to rearrange my Vietnam flight for early tomorrow cutting short my time in Laos and increasing my time in Hanoi by two days after realising I needed more time for travel in Vietnam. After a lazy café breakfast reading the paper I returned to the shooting range to try out the beginners pistol and rifle (0.22 calibre) – five bullets for each firearm for about $3. I managed one bull's-eye with the pistol but was not so good with the rifle. As you walk along the pavement every so often there is a large pile of sand indicating more building work. I spent the rest of the afternoon flicking through DVD catalogues – I needed to sit down. The traditional Lao food was half chicken and half fresh green-leaved spice. I was disturbed last night by the random noises coming from the washing machines so I switched on the extractor fan which masked the noises and allowed me to relax. The downside was that in the morning there were sixteen mosquitoes in the room.

Vientiane, Thursday 11th January

I messed up today. The Vietnam visa was the type where the start date is fixed so bringing my flight forward one day made my entry into Vietnam invalid. So I

Luang Prabang Sunset and Tourist Market, Laos

made a wasted journey to the airport. Remember whatever tuk-tuk price is agreed, you stick to it, regardless of any notional printed prices. About four hostels were closed or full at such an early hour before I secured a room at Joe's. I rearranged my flight to the original times and the booking girl said "see you tomorrow". I visited the National Museum (lots of propaganda, status assertion and photos) and quickly photographed the shooting gallery that I forgot to record yesterday. I must alter my mindset to remember to record my surroundings much more than I do – with "infinite" digital there is no excuse. I felt quite grumpy with the early pointless rise that the morning became a lazy time. The new place is much friendlier and maybe I should not commit to accommodation for more than a day however tired I am when I arrive. It does not take that much energy to make a few quick comparisons. Due to limited time in Vietnam, I plan to spend tomorrow researching so that I am fully prepared for the next ten days. I believe my spell in Laos is my recovery period as I will be busy on my return home with little opportunity to relax.

Vientiane (Laos) to Hanoi (Vietnam), Friday 12th January

The morning was a drift between cafes, reading the Asian papers and business magazines about property and Googling. I was offended in the café when they did not accept my ten dollar note. It was a weird incident and I had a potential spell of paranoia thinking they had switched it for a tatty unusable note after disappearing off on a moped. The situation was diffused when I just exchanged the note with another tourist. The staff recognised me at the airport and the plane left 20 minutes early. The minibus from Hanoi Airport was full of Russians. The driver took everyone to a restaurant rather than the city centre and just waited outside before being pressured to actually take us to the centre as expected. I quickly found my second choice, a room at the back, booked my train trip down to Hue (flights were full) and a two-day tour to Halong Bay. It was so much busier and I felt more warmth from the people compared to Vientiane. I enjoyed some traditional Vietnamese food in a cosy restaurant next to a table of French. CD shops are everywhere. The mopeds are chaotic and so is the act of crossing the road.

Hanoi, Saturday 13th January

There are distinct product streets when you go shopping in Hanoi: shoes, clothes, jewellery, metal goods and spices. The greatest tourist site of the city is the general atmosphere with streams of mopeds. I feel immune from the constant hawkers which at other times I would find annoying. Some boys were playing bowls using their sandals and others were battling with wooden tops, spun using a thick string. I captured the challenge of walking across the street on video. With brief rests away from the noise I spent all day walking. Of course the barbers shop is found opposite the Revolutionary Museum! The postcard of a moped with a large bunch of ducks and chickens tied on the back is striking. I sat at the restaurant next to some young Australians and another French couple.

Hanoi, Sunday 14th January

Paying respects at the Ho Chi Minh mausoleum was a cultural activity engaged in by many local Vietnamese – people shuffle past a spot-lighted body. The museum nearby seemed to combine modern sculpture with important political documents in history. I sat at the café table and young Vietnamese practised their English and asked interesting questions. I met Irish Ciara and shared a small cyclo to the Temple of Literature with the driver playing the usual dramatic payment outbursts, trying to take advantage of similar sounding numbers "fourteen" and "forty". After a circuit of the temple grounds it was next by moped to the Ethnology Museum presenting outdoor reconstructions of traditional houses with bamboo strutted floors and walls. Later I had coffee on the balcony overlooking the lake and attended a cultural performance of the traditional and skilful water puppets. Steffen (who recalled his intense annoyance with Macao and the aggressive hawkers in Asia) and Ciara were both entertaining company which has been lacking recently.

Hanoi (Halong Bay), Monday 15th January

Unusually I am writing from a boat in Halong Bay with card players to my left and right. The tour bus picked me up and we headed towards the bay with grey low contrast skies. All the tour buses stop at a craft and restaurant place en route. The port was chaotic with about five layers of boat randomly arranged between land and open sea. Boats bump each other when arriving and leaving. Early in the day the limestone karst scenery was barely visible in the mist. Kayaking under the cave was stable. Some jumped in the water from the top deck and more brightly lit boats are now arriving. Thankfully the sea is calm. One of the pinnacles had a few caves inside and a great view of the bay. Naturally hawkers arrive by boat. Some staff are sleeping in the communal area. The sliding door needs constant adjustment. The three Irish girls have been travelling together for a year and there is a Korean bloke who found some oysters but none with pearls inside. The London carpenter dreamed of motorbike adventures. It is only 9.30pm and most have gone to bed. It would be better if the beer was free. I am sleeping on a boat tonight and on a train tomorrow night.

Halong to Hanoi to Hue, Tuesday 16th January

This only happens in Vietnam: you enter a train station and someone asks your destination (Hue) and then advises that you need to go to a train station far away with a moto but in fact you actually just need to walk for a minute across to platform one! After a relaxed breakfast there was a floating village with a school and short boat trip to the lagoon entered via a cave archway when the tide is just right: too low and the boat grounds, too high and there is not enough height clearance. Fishermen trap their catch at the lagoon entrance. The three-day group were dropped off at the harbour to another boat and we were joined by a previous group. Vietnamese music is now blaring and distorting over the loud speaker of the train as I sit crouched in the corridor with others moving into the compartment. After lunch back in Halong city (at a restaurant in the process of being built) we returned through industrialised areas with narrow houses, finished on the front road-facing side but grey and unfinished on the other sides. A welcome power cut – silence, no music! Two minutes and the loud speaker is back again, destroying the melodic continuity of the "song". I decided to walk to the station via the café. A large tour group occupy most of the rest of the carriage. Will I be able to sleep tonight?

Hanoi to Hue, Wednesday 17th January

I talked to Le Ella and her grandparents from Israel who were occupying the other three beds in the compartment. I ended up playing badminton in the train corridor and going for a long walk to the restaurant car drinking beer. The motion of the train was just too erratic and sleep was intermittent, maybe less than an hour or two all night. A few nuts and dates for breakfast, a long wait and we eventually arrived in drizzly Hue. I walked to the hotel and quickly set off on a moto tour of the local citadel, pagoda and royal tomb, feeling wet and uncomfortable on the way. I only recovered after a snooze and some food. If my trip was ending this week I would be feeling depressed now. I actually feel very happy, satisfied and healthy. In the internet café the Vietnamese girl next to me was singing out loud.

Hanoi Traffic Junction and Historical Wooden House, Vietnam

Hue to Hoi An, Thursday 18th January

I had to really think hard at the bank about which hotel I was actually staying in at the moment. I was picked up by a large coach soon after breakfast. The rain splashed through the underside of the bus window pane. One passenger thought we might be going the wrong way because the "sea" was on the wrong side. There was a brief stop at some marble shops and as it was raining, the planned sightseeing stops were cancelled. There is no point in accepting any navigational advice from people that enter the bus promoting hotels. My hotel was in a state of refurbishment but still open. The fish in banana leaf lunch is worth mentioning. I wandered until the rain began. Children wander around freely and chat with foreigners who gather at cafes. I can not see myself going on any of the local excursions and so I am likely just to walk around town, trying to have fun haggling conversations with the locals. I managed to book a cheap Paris hostel dorm bed near the Eiffel Tower. I bumped into the Korean bloke again whose main priority is drinking alcohol (beer mixed with vodka). My mp3 player display has given up, not being able to cope with the high humidity in the rain.

Hoi An, Friday 19th January

I managed to lose two underpants (now replenished) and gain a towel accidentally. I enjoyed a refreshing shave just past the Japanese bridge and am beginning to recognise the faces of the moped taxi blokes. I quickly bought some rucksacks (large and small) and CDs on my meanderings with just two days before my first trip ends. Thank god it is not the last one. I record rather than attempt to select exciting artistic images from the environment. The hotel refurbishments appear complete and the lobby is tidy. I am writing in my pink completely tiled room where the fan is drying my clothes and the mosquito nets above me remain unused. There is a bath in the room so I might as well make use of it after the water heater has done its job (but it has no plug so I will have to shower). I have now moved to the restaurant opposite the hotel to sit on the mezzanine balcony overlooking some tables with a more conventional holiday atmosphere. So what are my overall conclusions and feelings? Simple really, have a great diet (varied and fresh), plenty of exercise and no financial worries and your life improves. Remember that in your working life you are not spending all your daylight hours in a paddy field.

Halong Bay with Floating Fruit Stall, Vietnam

Halong Bay Boats and Cave, Vietnam

Halong Bay Fishing and Hoi An Flower Seller, Vietnam

Hoi An Ferry and Town Centre, Vietnam

Wood Carving and Cat and Dog, Hoi An, Vietnam

Hoi An to Hanoi, Saturday 20th January

Well it had to end some time. I lingered and did very little around town. I spotted the Israeli family on cyclos, the Yorkshire women from the tour group, some amazing cakes in the café and walked along the opposite riverbank and through the market again. The centre of town is blocked to traffic at weekends so suddenly becomes very quiet and pedestrian friendly – and probably increases sales. There are so many puppies around. I arrived at Danang early by car and was soon in dark drizzly Hanoi. Being in Vietnam for so long I have developed more paranoia and was cautious paying for the airport bus in advance, which dropped me off somewhere that required a further moto ride to my hotel. Only the expensive room with a balcony was available (not that useful at night) which I haggled down seeing as I also booked a taxi back to the airport for early tomorrow morning. Most restaurants were closed by 10.00pm. The big red rucksack is fully loaded and I am comfortable after a long hot shower.

Jump forward to the next trip.

2. London (England) to Nairobi (Kenya) transit and back to Bamako (Mali), Friday 2nd February 2007

The shock of poverty and basic infrastructure is still strong as I sit here in Mali at the Lafia Auberge (a place that I believe to be the Auberge but with such a low level of building refinement there is no identifying sign). Recently coming from the beauty and glamour of Paris, this shock is multiplied. The staff are just acquiring a bed to put in my room.

So I returned to London from my first trip covering Central America and Asia. The flight from Vietnam crossed icy mountains in Afghanistan and London looked like a jewel in the cold clear night with the cluster of Canary Wharf skyscrapers visible. I had a day to sort out things like the Ghana visa, checking and responding to accumulated post at the flat, rearranging and collecting reissued air tickets from High Street Kensington, picking up a Paris travel guide, US dollars and checking email and internet information about forthcoming trip details. My father's breathing was wheezy and coughy.

Paris was amazing and it really is so close. The Mali visa application was quickly processed after I had located the correct Mali embassy building. The metro is fast, efficient and fun to use. I had some doubts about the Three Ducks Hostel where I secured a dormitory bed with breakfast and free internet for US $20 – very cheap for Paris. I had to move to a different dorm after the first night and sleeping was variable but I met a lively group of Brazilians who kept me up one night and partied with me the following night, refilling my cup with Smirnoff Ice. Elena from Russia doing some kind of apprenticeship at HP in Germany was lively intermittent company, returning to Moscow to do exams. Amazingly the bar is open until 2.00am and there is a hostel lockout during the day when it is cleaned.

During this my second visit to Paris I am old enough to appreciate the museums and architecture which are all very impressive. I met up with Stuart and Jane for dinner and walks and Sushil for a jazz club. Note for the future: must visit Paris more, even just for a sit down coffee in a café. The quality of food is a step above the UK. A week means a relaxing pace to visit the sites of interest. The bitter cold forced me to buy a balaclava.

So after my 8-hour flight from London to Nairobi and a 6.5-hour flight back across Africa to Bamako, I feel ok. I am quite glad that this trip is organised and I will not have to battle the primitive infrastructure every step of the way. Cheaper air routes are often geographically illogical. This really is one

Stained Glass and Indoor Market, Paris, France

Champs Elysees and Louvre Grounds, Paris, France

Pompidou Centre and Napoleonic State Room, Paris, France

of the poorest countries I have visited and at the moment I am not quite 100% comfortable with the shanty atmosphere.

Bamako, Saturday 3rd February

The poverty is humbling. I managed to sleep ok on the hard bed placed centrally in the yellow room. By 6.00am it had cooled and the ceiling fan was no longer necessary. Last night I just had to go out for more water, past gangs of playing and noisy young children and immediately drank a litre before going to sleep. The plus 30°C temperatures and fan meant I was losing water fast. My only task was to change money and I was led by one of the hostel staff to the bank near the roundabout, an air-conditioned and clean refuge from the dusty streets. The open sewers, boys carrying plastic goods on their heads, families sitting in the streets and the heat surround you. The people have nothing – although some seem to have Mercedes. A couple staying at the hostel had driven from Holland. A taxi transported me to the more upmarket Rabelais Hotel (no numbers, just names on hotel room doors), isolated from the street atmosphere outside. After the beds were separated and I relaxed with French TV, I had little energy but to take advantage of the free internet in this deep hotel. I went for a walk towards the garage and small supermarket and purchased a malt soft drink, receiving sweets in place of small change. Consulting the travel guide bible, I determined the exact location of the hotel and walked to the nearby bar where friendly locals made sure I was looked after (tasty brochettes and grand bière) and my French comprehension and fluency improved. I ventured further to the fast food place right past the roundabout in the dark. The lack of street lighting adds to the gloom – but the people are happy and I do not feel threatened. In my past trips I have been isolated from the local African culture with a tour guide always acting as an intermediary. My experiences this time have been more real and authentic. I have no expectation of the group I am going to travel with. I just appreciate how the travel hassles will be minimised and sightseeing maximised.

Bamako to Segou, Sunday 4th February

I was disturbed by my tour roommate Charley from the States at about 11.15pm. I was later disturbed by mosquitoes and deployed the net – mosquitoes do not mind whether the room is decorated in a fancy way or not. The group were on first impression much older and less used to independent travel – making decisions, taking initiative and doing things out of the ordinary and spontaneously. I guess I chose this easy mode of travel myself and am fully aware of the pros and cons and am aware of the difficulty of travel in Africa in

Market and Petrol Stations, on the way to Segou, Mali

Hairdresser, Road Transport and Carved Figures, Mali

general. After lots of form filling in reception the 3-hour trip, past a market and through country resembling dry northern Australia we arrived at the posh Hotel Independence, the menu choices being phoned through in advance. The waiter found the name John amusing and the other members of the group were finding their feet. The last day of the festival in Segou involved giant puppets, drumming, music, dancing in a line and people generally milling about in a friendly atmosphere. The young kid asked for my empty plastic water bottle. After walking along dark dusty streets I was unable to find a suitable restaurant and bought some supermarket snacks. The hotel has a pool (as did the last one) but there is just no time.

Segou to Djenne, Monday 5th February

An early breakfast was set up in the courtyard of the hotel. The rest of the group really seem to be dependent on the rest of the group. Bags were piled on top of the bus and we were ready to go later than planned – inevitable when steering a group of thirteen. After walking across a bridge kids gathered and held my fingers. The kids asked for empty bottles of water at a village where we stopped with primitive granary hut structures and a beer making centre. The chief of the village was paid a token amount for the imposition of this group of tourists. Using cliché terms such as bustling and colourful seem the only correct terms for a market on the way, near an adobe mud constructed mosque, a smaller version of the one at Djenne where I am now. The light does not work in the bathroom but the hotel itself is the most upmarket in town. The walk around the mosque, market and side street was one of the most culturally different I have ever experienced – goats, turbans, mud bricks, weird unidentifiable medical cures, dust – and a view of the adobe mud architecture in the dying sun. One member of the group had multiple mobile calls indicating some kind of developing crisis back home. The journey involved a little snoozing and a stop at a granary with many huts. I felt no great need to communicate continuously with the other members of the group and maybe I should develop some stock responses when they comment on my quietness, to make them feel more comfortable: "I'm learning to relax", "Don't worry I'm very happy" and so on. "I try not to be too intense", "I'm content and have got no worries". There was drum accompaniment with the bony chicken dinner in the evening.

Djenne to Dogon Villages, Tuesday 6th February

The hotel room light flickered continuously, as did the light from the other hotel rooms. A super warm night and I am glad the fan was working. I am sitting on the dusty terrace where the tents are positioned with faint generator noise, children playing and French conversation in the background. After weeks of good health my stomach is now not 100%. At every stop there are hawkers that do not bother me as much as they bother others. There was weaving of strips of cloth and a description of coming of age ceremonies under the red rock, reminiscent of Australia but a living culture with herds of goats and braying donkeys. After an interesting walk down the rocky path into the valleys, we continued with the air-conditioned jeep journey (which is a secret luxury because not all the jeeps have it) along sandy roads. There is less bickering and complaining in the group and sometimes I feel like a diplomat. Strangely past experience with computer games helps with navigating the special warren-like arrangement of the hotel.

Dogon Villages, Wednesday 7th February

My stomach felt a bit poorly before I went to bed and I tried to induce throwing up but nothing happened – but later twice woke up in the night to throw up into plastic bags (one with a few holes!). The night was warm and lit by the moon. Some conversations could be heard late into the night and adding the stomach problems, I had little sleep. The trek was strenuous, climbing up rocks through villages, up tree ladders and what made the walk most challenging was the heat – about 34°C in the shade. The views again reminded me of Australia but here the people still live the traditional life style. There was a stop for melon under the shade of a tree but there was only rehydration solution for me this time. But amazingly seventy year old Cynthia managed the trek with help from the local boys who supported her and helped carry day packs and water. I could only rest in the afternoon heat back at the hotel where we were camped, my body leaving a sweaty imprint on the camping mattress. We visited another Dogon village in the late afternoon where they were grinding millet, four women each pounding in rotation with a large stick. It is a bit breezier compared to last night so hopefully I will be more comfortable. My hands feel cleaner with the alcohol gel I have been given.

Dogon Villages to Sevare, Thursday 8th February

The gusty wind buffeted the tent regularly during the night and I managed to sleep in the cooler temperature. Fried bread dough (doughnuts!) for breakfast and we were off. One Dogon village seems to merge into the next but after climbing the rocky paths we reached a very colourfully painted parliament house where debates take place under a low roof. The locals put on a mask performance and I felt like Prince Charles. It was entertaining and colourful and

Segou Procession and Festivities, Mali

Dancing, Singing and Sunset, Segou, Mali

I kept taking photos of this traditional dance which would normally be performed on special occasions but is now pre-arranged for tourists. After lunch on the terrace with usual negotiation paying for the drinks (with little small change) we stopped to look at the crocodiles. A moment of neurosis and I mistakenly thought my 2x converter lens had been stolen. The jeep behind gave us a gentle nudge on the way along bumpy sandy roads to the isolated hotel between towns. There was a horse next to the swimming pool.

Mopti, heading north along the Niger River, Friday 9th February

This was written retrospectively while heading north on the Niger river with a strong breeze. There was no running water in the morning to wash so I used the shower by the pool. The Spanish owned hotel provided a high quality pastry breakfast. After a pottery demonstration the Mopti market was chaotic with flies covering all the produce including the fruit. The upper level of the market provided a good vantage point for taking photographs and I succumbed to purchasing a small bronze figure souvenir. After buying beer supplies at the river bank we boarded the pinasse or narrow boat and smoothly and gently travelled north with slight splashing from the bow. Large colourful sailboats moved in the opposite direction and we passed many narrow fishing boats. To break up the journey we stopped at towns on the way, one with a Disneyland style mosque and one where we greeted the chief and founder of the village. Most were happy to have their photograph taken. There were the usual kids on a donkey, carrying of babies, marshalling old tyres with a stick and requests for gifts – bottles and sweets. There was a desperate struggle to grab pens given by one member of the group. We reached the campsite just before sunset near a ditch and much cow dung. I attempted a photo of the stars but my camera's exposure with widest aperture is not quite good enough. Everyone went to bed early and my sleeping bag proved just warm enough for the cool night.

Somewhere along the Niger River, Saturday 10th February

As the boat is stranded here for a short time waiting for the sandstorm to subside I am struggling to remember what happened yesterday (on the 10th). We set off soon after sunrise and passed waving children, basic settlements and cows. The river narrowed for a time and then expanded into a vast lake where the wind picked up and the front of the boat became soaked by successive waves. The back of my neck is being splashed as I write this entry retrospectively. A couple of stops for supplies of fish and meat and we continued downstream with the view from the roof of the boat for variation. At the campsite near four metre high termite mounds just past a village some hippos made an appearance. The camp chair sank in the sandy riverbank as the sun set, ready for dinner and chaotic conversation around an oil lamp. Amadou our guide broke the plastic plate while trying to cut the fish. Others reported hearing the hippos overnight. As the only representative of the USA, Charley defended his country's reputation.

Along the Niger River towards Timbuktu, Sunday 11th February

Essentially more of the same, moving past the bank with some tree roots exposed, the river remained wide. Distant sandstorms obscured the banks. My foot is resting against the blue ledge of the boat and as the boat picks up speed there is more splashing as I face backwards, facing the rest of the group – doctor, potter, ex-nurse, ex-pilot now tax assessor, government employee, retired ex-TV vision engineer, ex safari tour organiser and I do not know the rest. This river trip up the Niger is better than following a dusty track with 4x4 vehicles but not particularly eventful, apart from the odd conversation with the group – some played Connect 4, number puzzles, ate sweets and took photos. The purr of the engine is soft and the waves continue to lap. Some are wearing scarves that completely cover the face, leaving only the eyes exposed. The boy at the back is bailing out the boat. I have adventurous and entertaining dreams while camping, enhancing normal travel reality. Josephine is impressed with people who have been to Bhutan. The campsite was near a large herd of goats and the sky remained sandy! The wind died down during the night to leave a calm lake-like view.

Niger River to Timbuktu, Monday 12th February

I am writing this under torchlight in a tent just outside Timbuktu. There was one stop to drop off some pens at a school in a village. The smell of the village sewers hits you before you come ashore. I felt a little uncomfortable walking through the village, again mainly due to the level of poverty. I was a "tubabu" or foreign tourist, invading their life with a camera. Number puzzles, biscuits, coffee, wine gums, sweets and a fish lunch helped to pass the time, a further 6 hours to a river point about 10 kilometres from Timbuktu. It was essential to have your photo taken in front of the "Welcome to Timbuktu" sign. Being a part of a tour is a bit surreal and you just have to go with the flow and accept some of the administrative delays. I played table football with the locals near the hotel before we embarked on a 2-hour camel ride which was surprisingly comfortable. Amadou made a mobile phone call while riding his camel. The meal was a full roast sheep with ululating and dancing as entertainment - touristy but enjoyable. I am often surprised at the range of characters you find on a tour. Some have such heavy irritating personalities it is difficult to believe they do not realise the effect they have on people. Timbuktu is such a landmark it feels great to be here. Dr Jennifer has quite a scatty personality.

Timbuktu, Tuesday 13th February

Today the group fragmented. After the cheese and jam breakfast, some walked, some returned with jeeps and the majority returned with camels, past a donkey lying on the ground almost dead. I felt quite comfortable in my saddle. We toured the small museums, past the mosque and explorer houses, past mud bricks and the inevitable market. A restaurant wait was so long that I only had a coffee and departed early to do some internetting, send emails and a photo from this special place. It was soon time to go out again to the Tuareg market but nothing appealed. We are driving back instead of flying as I understand the situation. Jennifer and West had dinner together at the place where a group of us had steak and chips. Some bought a solid slab of salt as a souvenir. The streets are dusty and full of droppings and the atmosphere is friendly. I haggled for my postcards before sending them at the post office, making sure that they were stamped – I hope they arrive. It is good to be clean again after the camping and not to have to put up the room. At times the group seems to be mired in inertia and indecision but on balance this is a good introduction to West Africa.

Timbuktu to Sevare, Wednesday 14th February

I have low energy. I am not entertained by the evening conversation and can not even be bothered to walk 15 minutes into town to have dinner. I almost feel guilty remaining in the hotel rather than exploring this small town transport hub. It could be the company that I am bored with too, without sounding impolite. I suppose I could regard this as a gentle introduction to Africa in the sense that I am shrouded by relative luxury and a familiar group culture before I hit the real Ghana. After breakfast on the terrace in the dark and a short drive to the ferry, we were soon on our way along bumpy roads through a dry dusty landscape. The Toyota Land Cruiser punctured a tyre after hitting a rock. We changed from jeeps to a bus and arrived in Sevare in the late afternoon, a tiring journey. I slumped on the bed with a French 24-hour news channel and unadventurously and unimaginatively had food at the hotel. I find myself becoming more like this safe tour group – quite worrying. I crave meeting a livelier, more adventurous and less safe group.

Meat and Spices, Mopti Market, Mali

Djenne Mosque and Dogon Grain Stores, Mali

Intense Gaze and Traditional Adobe Mud Constructed Mosque, Mali

Granary Hut and Medical Cures?, Djenne, Mali

Fulani Conversation and African Pot Carrying, Djenne, Mali

What Rooftops? Djenne, Mali

Dogon Souvenirs and Village, Mali

Dogon Parliamentarians and Rhythm Section, Mali

Children watching Traditional Mask Celebration, Dogon Village, Mali

Mopti Market, Mali

Fish and Vegetables, Mopti Market, Mali

Mopti Market and Mosque along the Niger River, Mali

Mopti Resident and Riverside, Mali

Along the Niger River, Mali

Niger River Villages and Overnight Stop, Mali

Niger River Village Scene and Children Playing in Timbuktu, Mali

Sevare to Bamako, Thursday 15th February

There was bread (with no sand) and "fruitless jam" for breakfast and an early start with all day spent on the bus. Although many vehicles are equipped with air-conditioning, it rarely works for long periods. I was sitting by the back emergency exit and was able to open the door on a latch to let some air through. We stopped for lunch at the hotel we stayed at on the way up. Again I am surprised at how caustic some personalities are and wonder if there really is an endearing warm character hidden underneath. Life is too short to figure out what made them that way. Some people are leaving very early in the morning, just after midnight, some tomorrow morning and most by Saturday. I had a fast food falafel (very generous portions) at the place near the roundabout. Accustomed to the poverty in the countryside, the city seems wealthy in complete contrast to my opinion when I first arrived. As the journey was unplanned (taking the place of a plane journey) there was some hassle at a checkpoint and Amadou our guide was forced to pay a bribe. The journey was tiring with the temperature in the bus around 35°C. The group has fragmented but there is still a city tour tomorrow with the remainder. I savour my last taste of luxury before moving to a cheaper hotel across town.

Bamako, Friday 16th February

It really is such a shock moving from a luxurious well lit and decorated hotel with pool to the Lebanese Mission dormitory – concrete floors, neon lights, smoke from a fire and old trucks outside and bare walls. The place with a very rusty main door looks as if it has been derelict for years. The only welcoming feature was a fellow human being in the dormitory. There is a dark dirt road at the front and the taxi driver had to ask a couple of times for directions. There are no in-hotel boutiques or internet access points. I suppose the key to staying here is to spend as little time awake as possible. The day tour of Bamako city was interesting, particularly the blacksmith's market. The view from "Point C" near the satellite dishes was hazy. After the murals depicting Mali culture were explained near the map and watered gardens, we visited the museum with an extensive explanation of all the textiles, patterns and sculptures. There was a ginger drink at lunch and after the meal a visit to the craft and food market. Jennifer received lots of hassle from the locals and asked us to accompany her while shopping and taking photographs. This basic dorm has mosquito nets and fan and the bathroom is across the yard. It may have been popular with backpackers many years ago. I was in two minds about staying here and I can also verify that there is a big difference between $90 and $5 a night. After spending time in Africa I need to learn to appreciate the basic things in life:

Street Food and Table Football, Timbuktu, Mali

Camel Fun, Timbuktu, Mali

Camel and Donkey Transport, Timbuktu, Mali

Blacksmith's Market with Sculptures, Bamako, Mali

running water, electricity, pavements, kerbs, crossings, covered sewers, mild temperatures, lack of mosquitoes and not getting sand everywhere.

Bamako, Saturday 17th February

Where to begin! The mosquito net had enough holes to let in at least twelve mosquitoes which was annoying but by daylight they were just poised on the netting surrounding my pillow. With little sleep I enjoyed a breakfast in the patisserie nearby, where a power cut meant no coffee for now. I caught up on sleep later. The dormitory manager and friends had lunch using their hands to scoop rice and chicken from a large communal bowl. On a recommendation I transferred to another hotel north of the railway tracks, a long walk in the heat. After a final afternoon walk through the maze of the main market, past the church, I coincidentally met up with Sara at the same place I had breakfast this morning. There was a vague plan to find a place for dinner via a photo shop and while walking Sara noticed an Algerian businessman she had met on a long bus journey who recommended a place just around the corner. Conversation was difficult with no common fluent language. There did not seem to be many live music options for the evening but we followed the recommendation of the manager for a bar called Balafon near the railway tracks with the occasional noisy train rumbling past. The atmosphere was friendly and I was entertained by many conversations, some had strange laughs, one person fell asleep on his chair and one kept banging his beer on the table. A closing nearby club filled the bar with more lively people. Everything was done in a friendly boisterous manner and I was thoroughly charmed by the company until 4.30am. This normal sociable and playful side of Africa is an image you rarely see. I felt satisfied that I managed to express myself and it was a fitting evening to end my time in Mali.

Bamako (Mali) to Abidjan (Côte d'Ivoire) transit to Accra (Ghana), Sunday 18th February

I got up at 11.00am, enough time for breakfast and it was soon time to walk towards town and flag down a yellow Mercedes taxi. Abidjan airport looks quite new and modern and I had difficulty using my last thousand note of CFA currency because it was too tatty and taped up – which I am now using as a book mark. At Accra I had to backtrack to exchange money for transport into town – with the usual initial over-inflated quote. Compared to Mali the infrastructure appeared modern but with few cars on the road. All the hotels in Accra were in darkness as there is some kind of power saving where one in five days is a scheduled power cut – which has been happening for many months.

Recycling Metal and Regional Map, Mali

Bamako Souvenir Carvings, Mali to the Accra Coast, Ghana

The upstairs room which I am writing from now is quite dingy and small but good enough. In my tiredness I forgot the name of the bloke who provided me with assistance. As there was no power there was no fan and it was a sweaty night.

Accra, Monday 19th February

Africa seems more sociable than Europe with people happy to talk to complete strangers. The intention was to walk around and do some basic tasks. I found a balcony breakfast place. The English here is a strange Pidgin English so I have to listen carefully, speak slowly and repeat myself to be understood. There is a low ATM limit so I had to obtain a visa advance of two million Cedi (!) at the main branch of the bank, a reasonable amount for three weeks. My t-shirt was soaked with sweat as I burned my photos to CD and later posted them at the main post office. There are a few holes in the pavements and people carry goods on their heads. The heat is oppressive but bearable. If I had come directly from the UK I would have been shocked culturally but coming from Mali, the place seems familiar with many similarities with England – for example there was a similar style button for the pedestrian crossing. I walked down to an area overlooking the beach near a cheap rice and chicken place and had enough energy to walk back to the hotel before dark.

Accra, Tuesday 20th February

I checked at the Date Hotel whether there were any rooms free but there were none. I waited for a while across the road at a breakfast stall just in case any rooms became available. I met this bloke (with skinhead cut and beard) who had taken a year and a half to cycle from London to Accra and who was on his way to Ethiopia! His slow speech, perhaps due to the solitary nature of the trip at first made me think that he was not English and from Wembley at all. He had replaced most of his bicycle parts, drank well water on the way and found muddy roads most frustrating - a 10-minute conversation during an egg sandwich breakfast but one of those amazing traveller moments that rarely occurs on an organised tour. As I have mentioned in the past, the more challenging and difficult to reach destinations seem to attract more interesting people. The National Museum was small and I bought some posters explaining tribal symbols. I feel some of the pollution in my throat as I write this. The arts centre was a small gallery, a stage where some dancing and drumming rehearsals were taking place and an artisan market with a large number of aggressive sellers. I walked to the lighthouse but was insulted at the initial cost to climb up and take photos so refused and was accompanied to the timber market (with fetish stalls) walking through a poor shanty town area. A taxi back for simple rice and beef with a physics and chemistry lesson showing on the TV ended the day.

Accra to Kokrobite, Wednesday 21st February

The receptionist at the Date did not appear friendly: after asking about reservations there was no answer but "we're busy", without referring to or discussing any booking possibilities. I have reserved a room for the time around Independence Day at the hotel on the corner nearby. The traffic was gridlocked as usual but I made it to the motor park for buses to Kokrobite. All the minivans are arranged haphazardly. The vehicle takes about 30 minutes to fill completely and then a path out of the parking area magically forms. A man was selling an historical quiz book on the bus and there was some dispute over the number of continents. Big Milly's is a resort on the beach with a central bar and restaurant. Everything is on a tab, run by a posh lady called Wendy dressed in bright colours. The waves are quite high and young boys play between the narrow fishing boats on the beach. I have not spotted any lively personalities. There is no running water and washing is from buckets. I seem to have a bit of a cough.

Kokrobite, Thursday 22nd February

I decided to write my journal in a public place but all the seats around the bar are occupied so I am sitting here on the periphery able to listen to any quality conversations – one long one about excessive UK tax. Long term travellers tend to grow a beard. The very long term travellers fashion the beard into some type of pony tail. I forgot to mention the large number of cats, dogs and chickens that wander around the yard. I understand the economics of a resort and if you are looking for a rest from the hustle-and-bustle then it is great. I have just thoroughly enjoyed a bucket shower in a stone outdoor enclosure. I spent most of the day reading the travel book propped up against a log, attracting curiosity from the children and watching the communal effort in gathering up the fishing nets. I am happy just listening to the conversation behind me without participating. It is certainly cooler today so I am not drinking as much water. Last night it rained heavily and due to a hole in the roof I was sprinkled upon so I had to reverse my sleeping direction and use my rain cape for about an hour – the hole was repaired during the day. I am thinking more about leaving after three nights as although this enclave is comfortable, I need to do some independent exploring. The workers spray the yard and there are small flares scattered about which may explain the lack of mosquitoes.

Kokrobite, Friday 23rd February

I have fulfilled my intention of not doing much in Kokrobite. The old German bloke with young Ghanaian next door played a little mouth organ last night. It was cool enough not to have the ceiling fan on. Essentially a lazy repeat of yesterday but I did go into the sea with the powerful waves hitting me every few seconds and my short pockets filling with sand very quickly. I watched some skilful table tennis and enjoyed the barbeque dinner with drumming, dancing and acrobatic entertainment. Where did the day go? I read a little, chatted a little and snoozed a little. I managed to hit my head on the roof beam and read about all the diseases you can be afflicted with in Africa.

Kokrobite to Cape Coast, Saturday 24th February

After a restful few days it was time to leave. I spoke to some friendly Danish who had a whole two-and-a-half month's holiday in Ghana. Talking of Ghana my t-shirt emblazoned with the Ghanaian flag receives some friendly reactions from people. After waving goodbye the journey was relatively painless. I mistakenly missed buying a ticket at the window so had to get off the bus and get on the next. For most of the 3-hour journey there was a forceful and shouting evangelist at the front of the bus, quoting the bible and even leading hymnal singing. Most of the bus was indifferent but a few willingly participated, singing and answering questions. The orator was irritating because of the volume of his utterances. Most passengers got off when the progress of the bus slowed around the market. I walked past the coastal castle and looped too far north before finding the "Sammo" Hotel – I am now satisfied with a room if there is running water! As always, there is a shed-like stall outside with sociable vendor ready to chat and give advice. I walked to town for some energy food and returned at dusk.

Cape Coast, Sunday 25th February

Having some food at the beginning of the day is important for sightseeing energy. I sat looking at the sea in the restaurant by the large white Cape Castle. The views of the fishing boats along the coast were amazing. The museum covered the history of the slave trade and how a triangular route of goods between America, Europe and Africa kept everyone happily trading. I did not find the dungeon as moving as I ought to have done – distracted by the bats on the ceiling. After a minute of conversation the locals ask for your email or telephone number – so everyone is super friendly? Even in Ghana they watch English Premiership football on a Sunday. I had lunch in a noisy bar and I was

Cape Coast Fishing and Bus Journey Sermon, Ghana

kept entertained by the locals who were curious and wanted to keep me happy. I forgot to mention all the religious names of the shops such as "God is Great Hair Salon". The shack across the road supplied a great pasta and malt drink and I am lying here under the rotating stand-alone fan.

Cape Coast to Kumasi, Monday 26th February

The fan is wafting warm air around the multicoloured hotel room here in Kumasi. After a roadside breakfast in the morning heat I reached the motor park for a bus to Kumasi. As is the usual protocol the bus does not leave until it is full. I sat near the back in the middle with my bag on my lap. Entertainment included the many sellers outside with goods (biscuits, bread, fish, and water) balanced on their heads. On the bus during the journey were two evangelists, a bible seller, a religious magazine seller and the second evangelist also sold small packets of what looked like sweets; towards the end of the journey a few passengers went off so I had a bit more room to breath. Coffins next to hi-fi separates were on sale by the side of the roundabout. After a short walk I found the hotel area but the first two hotels were full. I met some Dutch in the local café who were doing volunteer teacher training for an extended period. They had had a nightmare overnight train journey which only takes 4 hours by bus! A power cut in the internet café cut short my session temporarily.

Kumasi, Tuesday 27th February

I am writing this with a traditional Ghanaian multicoloured bracelet around my wrist. I checked the adjacent hotels. Some were full or only had an expensive room available. The Guestline Lodge seemed to be clean and much cooler so I moved there. After withdrawing three million Cedi (!) using my visa card and a breakfast pasty with no meat, I could only snooze. My target was the National Cultural Centre with a small museum with guide and some craft shops – a relaxing place away from the busy traffic. The insect repellent seems to have dissolved my plastic wash bag. I could not find a small shampoo for while and a local woman said she had some spare at home to offer – an example of the general attitude towards tourists. I updated TheTravelMap.com with the camel photo from Timbuktu, checking that the command line can see the ftp site and that the ftp transfer is in binary for the upload of the image. I will tackle the other museum and the colossal market tomorrow.

Kumasi, Wednesday 28th February

After breakfast in the white-walled courtyard I walked towards the other museum. Walking across the railway overpass there was some kind of commotion with a large group of women carrying metal pots. Someone asked me if I had a permit to take photographs and I questioned which areas required a permit with no answer in response. Past the chaotic market and to the calm grounds of the palace museum with serene peacocks roaming the grounds. The museum tour was compulsory with interesting descriptions of the King's residence and history. I sat relaxing with the groundsman listening to the radio before tackling the periphery of the main market – following the railway tracks. It was quite intense. At regular intervals I stopped for drink. I talked to William who was considering a route east across Africa but with only politically unstable countries along the route to Ethiopia. Dutch Joyce was a fine dinner companion who had done some fundraising work in Ghana. The fan on the wall keeps cutting out due to a dodgy switch. I may rest tomorrow.

Kumasi, Thursday 1st March

It was a rest day and apart from making a long phone call home, internetting, eating and drinking, there was little activity. I had difficulty obtaining US dollar cash from the banks – probably quite a rare transaction here. The heat is quite exhausting but I am slowly becoming acclimatised. Everyone was watching a sponsored African awards ceremony on TV.

Kumasi (Bosumtwi Lake), Friday 2nd March

I had arranged a day trip to a local lake with Joyce. Her guidebook on just the country Ghana supplied more detail about the place and mentioned a lake view guesthouse stop for lunch. The tro-tro ride (large shared taxi) was painless and a further negotiated taxi ride to the lakeside village was quick – but the extra fare to the guesthouse "along a very bad road" was far too much and walking was a more interesting option. With local hellos, some balancing a single large bottle of water on their heads, neutral colours of the calm lake, children swimming and fishermen on planks of floating wood rather than boats, it was a great contrast to noisy Kumasi. I am writing this in the white courtyard with staff conversation from the upper balcony and quiet reading and writing from other guests around me. The souvenirs in reception are looking more tempting. Apparently the Indian boss of the hotel was angrily telling off a staff member for being too friendly yesterday. I caught a little sun and feel pleasantly tired ready for any evening meal. As the large beer is the same price as some of the soft drinks, I am committed to choosing the beer. My coloured bracelet, perhaps signifying four months of completed travel is beginning to feel more appropriate on my wrist.

Kumasi to Akosombo, Saturday 3rd March

I spent all day on buses although I originally thought it would not be quite all day. The hotel employee who does the breakfasts had not turned up so I skipped, leaving relatively early at 8.45am. I am sure Joyce must have found someone to carry her bags to the bus station around the corner. I was destined for a bus station further away, by the overpass road works and across the railway. There was a choice of bus to Accra and I was ushered into the larger one. The sellers' eyes outside the bus were transfixed on the wrestling with Italian commentary being shown on the bus TV. One advantage of a longer bus is that the preacher is further away and not in your face. If you wait long enough breakfast comes to you in the form of a few boiled eggs. Small bags of drinking water are on sale at every stop. After an hour we set off and the bloke next to me was dropping his head asleep on my shoulder every so often. They were selling "sweets" on the bus again today and I found out that they were actually tablets for treating intestinal worms. There were delays en route with shared single lane sections. After a minor scrape with a vehicle (but could have been a roadside stall) the whole bus detoured to the police station with in total about a one-and-a-half hour delay. So an expected 5-hour journey turned into a 7-hour journey. I was splashed through the window by a water sprinkler used to dampen the dust of road construction. There was someone else going to Akosombo so I followed the brightly patterned dress to the next bus going to an intermediate destination. It is impossible to make visual sense of the minibus station or scrum as there is no signage and you have to rely on advice from the people around you. It was dark at the next bus station stop. Luggage was put on a cart and on to the next bus where I sat at the front. I only had some bananas for lunch and was feeling grumpy with hunger. The bus went part of the way so I had to catch another one competing with a large crowd at the roadside. I managed to get on the third bus after a scramble. I was walked almost all the way to the hotel but it was full and three times the price I was expecting. I was desperate for some drink at reception. After walking back to the corner petrol station where the taxis gather I reached the Sound Rest Motel down a dark drive. I was kindly made a breakfast meal in the evening and after spending all day on cramped seats am finally feeling comfortable under the dim motel room light bulb. Good night!

Akosombo, Sunday 4th March

I sat with a group under the shelter eating a second breakfast of food kindly offered to me: thousands of tiny spicy fish with a polenta-like addition eating with your hands. I headed for the Volta hotel with the aim of seeing or touring the dam but ended up just admiring the view of the dam from the terrace near the big football screen. I have been mistaken twice now for someone else, being offered change this time. I believe this is the phenomenon of not being able to discriminate between individuals of an ethnicity you are not used to seeing. I internetted and my site is actually receiving non-spam comments! I need to find an easy way of uploading pictures. I walked back to town and taxied to the next town for some food but ended up just drinking a beer as my stomach was not quite right. Financially I gain nothing by walking as the amount I would have spent on a taxi I spend on satisfying my thirst. I had to rush to the toilet and when I had to clean myself up it was quite frustrating that no water came out of the tap. I have hardly taken any photos these past few days. Even the misty dam would not have made a good photo. According to the hotel manager there is a ferry to the island tomorrow so I will try that and hopefully get back to Accra in good time.

Akosombo to Dodi Island to Accra, Monday 5th March

The cruise up the misty lake was uneventful. The barbequed fish was excellent and I spent most of the time just drinking, relaxing and watching the draughts players. There was nothing on the island apart from fish sellers, a band and begging children. The band on the boat did not come alive until they dropped the covers and attempted more traditional African songs. There were lots of older African Americans. It was a reasonable way to spend a day. The bus back to Accra was quite speedy but the terminal was dark and unfriendly. No-one could point out where we were on a map. I was intensely annoyed when I finally discovered my location and decided on a taxi and he quoted four times the normal price. This really cancels out some of the friendliness of the other Ghanaians and is a real insult. I walked to the hotel and luckily my reservation stood but in a noisy room next to the main road – the whipping fan should mask some of the noise. Someone at the hotel accompanied me to the nearest drinking place and restaurant only to request I pay for half his soup while relating his story about a potential wife from Denmark. My negativity was probably irrationally triggered by the taxi driver but I made it to Accra with a place to stay so that is a basic success.

Accra, Tuesday 6th March

Most people were watching the Independence Day celebration on TV and I decided to head to Independence Square to see for myself. The taxi driver dropped me as close as possible to the Square; having a white "Ubonu" (white man or foreigner) in his taxi allowed him access to a closed road. The square area was full of colours and I ventured through the crowd to have a clear view of the assembled people behind the military vehicles. The crowd was uncontrolled and I had to escape across the drainage ditch to an emptier area. It is unfortunate that despite the kindness of the people I have met in Ghana, a lasting memory I will carry is being pick pocketed in the crowd. I thought I was careful with my wallet in a zipped compartment and difficult to remove but some deft fingers still managed to remove just the cash without removing the held wallet. Although the amount of cash was small by European standards (less than $15) my enthusiasm for the celebrations was dampened for a few hours. I walked along the crowded coastal road and relaxed at the hotel near the beach where they were painting the pillars yellow. Isolated and away from the crowds I relaxed. I met this helpful bloke a couple of times during the day but was in no mood to follow up friendly invitations. I taxied to the OSU area for some sit down fast food with various people sitting opposite and saw some carnival dancing and hip-hop set up on a stage. A live microphone broadcasting on local radio was directed towards me and I tried to sound enthusiastic about all the celebrations. I could not understand the hip-hop words on the PA system. I feel a bit of low budget trauma with the poor bathroom facilities at the hotel.

Accra, Wednesday 7th March

I dropped off my sleeping bag for alterations to add a zip and I had a haircut. My temporary "helper" expected payment and I refused and believe I insulted him because he departed shaking hands with his left hand. I had an early lunch but the familiar internet café was closed so I had to enter one further down the road – I booked the train ticket for my parents to visit my sister on my return. I still find it amazing that I can do this from anywhere in the world if the connection is fast enough. The temperature here seems to be about 32°C at any time of day. Although more acclimatised compared to my first day, heat has a tiring effect. I was expecting celebrations to last for a few days but I am told that there was nothing to see today. I moved to a slightly less noisy room and my shampoo seems to have disappeared. I am looking forward to my next destination and can not see myself doing much in my last two days in Ghana. The design of the hotel really does not encourage much social interaction. The hotel employee writing receipts seemed drunk or drugged up from yesterday's celebrations. I believe I have enough energy to wander up to the White Bell balcony restaurant for dinner. I miss not having a music player which would make me feel more homely in what can be described as "raw" surroundings – but I suppose listening to music is a deliberate distraction to remove myself from the immediate environment.

Accra, Thursday 8th March

I have got used to: large holes in the pavement, choosing straws for drinks, drinking from small plastic bags of water, people carrying goods on their heads, hissing when trying to attract someone's attention, being called white man, the high temperature, unpredictability of plumbing, twenty thousand Cedi notes, the smell of open sewers, babies carried on slings on mother's backs and school girls with short haircuts. I spent the day away from my surroundings on the internet. The "Busy" internet place had a few restaurants close by and a café on site that serves food. I did my admin and returned in the evening to relax on my hotel branded bed sheet. I tried to find out about films currently showing from the information centre but was unsuccessful in my search. A familiar American sci-fi action film was a welcome distraction at the open air Roxy Cinema with a few drops of rain during the presentation.

Accra (Ghana) to Nairobi (Kenya), Friday 9th March

I had a jam sandwich at the usual roadside stall and visited the tailor to give him money to buy the zip. The Akuma village hotel no longer provided internet access so I killed time at an internet café near the post office, giving audio updates of the session status. I wandered through the market with no intention of buying anything, a long lunch and my last day in Ghana was almost over. There was so much traffic on the way to the airport that I was glad I had left very early.

Nairobi, Saturday 10th March

The bloke sitting to my left on the plane had malaria and was taking medication for it. The 5-hour-15-minute journey was painless but with a long taxiing delay at Nairobi Airport. There was some frustration at the hotel where the receptionist rather than checking I was booked into the hotel, just directed me to the shuttle tour service to verify I had a shuttle booking. I had no vouchers (could not be sent to me on the road) and there seemed to be no record of my booking. I cut through the apathy and inefficiency and finally in my tired state confirmed that the hotel had my booking and was able to crash in my posh

Masai Village and Jumping, Tanzania

Masai Necklaces, Tanzania

hotel room overlooking the pool. I met my tour roommate Andrew later (New Zealander originally from Birmingham) who seemed quite sane. To save tour costs rooms are shared. After resting I returned to the fast food place a short distance down the road past the roundabout and garage. The city feels far more modern than I remember it with more skyscrapers. It seems cooler and more comfortable here compared to Accra. I seem to be quite dependent on my regular dose of internet information although I may resist as it is a bit pricey here in the Silver Springs Hotel.

Nairobi (Kenya) to Arusha (Tanzania), Sunday 11th March

I have neglected my diary duties for a few days and now as I sit in a Serengeti camp chair, relaxing after lunch I will try and recall what happened. It is immediately apparent that this tour group is far friendlier than the last with people making an effort to be entertaining. Many of the group were together for a previous tour, which included an aspiring transsexual – well that is how he was described. They all complained that the Carnivore restaurant last night was far more expensive than expected. The large truck took us to Arusha. This is a trip I have done before and I will try and concentrate on the differences. It is difficult to tell whether some of the differences are due to me being different after so many trips or that the places have actually developed. Arusha seems more modern with more buildings, cars and people rushing around doing something. I suppose the puppy dogs I remember at the campsite are now fully grown. Because of the slightly rainier season we transfer to three four-wheel drive jeeps. I managed to miss eight shots at the black while playing pool at the campsite bar with acrobats in the background.

Arusha to Serengeti (Ngiri Camp), Monday 12th March

Sunday was a long drive and so was today. After buying supplies of water at the local supermarket, with hawkers present everywhere we set off. I bought some necklaces on an impulse at the lake viewpoint. I was sharing with a Polish couple and French Stephen with Sally. The green jeeps are double wheel base so they look sturdy and powerful and can accommodate seven passengers comfortably. We stopped at the entrance gates to the renamed Oldupai gorge. We stopped at viewpoints and toilet bushes and finally arrived at the campsite just before dark. Tents were arranged in a circle as a defence against curious wild animals. There was rain in the distance but it is actually difficult to believe it is the rainy season. Everything is green and the grass is very tall, a great hiding place for all the animals – oh dear! There was no campfire and the cooked dinners are always tasty and welcome even though very little exercise is done

Bird and Deer on Safari, Tanzania

140

during the day. Lunch was at the viewpoint of the crater, a convenient time to change the punctured tyre. There was another puncture later and I am not sure whether this is more likely due to a reckless driving style. Although not that authentic, we visited a Masai village, watched the traditional jumping dance, the school children and people selling spears. I recorded some good portrait shots. James from the group kissed one of the Masai girls and there was some reaction, a friendly response. One of the girls sitting opposite me on a camp chair is from Manchester, works for Trailfinders and I just cannot remember her name at the moment

Serengeti (Ngiri Camp), Tuesday 13th March

Activity begins at daylight with a simple breakfast. The light is perfect in the early mornings for spotting deer, giraffe with their heads hidden in the tree foliage, cheetahs far in the distance, gathering of tour jeeps and birds on the picnic tables. The heat is fine as after four months my body seems to have acclimatised to warm weather. I no longer use sun tan lotion and do not miss having a regular shower. It has been a relaxing 2-hour lunch break giving me a chance to catch up, ready for the afternoon game drive. The drive itself is still enjoyable even without wildlife as the scenery is still spectacular. Baboons and giraffe wander in and out of the camp.

I am trying to remember some of the animals. Lions are the most interesting and you can be quite close. At the river there was a decaying hippo that looked like a pink rock, being eaten by crocodiles – what a horrible smell! The other hippos were too far away for a decent shot, even with an eight times optical zoom. The campfire made a real difference to sleeping temperature but I was still cold for the last few hours of the night. There was talk of different customs in marriage and relationships and after a few beers talk of breaking wind. We stopped at the posh lodge in the rain for coffee and tried to guess the cost of the cheapest room ($300).

Serengeti (Ngorongoro crater), Lilongwe, Manyara National Park, Wednesday 14th March

I have so many shots of giraffe. I am not that great at spotting wildlife and usually notice the congregation of jeeps indicating something of interest ahead. We never got close to cheetah. Some of the group had an early morning balloon flight and we set off for the crater. Although I have been there before, the crater is always different with animals all over the place. Lines of zebra and some wildlife either keep their distance or run away from approaching jeeps. The deer

Lazy Lion and Tiny Deer, Tanzania

Watchful Deer and Elephant Road Hazard, Tanzania

and antelope seem to have got used to the jeeps. A fellow tourist could not stop laughing as we followed the steep road out of the crater with long drops – a genuine sign of fear. I rushed to use the flaps on the netted windows of the tent as it had started to rain. The chance to clean up in a shower was as welcome as the beer in the bar but there was no water in the pool due to renovation. I charged my camera batteries in the back office and was ready for more wildlife action.

Manyara to Arusha, Thursday 15th March

We left our tents to be picked up later by local staff and deposited bags in one of the rooms before starting a game drive. The path was much more forested with baboons and even elephants blocking the road. The small Dik Dik deer were gracefully arranged in a group, full of large watchful eyes. I am writing from the familiar Masai camp with a chandelier made from drinking glasses. After the morning game drive there was an opportunity for some shopping where I haggled for a full 30 minutes for a cheap t-shirt with Mzungu ("White Man" in Swahili) on the front. I bought a bowl, necklace and small mask. The drive back to Arusha was quick and one of the cans of beer in the cooler left behind seems to have rusted and developed a leak. The tipping of the drivers has finished and we are going to a local restaurant for an Indian barbeque later. It must be just the shaking about on the Land Cruiser that is enough to build up an appetite.

Arusha to Nairobi, Friday 16th March

Last night's dinner was at an Indian street barbeque restaurant with plenty of spices. I did not have the energy to stay long in the bar. Again I had to rush to close the tent flaps when the rain began. There was a whole pile of bicycles in the campsite belonging to a group cycling from Cairo to Cape Town in about four months, including a blind man on a tandem. Our tour reduced to four people with the rest taking a long bus journey to Dar es Salaam. The customised t-shirts that some people ordered seemed far bigger than the specified size. I was ravenous for the large pizza meal in the local shopping centre in Nairobi and the retail environment is such a contrast to the bush. The pre-arranged taxi did not turn up so we ordered another back to the hotel. I am so spoiled by the hotel and am forced to downgrade tomorrow to a cheaper one closer to the centre. I am writing from the bar and tomorrow I can theoretically eat two buffet breakfasts as Andy is leaving very early in the morning. I have a completely different impression of Nairobi this time, influenced by this hotel, its location and visiting modern shops in a shopping centre. I am staying here so long because there is only one weekly Wednesday flight to Madagascar. I hope I can find enough to keep me entertained for four days in the city. I need to check out as late as possible to make the most of this comfortable environment. I enjoy watching the different style of foreign adverts on TV.

Nairobi, Saturday 17th March

The buzz of a mosquito prompted me to unknot and deploy the net in the middle of the night. After the buffet breakfast I transferred my photos to a USB memory stick. The lost property department did not find my pants left in the room from my previous visit but I hope they make someone very happy. Today I feel a bit paranoid about malaria and I assume that if you have the disease that it is obvious that you have caught it. I am beginning to imagine mild symptoms of the disease. I transferred to the cheaper Terminal Hotel, a short walk from the centre of town. My Mzungu t-shirt is receiving a good reaction of smiles and laughs as I walk through the city. I did originally intend to walk to the National Museum but ended up snoozing and doing a circuit of downtown. I stopped for a meal at a corner restaurant where someone offered to buy me a drink but I refused (my general policy with drinks from strangers). I found a café and cinema. I began to feel more comfortable and distracted from the dangerous image described by the guidebook. I replaced my lost pants at a shopping centre opposite the hotel. I will heed the advice from the book about not walking after dark, even short distances although I should be ok to reach the fast food restaurant on the corner of the street.

Nairobi, Sunday 18th March

After a relaxed breakfast across the road and a barrage of questions from the taxi driver about my itinerary, I set off for the National Museum. I must be of such an age that people think I have lots of money. I noticed someone was following, looking down when I looked back and seconds later there was a hand in my pocket. Because of my deep pockets he did not get purchase on my wallet and then he quickly disappeared through the wall, which was actually an opening for the sewer channel. Apart from shouting in anger I did nothing. Next time I feel I may be more violent, however irrational this seems and generally lack of action is never seen as damaging as it always has only speculative consequences. As the workmen further down the road said, the pickpockets were just too lazy to do any work. The policemen's advice was to "box them". The main passive defence against pickpockets is the redistribution of money in multiple pockets. I carried my camera in a plastic carrier bag. I was less affected by the incident as it is my second time. The museum past the

Boulevard Hotel was closed for renovation and I was in no mood to pay eight times the price compared to a local for entry into the snake park. I wandered back, internetted in an office block (a home away from home), relaxed with a coffee and then watched the film "Dreamgirls", the early showing before it gets dark. It is likely I will go and see a film tomorrow too. I do not seem to suffer from loneliness as much as other people and am quite content looking at the sunlit high-rise downtown view from my third floor room. There is no point in getting angry at mosquitoes or pickpockets. A more sensible approach is to take preventative action – repellent, net or even invest in malaria research.

Nairobi, Monday 19th March

I am effectively killing time here in Nairobi without experiencing anything uniquely Kenyan. Every so often I have to do my travel chores (burn and send a photo CD, postcards). I had such a small amount of Tanzanian money left (about $10) and was stung by the transaction fee. I was looking for those forehead LED camping lights but without success. I walked towards the Hilton to catch a Matatu (minibus) to a shopping centre to the west of town. There were more white faces there. In big cities I seem to end up looking in shops and entertaining myself in the cinema. So if everyone was rich would they converge to a Paris Hilton lifestyle? I am now taking my anti-malarial medicine regularly. I suppose when there is not much happening on the travel front it becomes a time for introspection: What a joy it is to wake up and get up when my body wants to. I feel generally quite satisfied and not in need of anything.

Nairobi, Tuesday 20th March

I guess it is a fact of life here in Nairobi that you have to take taxis at night, even for short distances. I have just come back from watching a film about Idi Amin. I did not do much in my last day in the city apart from consume entertaining media. I updated my site with a couple of photos although at the first place I could not ftp as it was disabled at the router level (I could log on and make a connection but not transfer data). The only plan was to wander around the centre of town, looking at shops and anything else that was interesting. There always seems to be bus chaos in the Hilton area. I narrowly missed being gently bumped by a van while trying to avoid a motorcycle going fast on the inside. The Kenchic place on the corner has become my regular for half a grilled chicken. The smartness of the streets in Nairobi is variable.

Baboons in Tanzania to a Ranomfana Shop, Madagascar

Nairobi (Kenya) to Antananarivo (Madagascar), Wednesday 21st March

I had to get out of Nairobi, past the gloomy crowds of people waiting for buses to get to work. There was a fancy café at the airport where I had breakfast and also where I have about 14 hours transit time before I return to London – I will miss my mp3 player which is currently broken. After changing to the adjacent exit gate at the last minute and some turbulence on the way I arrived in Tana (Antananarivo). The brick buildings looked familiar and reminded me of the poverty level in Central America. I was followed by a crowd to the money exchange – a little surprise: There is a new currency called Ariary, which is worth five times the old FMG currency I was expecting. Changing currencies so often recently I find it easy to adjust and understand a value translation. There were more children wandering the city streets. No room at the first choice so I had a short walk to a hotel nearby just as it was beginning to rain. I braved the steep steps to a local café. No-one reacted to the short power cut so it is probably a regular occurrence. The bathroom has no toilet. I just need to firm up my schedule tomorrow with advice from the tourist information place. Two nights here and I need to think about heading down south to the national park and then to the south-west coast, flying back and giving me plenty of guard space in case there are problems with the flight and I need to return by land. The Malagasy language sounds a bit Portuguese to me.

Antananarivo, Thursday 22nd March

I admired the panoramic view at breakfast on the top floor of the hotel and quickly noted any useful information from the French copy of a travel guide to Madagascar on the table. After travelling for a while you develop a sense of moderate scavenging for resources. I bought my single air ticket from the south-west back to the capital (after missing my ticket queuing slot), sought advice from tourist information, walked around town by the lake, remained in the combined post office and internet place for longer due to heavy rain and drank. The frequency of approaching hawkers and begging children is high but not aggressive or persistent. Antananarivo is quite an attractive town with traffic pollution not as bad as I thought it would be. I bought a cheap LED forehead lamp for later in my next trip. The city is quite hilly with steep steps connecting different areas. It is easy to speak French but it is quick comprehension that is difficult. I am taking a "Taxi Brousse" down south tomorrow which is a generic term for some kind of public transport: it could be a lorry, car or a minibus. I felt comfortable walking around town. I reserved my last three nights in Madagascar in the popular hotel just down the road past the steps. I will have a full three days at the end of my stay to investigate the capital thoroughly. In places classed as high risk areas after dark I tend to do little in the evening. My nomadic lifestyle seems quite normal now.

Antananarivo to Fianarantsoa, Friday 23rd March

I had so much trouble remembering the six syllable destination today. Entering the southern transport station was chaotic as two people sandwiched the taxi on each side, hoping to persuade the driver to take me to their bus service. The process was painless, buying a ticket, exchanging it for a seat place ticket with mobile sellers holding boards of sunglasses, lighters, toothpaste, torches, calculators and other little bits. After an hour of waiting the journey began, a long one, about 8 hours in total, finally arriving in the dark. The countryside on the way was very cultivated with rice fields, pleasant villages on the hillsides and not much forest. The waiting taxi drivers respected my request to wait a few minutes as the luggage was being unloaded. Again I am unlucky with the first choice being full but the second choice right in the centre of town close to restaurants may be better. The taxi driver left me his number hoping for repeat business tomorrow. The big room with wooden floor is comfortable. I do not think that they have many guests. I am feeling quite fat after a full meal at the Panda restaurant. I just need to figure out tomorrow's logistics: how to get to the lemur park and whether to stay in the adjacent village – it should not take too long to figure out. The twisting route with loud music and video in the minibus was quite tiring.

Fianarantsoa to Ranomafana, Saturday 24th March

It was sensible for me to wake reasonably early to secure transport but I did not feel like it. The owner of the hotel showed me the building plans of the hotel he is currently building in my destination town of Ranomafana. The transport system works like this: a spotter sees a foreigner walking to the taxi Brousse station with baggage, asks about their travel plans and receives a commission from the conductor they lead me to. The system works. An hour seems the average time to wait for the minibus to fill up and go. We sailed past the park entrance and straight into this small town where I secured accommodation with attached restaurant that felt as if it only opened up for me. I had a guide for the lemur walk and we eventually spotted some. They behave a bit like monkeys and sloths and with shelter from the canopy there is little light to take a decent photo (my flash is not powerful enough). After 3 hours walk through the forest I was expended and needed the carbohydrates back at the restaurant. I feel I have a rough idea about lemurs and a visit to the capital's zoo may be my source of close-ups. This is the largest forested area I have seen so far in

Dragon Fly and Baby Lemur, Madagascar

Madagascar. It is a warm night under this double bed mosquito net. I am having too many negative thoughts about work. The bed is long enough for me. Are baby leeches cute when they try and suck your little toes? No! I applied insect repellent quickly.

Ranomafana to Fianarantsoa, Sunday 25th March

I decided to return to Fianarantsoa and after waiting a short time in the centre of town with a helper (who enquired about places on a passing minibuses) I was soon back in the main town. Most people on the minibus seemed to be carrying babies. I apologised for not having one. I secured my room with a small back-and-white TV and walked to the Haute Ville area with views near the church, surrounded by kids who acted as guides describing everything of interest in the area. I felt quite comfortable walking about on this quiet Sunday with most places closed. After my circuit and walk to the eastern side I returned to rest my feet. How am I going to do the Everest Base Camp trek if I am tired after 3 hours of slow walking? Although there were lots of poor people living on the street, I felt comfortable. The combined internet and gift shop around the corner was run by a French bloke addicted to surfing and jazz music – the speed of the connection was frustratingly slow. The adjacent restaurants were closed so I headed for the lights to where locals seemed to frequent - often a good sign. I have an all day bus journey tomorrow so need to rise reasonably early.

Fianarantsoa to Toliara, Monday 26th March

I spent all day on the bus again but it was interesting and eventful all the same. It is often difficult to separate the transport part of travel and the more formal tourist site experiences of travel. I had coffee with the friendly hotel owner after a sleepless night – too much coffee last night. I knew I had a long minibus day ahead of me and as before, a helper directed me to a bus that was leaving very soon in the direction I was going, to a place called Ilakaka (I cannot find this on a map!). In return for help, buying a coffee for breakfast was appropriate protocol. I commented that he had more coffee but it was just the effect of the bowl, compared to a normal small coffee cup (as was demonstrated when they gave me a replacement bowl and transferred the contents). The bus broke down leaving a trail of oil down the road - an opportunity for some macro photography of insects. A replacement vehicle arrived, roof luggage transferred and we were soon on our way after about a 90-minute delay. The twisty roads transformed to straight roads along green grassy valleys. It seems to be ideal motorbike country. Maybe the point of all the military checkpoints near towns

Lemur and Cart, Ilfaty, Madagascar

Comfortable Lemur, Ilfaty, Madagascar

is more to do with early warning of any coup attempt rather than anything to do with traffic regulation. After a stop for traditional rice and chicken, we continued the journey. The valleys expanded to grassy plains to the horizon with rock outcrops and a gradual yellowing of the grass. The intermediate destination looked a bit primitive with people staring at street life and the buildings principally looked like a collection of sheds. I was lucky to catch a connecting crowded minibus to my final destination of Toliara, receiving directions from a friendly soldier. The last part of the journey was at night with a warm breeze, passing people walking in complete darkness and gathered at the roadside in villages, just chatting and playing. I knew the higher quality hotel (with art on the room wall) was just around the corner but it does not prevent offers of pousse pousse or the Madagascan rickshaw. I am relaxing just near the live music and writing my journal in a hotel restaurant for a change. It is a bit late so I am actually on my own here waiting for my food but I do not feel too exhausted.

Toliara to Ilfaty, Tuesday 27th March

I took the pousse pousse (Rickshaw or man powered cart) from the centre of town after walking around a bit. My luggage was on top of a minibus before I had a chance to make a choice – but unfortunately it broke down with clutch problems later so I had to jump on the crowded converted lorry, sitting on a full beer crate – this was my chicken bus. A helper escorted me to various hostels. The higher temperature here down south meant I needed to hydrate more often. I stopped at an inn that had some baby lemurs and I later returned to take some more good photos. The Mora Mora Place was right on the beach and I am writing from bungalow No 9, a pleasant hut with mosquito net and light bulb. A parrot entered my hut and wanted it as a nest and would only leave reluctantly – it landed on my head. I walked along the beach to the dive place and arranged diving with South African Richard. The sea is calm. I eventually found "Chez Freddy's" for a smoked fish starter and Zebu (beef) kebabs main course and crème caramel and on-the-house coco rum to finish – really excellent and delicious. The infrastructure had taken a step down with fences and huts made from branches of wood and sand roads. The people in the village are super friendly.

Ilfaty, Wednesday 28th March

I found out that the dive club organiser did not decide to settle here but was actually stranded – his boat broke down many years ago. The visibility was poor descending the anchor rope but surprisingly improved near the sea bed. The

Tortoise Art and a Quiet Beach, Ilfaty, Madagascar

Ilfaty Shop and Beach Activities, Madagascar

Ilfaty Fishing Boats and Chicken in Antananarivo, Madagascar

tanks were aluminium and so much lighter than usual. I saw my biggest shoal of yellow snapper ever, a group consistently around a particular spot. The salty nuts in a little wooden bowl have arrived. I snoozed most of the afternoon. After paying for the two dives with my emergency money (there are no cash machines) I decided to just laze for the remaining two days here, taking photos with perhaps a walk and swim. Maybe the same parrot returned to raid the sugar bowl in the bar area at sunset. One mosquito managed to penetrate the net last night. After a super calm morning where the sea resembles a lake it is a little windier and cooler now. The fresh grilled fish at lunch was absolutely superb and the dinner in the usual place is far better than I could normally eat. It feels like a little corner of France.

Ilfaty, Thursday 29th March

I have been changing countries every ten days on average so eating at the same restaurant for the past three days is quite consistent – although I always sit in a different place as the owner noticed. After breakfast with a gecko for company I walked left at the t-junction, past cow carts and cacti. I visited the tortoise conservation area with guide and saw the fat baobab trees, a bee's nest and tortoises of various sizes. I still need to take a good photo of the bus-lorries. Walking to the right of the t-junction (south towards Toliara) was less interesting. There are only hotels, restaurants, basic food stalls, bicycle shops and I discovered a hairdresser – a simple life. I did not have many Ariary left so was toying my budget between another dive, souvenirs and food – food won although there was room for some token miniature souvenir pots. The dive owner totally underestimated the value of the US dollar. Tomorrow will be more of the same, winding down my time in Africa. They offer free rum here with a wide selection of flavours (for example coconut and ginger) a great idea for drinking lots of rum.

Ilfaty, Friday 30th March

I am not sure whether it is a good thing or not but during this year I will not be employed or used by anyone, have no responsibilities for anyone but myself, not be dependent on anyone and have no examinations at the end of the period. It is shockingly enjoyable and will be quite an achievement. I tried to capture the relaxing beach life with photos. In the village I was immediately surrounded by children who wanted their group photo taken but my main interest is authenticity without posing. A couple of boys were racing model sail boats. Sand is accumulating in the bungalow. I return to civilisation tomorrow, perhaps nowadays defined as a place with an internet connection. Even in my short time here the locals know and call out my name. The shell vendors were quite persistent. The geckos seem to project a friendly persona. I am sitting at my dinner table at the Mora Mora for my last dinner here, listening to interesting drumming over the speakers and looking at a dark sea with a single bright star in the sky. I am sure the atmosphere here improves with a lot more guests. The moisturising insect repellent works but has a slight warming effect.

Ilfaty back to Toliara, Saturday 31st March

I am back in civilisation but the electricity is temporarily off at the restaurant as I write this under candlelight. I left my key at reception and waited for my mystery form of transport back to town, this time an old French car, following the least rough sandy trail to the centre of town. I booked the place recommended by the Ideal Hotel owner and headed for some lunch in a cavernous restaurant. When I finished my meal all shops were shut down for the midday break so I did the same back at the hotel. After cleaning myself up and finding out what was going on in the world I poussed (rickshawed) to this restaurant. I am retracing my steps back to the capital, allowing myself plenty of time for any potential delays. I was down to my last few Ariary. There was a low maximum limit on the cash machine but enough for me to feel comfortable over the last few days in Madagascar. Apart from one persistent beggar I felt comfortable walking around here – you just hear the regular offer of pousse transport, which feels like a mild form of slavery in use. The heat is bearable. There was some misunderstanding at the internet café where I almost paid too much (the price was still in the old less valuable currency). I can see why people can become interested in Africa and travel in Africa: once you accept the level of poverty and all it implies the culture is there, rich and open to exploration. I must admit I am enjoying myself!

Toliara to Tana (Antananarivo), Sunday 1st April

Strangely I could not sleep so turned on the TV and watched the end of the latest Bond film in French. I was too early for my flight but time soon passed and I quickly arrived and was installed in my hotel. On the way I had a philosophical conversation with the taxi driver about the luck of being born in different countries. I sat on the terrace for a short while waiting for my room to be made ready. There are often tourist ghettos that stay open on Sundays and I found one so I could relax. I really enjoy updating my website and in a controlled cyber cafe setting up a batch file to trigger dos for FTPing is easy. I am now updating about every two weeks and it no longer feels like a chore. It was dark when I finished and remember if you cut across the grass you may get your feet muddy. The restaurant I intended to visit was privately booked so a takeaway pizza was my choice today. I am writing from the same terrace I rested in earlier with noisy street activity below. Begging is frequent here and I am becoming accustomed to it having little reaction apart from feeling minor irritation and inconvenience - they beg for the food I am eating at the time. The moon is full and my legs are resting on the bamboo coffee table,

Antananarivo, Monday 2nd April

Museums are often closed on Mondays as I found out from the guidebook so I postponed my touristy intentions until tomorrow. All the specialist tourist shops had western prices. I enjoyed cheap fancy cakes in a patisserie and just walked down the shady side of the street. I searched for a music CD for a while and peered in the popular hi-fi and video shops. My activity boils down to sipping coffee and more internetting. The drop in temperature from 35°C (down south) to 27°C here means that I am far more comfortable.

Antananarivo, Tuesday 3rd April

I have 14 hours to kill in transit at Nairobi airport on the way back to London. I visited the palace area for a panoramic view of the city (with a chicken perched on the railing) and the museum close by containing royal objects. I found the familiar Haute Ville area and desperately tried to find something to buy to use up my Ariary currency. There was a street full of jewellers. It was quite an aimless day. A street seller tempted me with some shirts without advertising logos. The only task I have left to do is pack my small rucksack which should not be difficult as I have been quite restrained with my shopping. The point of my trip was to do and see as many interesting things as possible. My African trip is almost over. Another success! I feel very healthy. I have to get up at 3.30am but I am sure I will survive. There were lots of businessmen in the Chinese restaurant earlier. The rain in the afternoon meant that all the street sellers sheltered under the covered archways in the centre of town. Kids were using some kind of fruit as a keep-it-up football. As I was walking along I was offered TV aerials, vanilla sticks, a lobster, a stringed musical instrument, a drum, music CDs, pornography, DVDs, apples, avocados, lemons, lychees, maps, postcards, magazines, newspapers, shirts, belts, mobile phone accessories, plastic bags, carved figures and toys, wooden printing stamps, table cloths, socks, a taxi ride, vests, sunglasses, a service to change money, offered coins to change, batteries, torches that did not need batteries, spices, paintings, bracelets, books and watches. I could even buy communion hosts in a religious shop if I had wanted to.

Jump forward to the next trip.

3. London (England) to Dubai (UAE) transit to Amman (Jordan), Sunday 22nd April 2007

It is 3.00am and I have just arrived at Dubai airport and the place is buzzing. Most airports at this time in the morning are tranquil dark places but here all the shops are open and it is almost crowded under bright lights and large TV screens.

I had about two weeks staying at my parents after the African trip, enough time to switch off from active travel and confirm the final round-the-world trip. I felt the need to visit different areas of London that I had not seen for a long time and combine my visit with travel chores such as obtaining my Indian visa, email queries, internetting and repairs. Watching DVDs filled my time. I fitted in a visit to my sister's new house in Shropshire with large garden and fields and almost human pet dog called George. Living with my parents (aged 80 and 70) proved not to be too traumatic but it would be inaccurate to describe my state as very relaxed. Anyway, I have set off again, roughly at the halfway point of my year of travel and the prospect of experiencing a new place still excites me. Now I feel a bit tired but have enough energy to explore before my flight departs in 4 hours. The carpet here has a wavy sand dune design.

There must be something about the climate that makes the traditional food of falafel, fuul (mashed beans) and hummus (all containing chick peas) and sweet tea a fitting experience. The transfer from the airport by bus and taxi seemed painless and I sensed that there was more honesty with the people I met, less of a feeling that I must always be on guard and that I am not being ripped off all the time. The taxi was less than fifty pence from the bus station to the downtown Cliff Hotel, down an alleyway but well signposted. I was lead by the friendly proprietor to the room with balcony at the end of the corridor. As I had not slept on the journey I had to catch up with about 4 hours. I made an effort to walk to the city lookout point and grab a meal. I feel comfortable walking the streets, far more comfortable than in Africa. I have limited time in Jordan but there should be enough time to pick out the highlights of Petra and the Wadi Rum desert area.

Amman, Monday 23rd April

I had little energy today and managed to exit the hotel at around 11.00am. There was a religious pamphlet in my hotel room with the aim of converting people to Islam. I visited the Roman amphitheatre and small museum on either side. Jordan seems far more organised and modern than Egypt. The brighter sun was

Amman Amphitheatre and Petra Landscape, Jordan

not too warm as I sipped my syrupy coffee. I wandered along the main shopping streets, stopped for lunch down a side road, (restaurants always seem to be upstairs) had pastry sweets, internetted and slept back at the hotel. The low season means that joining organised tours with a minimum of four interested people is unlikely.

Amman to Petra, Tuesday 24th April

I roused myself and again left the hotel late at around 11.00am. The taxi driver took me to another bus station for buses heading south and I was soon on my way. Everything seems so civilised and organised, particularly with the reference point of Africa still in my mind. I was greeted with the usual lies, anything to encourage my patronage of a particular hotel. I walked down the hill to the Petra entrance, dropping my stuff at a mid-range hotel close by. It was late afternoon so I had to make use of the time and briskly walked to see as much of the carved ruins as possible. Many people were assisted by camels, horses and donkeys. The young kids wandering about learn by mimicking what the foreign tourists tell them. It was quite a climb to the monastery and far reaching views. Most of the stalls were in the process of clearing up as I ascended. All the restaurant places near the entrance have inflated prices so I whizzed back up to town for traditional Arabic food. The walk back was cold and I wallowed in the relative luxury of the hotel room, quiet, isolated, smart and with breakfast included. I bought a two day Petra ticket and will hike along another path tomorrow. There is no rush but it feels like a warm up for the Nepal trek. I managed about 4 hours of walking today!

Petra, Wednesday 25th April

There was a group of Italians at the buffet breakfast. It is a rare event to stay at such a pricey hotel. What a contrast it is here at the Cleopatra Hotel, far away from the overpriced ghetto near the entrance to the famous site. I am close to town where the locals eat and shop. I walked to the sacrificial point and followed the steep steps down towards the museum, a little less strenuous than yesterday's walks. The site was busier during the day with lots of school parties, mainly Muslim girls excitedly trying their first camel ride. I taxied to town and unusually followed the drivers recommended choice (which was also mentioned in the guide). The hotelier was super friendly and helpful and as I always seem to land on my feet, I hooked up with an Andorran couple (Laia and Joseph) going to Wadi Rum, implying that a ridiculously early start tomorrow was no longer necessary. A jeep safari in the famous desert would also have been prohibitively expensive if I had not found someone else to share the cost.

Tea Break and Tourists, Petra, Jordan

I met an American family with young children on a long tour which included four months in India. The hotelier was engrossed in an American TV series which included lots of actors who looked like fashion models.

Petra to Wadi Rum, Thursday 26th April

The late morning taxi from Petra was painless but the misty (or sandy?) skies meant that there was no point in doing a jeep safari without being able to see the views. It is important to clarify exactly what transport is included in the price of a tour. I am writing from inside a light brown tent at the Rest House in Wadi Rum bathed in light from my newly acquired head torch. Joseph happens to be a mountain instructor (climbing, skiing and canyoning) and I was given 5 minutes to decide whether I wanted to join them for a grade II mountaineering hike. The answer was yes! There was one point where it was wise and cautious to be attached by a safety rope and I managed my first abseil (rappelling) of 40 metres. I felt a little uncomfortable in the makeshift harness and I did sweat a lot but it was on the whole an enjoyable experience. The tent has a proper mattress and sheets. After 6 hours of strenuous climbing, hiking on sand and lowering myself down narrow crevices I made it back alive. It was quite an unplanned adventure experience that I feel good about. The late dinner at the large table went down well and I listened to the ambient Spanish conversation for a while. I believe the heat from the sun will force me out of bed in the morning.

Wadi Rum Camp, Friday 27th April

All the walking the previous day ensured a good night's sleep, sometimes slipping between the two mattresses. After breakfast we tried to call our contact without success, during which another very tame and unconfident offer from another guide was rejected. We waited for our guide after a shopping trip at the place nearby for some cheap traditional sweets. We were joined by English and Turkish girls and visited some of the famous Lawrence of Arabia spots with a convoy of Spanish vehicles. The desert itself was the star. A walk to a bridge rock formation took in total about 2 hours while the others had lunch. More rocks, dunes, a small bridge that was easy to climb to and finally sunset at the camp. More people joined the campers, Italian, Spanish and even a Slovenian couple. With entertainment from an Arabic guitar and drum, the evening passed with jokes and a great meal cooked in a hole-in-the-sand oven. The sky was not clear enough for a view of the stars. The Arabic entertainer mentioned that he did not like the Japanese because they stayed up all night looking at the stars chatting away.

Wadi Rum and "Dinner is Ready!", Jordan

Wadi Rum to Aqaba, Saturday 28th April

There was a whispering breakfast at the camp before everyone had woken up. The Italian couple kindly offered us a lift to Aqaba. Due to a special holiday weekend the first five hotels I tried were all full. I returned to the original accepting the offer of a place on the roof which later changed to a room with a balcony view across to Eilat in Israel. I visited the small castle and museum near the tall flag past the beach with fully clothed women bathers. I met up with the Andorran couple for lunch and dinner, sitting at the corner window with the curtains flapping away in the wind. We walked through a more modern part of town with lots of tables outside and many ostentatious Hummer vehicles. I write this on the following day from an Amman hotel with a pneumatic drill working outside at 8.30pm. Rather a short entry so I will try and remember some fragments of conversation. Joseph does not like sand! He had also been to Mali and recalled an incident where some boys caught a rat, cut it open with half a tin can and as the guts were spilling out they licked their lips. The Andorran couple had originally met at school.

Aqaba to Amman, Sunday 29th April

My guidebook is at least four years out of date – bus stations sometimes move. There was a customs point (inside Jordan and not at the border!) where everyone got off the bus and bags were briefly searched. The journey back to the capital was around 4 hours. The taxi driver at the bus station could not speak English so phoned someone who could, passed me the mobile phone so I could declare my destination and then I passed it back to the driver – a novel use of mobile communications. It is a good policy to try different hotels so I tried the tall, recently renovated 6th floor Farah block with a tidy room. Near the mosque as I was taking a picture under moonlight some bloke guessed I was forty years old. The building noises did not stop until about 1.00am. The shawarma or wrapped chicken kebab was just not enough to eat. I am becoming addicted to Jordanian sweet biscuits or dessert, an important part of a male dominated culture?

Amman to Jerash to Ajlun to Irbid, Monday 30th April

After breakfast sitting on the chairs covered in plastic, I set off to Jerash by shared taxi then bus. The Roman site had the usual columns and an

Minaret and Restaurant View, Amman, Jordan

amphitheatre where schoolgirls were making lots of chanting noises and drumming with a bagpipe player. The contrast between old and new was photogenic. I could not be bothered with paying for the Roman re-enactment of battle and chariot racing. As I headed towards the bus station I accepted an offer of a taxi to Ajlun castle perched high on a hill. The driver had studied English in India. A couple of coachloads of schoolgirls arrived soon after and all were eager and excited to try out their English: "Hello, how are you? Where are you from? What's your name?" As I was walking back down the hill I was offered a lift to the bus station and was soon on my way to Irbid, the town centre being another short bus ride from the regional bus station. I temporarily memorised the phrase for town centre and was led to the hotel – the reception had a slight sewage smell but no matter. I was offered a cup of Turkish coffee. There is not much for tourists here apart from a reasonably priced hotel base for exploring the surrounding area. I walked up and down the street and bought some ankle supports anticipating my future need. The Jordanian people are one of the friendliest people towards tourists I have experienced.

Irbid to Umm Qais to Amman, Tuesday 1st May

They strike when you least suspect: mosquitoes. Perhaps because of the lake close by, a giant one created some islands on my back during the night. I watched some Aljazeera TV which looked familiar with many former BBC faces. There was a bloke coughing and spluttering while I was having breakfast in the laminate reception area. Writing the "north bus terminal" in Arabic on a card aided my navigation. Sleepy Umm Qais ruins were impressive because of the views over to the Sea of Galilee and surrounding area. Skilful negotiation with cups of coffee meant I bought a small oil lamp that I had no original intention of buying. Perhaps the key to negotiation is to talk about something entertaining and unrelated while making the financial part seem incidental. I waited for the bus for a while near a retarded bloke. I soon returned to familiar downtown surroundings. The hotel must be heavily publicised in Japan as there always seems to be a new Japanese person in the reception area. I replenished supplies of drink at the food shop next door to the hotel entrance. Street noise meant that I often woke up and my dreams were interrupted.

Amman, Wednesday 2nd May

Today was a rest day in preparation for a hectic one day visit to Dubai – I fly out late tomorrow but will have to leave my Amman hotel by 1.30pm. I stopped at different barbers asking for the price which varied from 3JD to 5JD to 1.5JD, a more reasonable amount. Strolling, internetting, buying food and drink with few targets filled my day. With Skype in internet cafes you can sometimes overhear other people's conversations – an American woman was having a marital crisis of trust. My body must now be 20% hummus. The locals now ask if I work here, probably because of my relaxed non-touristy manner. There were no significant events today, just ordinary living.

Amman (Jordan) to Dubai (UAE), Thursday 3rd May

I finally sorted out the right-hand margin problem with TheTravelMap.com website by removing the graphic that was slightly too wide. It is a full moon and I am writing from a relatively expensive hotel in Deira, central Dubai – not much choice. I was tempted by one last visit to Haschem's cheap food place. I had to walk across the car park to the other terminal for my flight. One of the hostesses at the passenger entry point was stunning. Four rows of taxis serviced four ordered queues of passengers. My driver from Ethiopia transported me through a super modern city to within 100m of my hotel by a pedestrianised street and after asking for a discount the rack price was reduced by almost a third. My Stomach was behaving negatively and I needed lots of water from the grocers nearby. I have a day of walking tomorrow, roughly a route through markets, dockside, across the "creek", museum and neighbourhood. At the moment I have little idea about what to do later in the evening but I need to be at the airport by 2.00am. The evening temperature here is a high 31°C so water will be my first purchase tomorrow morning.

Dubai, Friday 4th May

I feel exhausted sitting on the red cushioned airport chairs, mainly due to the heat. I am very early for my 4.00am flight but the only other option was probably another mall. The main activity here is shopping, entertainment and restaurants. My room rate did not include breakfast – no matter. I set off in the heat, an exhausting heat if you are not acclimatised. I was so surprised that Dubai seems to be full of Indians! It feels like Delhi and the Arabs probably own all the businesses. The area of town I was in effectively closes until late afternoon on a Friday. The tour bus was too expensive (equivalent to three significant taxi journeys) so I rejected that but the map I picked up gave me a better idea of the tourist sites around town. I sped to the famous sail-like skyscraper with helipad called "Burj al Arab" but entry is prohibited without proper dress and a reservation, rumoured to be US $1700 a night. There was a mall nearby and I walked there searching the shade of palm trees. The mall was indeed luxurious and I treated myself (this does not happen often enough) to

Modern Dubai and Busy River, UAE (United Arab Emirates)

dinner at the Dome. I sped back to the museum along the skyscraper avenue - really quite impressive. The heat was making me irritable as I was walking along dodging the crowds. A couple of hours at the airport in an air-conditioned environment feels like a heavenly respite. I cannot believe there are so many watch shops and cannot understand how the street of gold shops stays in business (Indians love gold). The cool silent atmosphere of the cab is a complete contrast to the noisy crowded streets. The light was perfect when crossing the creek by small boat back to the Deira side in the late afternoon. All the floors seem to be polished marble. Dubai is amazing for a city that did not really exist twenty years ago, a truly Arab and Indian Hong Kong.

Dubai (UAE) to Delhi to Kathmandu (Nepal), Saturday 5th May

I managed to sleep by the escalator for over an hour and soon left the space age Dubai airport. Sleep was a priority on the flight. Administration of transfers at Delhi seems just chaotic with no real confidence that the multitudes of staff know what they are doing: Multiple stamps of tags, tickets, scribbling notes on boarding passes, unnecessary questions and so on. I had the luxury of someone waiting for me at Kathmandu (initially with a very small sign) and of course a high standard hotel for an organised tour. I was sharing with Billy, a South African and the rest of the group were Cheryl (Canadian), Tony (Scottish), Clint (ex South African living in England) and Aaron (American). Due to lack of sleep my eyes felt heavy during the briefing and I was asleep in my room by 8.00pm

Kathmandu, Sunday 6th May

I walked to the bakery down the road for a cake breakfast which was open but with a closed sign on the door. The city tour was a quick taxi ride up to Monkey Temple, walking back though the city, past a central water source and fruit-laden bicycles to Durbar Square with sellers of intricate Buddhist philosophical designs. I could not resist returning to the area I stayed in during my visit thirteen years ago, Freak Street and the Snowman Café. It is interesting to see the developmental changes with more buildings and cars. Kathmandu is such a classic young backpacker destination. I stocked up on adventure gear – sunglasses, light rain jacket, rain trousers and sleeping bag liner. A meal of steak at an Irish owned restaurant was pleasant. I relaxed drinking coffee looking down from a balcony at the street life in front of the landmark Kathmandu Guesthouse. There was light rain. I stocked up on trekking food and suntan lotion. The communal evening meal was traditional Nepalese with many Indian-like dishes, accompanied by dancing and a band. Back at the hotel I had to

Dubai Airport at 3.00am, UAE and the Monkey Temple, Kathmandu, Nepal

Monkey Temple, Kathmandu, Nepal

separate my gear into stuff that I would carry while climbing and stuff that the porters would carry. I was entertained by the National Geographic channel about early aviation.

Kathmandu to Lukla (2860m) to Phakding, Monday 7th May

After an early 5.00am meeting in the lobby, the flight to Lukla in the mountains on a sixteen-seater plane carved a path through the valleys. There was a turn at the last minute with little clearance between the wing tip and the cliff with all the mountain peaks appearing slightly above the level of the aircraft. Breakfast was a short 10-minute walk away from the airport offering a view of planes taking off and helicopters landing. The skies began to clear and the 3-hour trek to the first lodge was easy. The young guide Mila was twenty-two years of age but looked about sixteen. Ten years ago most of the lodges would have been very basic (lack of electricity and no running water) but now they are more luxurious and numerous. Lunch and dinner were pre-ordered and written in a little book. Lemon tea is very appropriate. I walked to the metal bridge and watched horses and cows crossing. A charcoal heater was placed in the middle of the dining area. There was discussion about climbing Everest, cost of tours (much cheaper if self organised), war, America and medical facilities in different countries. The walls of the room are made of hardboard.

Phakding to Namche Bazar (3420m), Tuesday 8th May

After a hearty porridge and black coffee we set off towards the bridge. With intermittent cloud the hiking conditions were perfect. The Russian group seem to be travelling at the same pace on the same route. Apart from stopping for black teas, looking at mountains and valleys, yaks, cows, porters, kids going to school, a myriad of small food supply shops, bridges, steep steps, waterfalls, streams, rivers, small settlements, we just walked for a total of about 7 hours. The steep step climbs required the most effort with muesli bars and chocolate providing a psychological and physical boost. Namche Bazar is our place to acclimatise and the steps finally lead to a high quality, smart and simple lodge. I skipped into town to consume sugar in the form of cake and fizzy drink and also to update my blog from a very high altitude internet cafe. The effects of the altitude were subtle such as an increased pulse rate to 100 bpm but thankfully I had no sign of a headache. I feel a general muscular ache but no pain. The Vaseline really helps with rubbing clothing. Lemon and ginger teas are great in the slightly colder atmosphere. It is a rest day tomorrow but we are still going for a short walk at a similar altitude.

Metal Bridge near Phakding and Namche Bazar, Nepal

Namche Bazar and Tangboche Monastery, Nepal

Namche Bazar, Wednesday 9th May

The rest day was actually a 3-hour walk. I had severe diarrhoea and had to drink some rehydration salts during the night and in the morning and take Imodium before setting off. We visited the museum near the barracks and admired the view of Everest as the cloud cleared. There was a steep climb up to the tea house near the runway and then a descent back into town. Hopefully by doing this today the walk tomorrow will be easier. I skipped lunch and snoozed then strolled slowly around town, uploaded a photo, bought functional items such as toilet paper, water and knee supports for potential problems ahead. By dinner I had a massive appetite. I feel healthy at the moment without any aches or pains.

Namche Bazar to Tangboche (3860m), Thursday 10th May

There were steep climbs during today's hike. The distant peaks visible yesterday were covered by cloud. Cheryl had aching knees and Billy was still suffering from stomach problems. Thankfully my diarrhoea has reduced but not disappeared completely. There was a mountain goat perched on top of the hill. Physically it has been easier than I expected so far. I have no aching muscles. Egg and chips was a comforting lunch. I rested by the open window of the wooden conservatory. The afternoon walk was a steady climb and a fleece was necessary. The entrance to the settlement appeared and a monastery immediately after. The lodge had a cylindrical stove heater in the middle and the bedrooms are smaller, the dimensions about the length of the bed and the ceiling around my height – maybe rooms become smaller the higher the altitude? I had two dinners and talked a little with the Utah couple who had a small device to measure blood oxygen level and pulse rate. They also played some type of bluff game called "50 cents" and made lots of noise. I hope my stomach recovers fully by tomorrow. I might take a precautionary rehydration solution. I almost forgot the visit to the decorative monastery nearby. It is noticeably colder here. Clint and Tony arrived at Tangboche at around 2.00pm, Aaron around 2.20pm, me at 2.30pm, Cheryl and Billy at around 3.20pm.

Tangboche to Dingboche (4350m), Friday 11th May

It is a battle against the effects of altitude and stomach problems (diarrhoea). Yet again I had to cancel my porridge and just drink black tea. The morning was cloudy and cold so all the surrounding magnificent peaks were covered. It does not take long to warm up during the climbs. Two young local girls standing by a wall formed an excellent photo as did odd peaks along the way that suddenly

Tangboche Monastery and Curious Children on the Way, Nepal

Everest Base Camp Trek to Dingboche, Nepal

unveiled. After a lunch break spent talking to a Dutch finance director the weather turned colder with small hailstones. My rain resistant jacket performed well as I plodded along the white path and along paths where streams were flowing in the opposite direction. There were lots of Americans at the lodge in Dingboche. After warming up by the heater I needed a quick snooze. About an hour after arriving the weather cleared and I quickly photographed the surrounding peaks. Some socks were drying on a chair and the fluorescent lights barely lit the dining room. I am writing this in my sleeping bag with two warm blankets under head torch light as the room light does not work. I do not know when my stomach will be back to 100%. Tomorrow is a rest day where we will do a 3-hour climb then return to sleep at the original lower altitude. Billy is quite brash and unrefined "f**k, sh*t, cough cough" but a lively trekker who keeps borrowing my pen.

Dingboche (4350m), rest day to Chungkung, Saturday 12th May

Today was an acclimatisation rest day. The walk was about 400m elevation to Chungkung along the valley. This was second choice to a local steep climb rejected due to the misty weather. I wore three layers: t-shirt, fleece and waterproof. The walk was a gentle rise with more criss-crossing streams but just cloudy views either side. The lodge for lunch filled with UK climbers and a couple of Frenchmen. Chicken noodle soup was an appropriate mountain lunch, giving me liquids, energy and noodle carbohydrate. Rather than carrying large amounts of drinking water I need to carry no more than a litre and supplement my hydration with cups of hot lemon at the lodges. The walk back was a complete contrast with stunning views of all the major peaks in all directions with slight cloud for a bit of dramatic effect – the best part of the trek so far and being downhill it felt easy. The intransigent fluorescent tube in the dining room switches on if you run your finger along its length. The local Nepalese were playing cards in the corner and as usual we gathered around the heater fired by yak dung.

Dingboche to Loboche (4930m), Sunday 13th May

The sky was completely clear in the morning giving spectacular views of all the peaks. As I am writing this I am shivering in my lodge bed using my head lamp again. We passed a team of people attempting some kind of world altitude record for a motorised paraglider over the peak of Everest. Helicopters with suspended loads passed through the valley. This really is the most spectacular hiking scenery I have seen. We stopped for a while at a place full of memorials to people who have died on Everest – often experienced people. I had five cups

Trekking to Loboche, Nepal

Dingboche to Loboche, Nepal

of hot lemon at lunch to rehydrate myself for the afternoon part of the trek. At the lunch stop there was a boy trekker of about ten years of age. The bloke with the binoculars speculated that the load carried by the helicopter could have contained body bags. There was also guitar music and singing at lunch. Billy offered a glucose sweet. I have now warmed up a little in my sleeping bag covered with a blanket. We climbed the local ridge and Mila the assistant guide climbed even further up. There were lots of Indians in the dining room and I was warned that India at this time of year might not be enjoyable in the 45°C heat. I borrowed the Economist magazine from the previous lodge.

Loboche to Gorak Shep (5288m) to Everest Base (5380m) to Gorak Shep, Monday 14th May

It was an early 7.00am start with a three phase trek: The first part, about 2.5 hours to Gorak Shep for a quick lunch break, a long 2.5-hour trek to Base Camp and then the return trip. The large boulder section was quite tricky and my speed slowed significantly during the final icy screed section. There was a blue tent bakery at Base Camp, full of delicious cakes and lots of mountaineers about to climb the famous peak. The weather cleared slightly for the easier return part. Reaching the base camp felt like quite a dramatic achievement and due to the gradual altitude acclimatisation and muscular build up over a period of eight days, it felt less painful than I had expected. I am having difficulty remembering the name of the place I am staying in at the moment. There are no lights in the corridors and an upper and lower duvet will help to keep me warm during the night. Health is excellent. I have another early start tomorrow.

Gorak Shep to Kalapathar (5550m) to Pangboche (3900m), Tuesday 15th May

The highlight of the whole trek happened today with the view of the mountains from Kalapathar, a strenuous 2.5-hour climb with slow black rocky progress near the peak. The weather was perfect with great views of Everest and interesting scenery in all directions – well worth the effort in reaching this spot. The descent was quick, a short break before retracing our steps but at super speed because the path was generally downhill with increasing oxygen levels. Unfortunately I received some bad boiled eggs for breakfast and later Aaron had some rancid butter. Everyone's health improved while descending. The group actually split up today with Cheryl and Billy missing out on the peak and having a head start for the return trek. I actually walked about 8 hours - a long day. At no time did I feel that I would not be able to complete the trek. One thing I forgot to mention was that the price of food and drink in the

Approaching Everest Base Camp with On-site Bakery, Nepal

Base Camp and Trail, Nepal

Trekking Lodge and the Everest Peak, Nepal

Views from Kalapathar, Nepal

lodges rises with altitude. Again I need to borrow a couple of blankets to have a comfortable night. Tomorrow's target is back to Namche Bazar an estimated 6-hour walk. When you have completed Everest Base Camp and Kalapathar all other walks and climbs should be easy. Talk became increasingly political over beers at dinner in the cosy square conservatory heated by dry yak poo. I am still amazed that I feel no muscular or joint aches and pains.

Pangboche to Namche Bazar, Wednesday 16th May

The return trip generally downhill was not difficult. Everyone was motivated to walk at a fast pace. At one point we chose a steep downhill shortcut, ready to rejoin the main path at the end of the trail. We only stopped for a lunch of vegetable noodle soup. The undulating path was negotiable, especially with greater oxygen at lower altitudes. The boys ran the last section and I arrived in good time at the final destination of Namche, despite not taking the final downward path straightaway but luckily I spotted our porters walking just a little ahead. The place felt warm and familiar and the streets were easier to climb due to our increased fitness and acclimatisation. A yak toppled over a bowl of apples on display in one of the shops. I wandered down to the prayer wheels and stream outlets. During dinner there was talk of films with Santosh our capable guide facilitating well. On the TV news they announce how many people had summited Everest that day. Later there was pool in a pub with lots of t-shirts with graffiti on the walls and ceiling, commemorating past Base Camp treks. I returned after a couple of games along dark streets to the comfortable lodge. You can easily differentiate between the people who have returned and those yet to hike to Base Camp: no heavy breathing, a suntan and generally a glowing face.

Namche Bazar to Monjo (2950m), Thursday 17th May

The super bright morning revealed great views of the town with a mountainous backdrop. It was an easy day with only 2 hours of walking. Aaron was severely sick and Cheryl was poorly too so the estimated departure time was delayed until 2.00pm. I relaxed in the café with soothing Buddha Café music. Tony bought another two fleece jackets and I bought a couple of small karabiners for attaching items to my day pack. I gave away one of my knee supports to Clint who needed it having twisted his knee yesterday. The last possible opportunity to view Everest was obscured by cloud. We crossed about four bridges before arriving at Monjo. I watched the others play cricket through the net curtains, together with an audience consisting of a fascinated dog and local children

Back to Tangboche Prayer Wheels and Namche Bazar, Nepal

Namche Bazar and Trail Porter, Nepal

sitting on the wall. The young calves played together like puppies. The toilet has a wooden latch. I really do need a shower.

Monjo to Lukla, Friday 18th May

The final day of the trek was about 3.5 hours of walking and was quite tough because of the persistent uphill sections. There was a short period of rain before the entrance to Lukla, marking the finishing line of the longest trek I have ever done. The Mera guesthouse was of high standard with a TV living room where we all snoozed and watched weird Indian adverts and a Nepalese soap opera with simplistic sound effects. The tip process for the Sherpa guides and porters was very well organised and their happy characters shone through. I went for a walk and consumed some chocolate as quickly as possible. A hot shower (shared with a large spider) helps make me feel much better. I am sleeping in a real bed with sheets and blankets which makes a change. There was some dramatic speculation over whether the flight back to Kathmandu would leave on time tomorrow which is totally dependent on clear skies. I can hear music from the bar downstairs. Some Russians were playing pool. Earlier there was heavy porter traffic in the opposite direction due to market day in Namche Bazar. No more hiking!

Lukla to Kathmandu, Saturday 19th May

I have neglected my journal duties so now need to catch up on the past two days. Wake up time was 5.00am for the flight back to Kathmandu. Luckily the weather was clear so worries about being stranded disappeared. There was a separate search line for ladies and men at the small airport. Take off was exciting as the pilots reach up for the thrust levers and the landing was super smooth. It felt good to return to civilisation and a luxury hotel room. I spent a few hours internetting, finding out what has been happening in the world and trying to encode some video. I completed the transaction for the Tibet trip and handed in my passport for immigration formalities. I had anticipated the need for a recovery period but instead feel super fit and in no need of rest. BBC World on the TV felt familiar. I cleaned up with a haircut and shave and almost forgot lunch. There was an arranged meal in the evening at a restaurant with thousands of cardboard feet hanging on the ceiling and walls, each scribbled on by successful groups that had reached Base Camp or other peaks. The army boys were drunk and the meal was excellent. I managed to negotiate the uneven pavement on the way back to the hotel in the dark. Many shops were closed today.

Near the Kathmandu Guesthouse, Nepal

Snowman Café Cakes and Street, Kathmandu, Nepal

Kathmandu, Sunday 20th May

I had a late breakfast at Café New Orleans with four eggs – the peaceful courtyard location was relaxing. I reviewed my photos on CD and sent them home. I settled for pizza just before it started to rain. My table was near a couple of American students and the woman from the happy Ohio couple that I met on the trek said hello. I could not think of anything to do apart from try the cinema a short walk along the palace wall (Spiderman 3 in English with an interval). I wandered to the local supermarket for a snack dinner and settled watching news ("Have Your Say" from Oxford) and relaxing in the room. The circuit breaker tripped in the room and was reset by removing the hotel key from the holder for at least 30 seconds.

Kathmandu, Monday 21st May

I moved to the cheaper Horizon Hotel (about $6 a night) after sorting out the video on my website. I honestly need a break from the organised group and relish some solitude. I did not plan to have five days free in Kathmandu but it just happened that way mainly to allow for a comfortable passport processing time for my Tibet permit. I have handed in my laundry and am ready to relax further. For nostalgic reasons I headed towards Durbar Square and the Snowman Cafe and yes I believe it is still the best cake place in the world – the décor is primitive but the product is excellent. I wandered back and took photos of interesting people and buildings. The phone rang a couple of times hinting that my washing was ready. I tried an Italian restaurant, each floor with a different style and explored adventure clothing shops looking at fake but functional trousers and jackets. I bought some comfort food to take back to the room. What a contrast to when I was first here. Back then everything was such a rush and I had no time to absorb the atmosphere. This time I have an easy five days to experience the character of the place. I can hear dripping in the adjacent bathroom. When I first arrived I heard lots of poor guitar music and French conversation.

Kathmandu, Tuesday 22nd May

After a cheap set breakfast in Helena's, I set off on two walks in town trying to spot interesting things to photograph: temples and street scenes and so on. It is enjoyable to be guided by a book along streets and narrow alleys that I would not have discovered by accident. I relaxed at a breezy café overlooking Durbar Square. Finally after almost seven months of travel I feel I have learned how to

Fruit Seller and Rickshaw Taxi, Kathmandu, Nepal

Metal Goods and Flowers for Sale, Kathmandu, Nepal

Durbar Square, Kathmandu, Nepal

Kathmandu Street, Nepal

relax. I stopped and looked at lots of adventure clothing but all the copies I saw were of low quality. The recommended shop was closed unfortunately for three months. Most of the sand in my pocket has emptied from my pen. There was a power cut earlier in the evening – I am not surprised judging by the condition of the street wiring (or could be due to trouble with Maoist rebels?). The first part of dinner was under candlelight. Eating, internetting and walking summarises my activity for the day. I sent emails to confirm a flight, change a flight and enquire about purchasing a domestic ticket.

Kathmandu, Wednesday 23rd May

I decided to visit Patan with a similarly named historic Durbar Square. I wandered through the busy and noisy streets, across roundabout walkways past a pond to the chaotic bus station. I was advised to stand at the exit and my helper would warn me when my bus was approaching. I felt like a local wandering the narrow streets to the historic square. I stopped for drinks at the café with a view then entered the smart restored museum full of metallic deities. The attached café was excellent but additional taxes really add a lot to the bill. I am developing a routine where the day's sightseeing activities finish around 2.00pm and then I surf for a couple of hours. I bought some fake adventure trousers. I decided to wander to Freak Street to the cheaper restaurants, under candlelight due to a 2-hour (probably common) power outage and of course a visit to the best cake place in the world was in order. To be honest I am probably less sociable and less sensitive compared to when I visited here thirteen years ago. Phoning home from a booth was fine.

Kathmandu, Thursday 24th May

I retreated into a virtual surfing world paying little attention to my real surroundings apart from when needing to eat. I managed to upload my first video file to YouTube which serves video files efficiently. I felt comfortable sitting alone at restaurants as my mind was elsewhere. I thought about what jobs I might be good at. The mixed pedestrian and vehicular traffic feels normal now and I am becoming an expert local. How am I going to make my great internet fortune?

Kathmandu, Friday 25th May

The drifting continues for another day. I had two appointments, one for a briefing (unusually just for me) and another to pick up the air ticket and my

Snowman Café and Patan, Nepal

Patan, Nepal

passport. I need a token amount of Chinese Yuan and only a few places seemed to offer this currency. After a slight increase in stress I discovered the Dream Garden, a relaxing place near the multitier fountain. There was some disturbance on the street with lots of soldiers with sticks and the remnants of teargas in the air. I do not know what it was about (demonstrations against the king?) but I imagine it is part of everyday life here. I have not had such a lazy time in a long while. I still feel anger at some remembered work situations and negative feelings that I should have purged by now. Compared to trekking I have a relatively easy trip to Lhasa Tibet to look forward to beginning early tomorrow morning. Apparently there are fifty-two people in the group and it is buses instead of jeeps – less intimate but hopefully entertaining. My hotel room without fan seems to trap the day's heat. I will leave packing for tomorrow morning.

Kathmandu (Nepal) to Zhangmu (Tibet, China), Saturday 26th May

There was a gathering outside the tour office early in the morning. Most disappeared to do bungee jumping and white water rafting. I sat on the back seat of the small bus feeling quite excited about the trip. Breakfast was on a shady veranda – there are always delays with such a large group. At the border there were chaotic scenes with a scramble to offer porter services. Everything at the border is done so inefficiently. We even had our temperature measured with a gun-like device pointed at our foreheads. Everyone scattered to their three, five or six bed dorms. I am sharing with Dutch and Spanish. Following the snaky path up the mountain we found a cheap food place and ordered food by pointing to Chinese words in the guide and enjoyed pronouncing the names. You pay such a premium for an English text menu. The internet place was packed and I verified that the BBC News site was blocked, although you could still see the main general BBC page and news blogs. I have the bed by the window. Often large lorries negotiate the narrow road through town. The group is big enough to include some interesting faces - a Nepali-Thai girl.

Zhangmu to Lhatse, Sunday 27th May

I am trying to cast my mind back to yesterday's 14-hour bus journey! The early breakfast just after 5.00am consisted of watery eggs and brightly coloured sweet jam. It was pitch black outside and no-one knew what was happening or where the buses were (a short walk up the hill). I sat on the back seat. The road just inside Tibet was under construction which meant slow progress and an extremely bumpy ride. At one point we had to exit the bus and rocks were placed on the muddy tracks. There were steep climbs and descents with lots of

Kathmandu Garden Calm, Nepal and Tibetan Peak, China

prayer flags at the cold and breezy peaks. Lunch was in a one street town where many owned carts pulled by small tractors. The dining style was similar to Nepal with everyone sitting at "desks" facing inward. There was a ten-second sand storm when all the hats blew away. The journey continued with views of Everest in the distance from a brown sparse landscape. Apparently it is possible to drive directly to the Tibetan side of the Everest Base Camp. The grand decorative entrance of the hotel flattered the basic dorms behind it with no electric light and disgusting toilets – I do not think it is healthy talking too much about toilets but they deserved a special mention. I lost my appetite with the soup and yoghurt presented in front of me and I walked to the most expensive looking hotel in town in search of a loo – the electric power was switched off while I was in there and on the way back I threw up – again due to the sudden change in altitude rather than anything I ate. High altitude I theorise makes the brain work slower and when I eventually found the correct dorm I managed to sleep, despite the slight headache.

Lhatse to Shigatse, Monday 28th May

It was a much shorter drive today, only about 150 km along smooth roads. A Hebrew phrasebook was found on the bus. A planned visit to the local Lhatse monastery was cancelled because of some failed linkup with a Vietnamese group. At the large town of Shigatse we briefly stopped at a bank to change money and then split up into doubles at the two top hotels in town. What a contrast to last night's shack! There was some mix up with the room where the initial two singles were later deemed invalid and I was forced to share. Francois and Narissa (French guy and Thai-Nepalese girl) seemed to be getting along fine romantically. The hotel was a short walk away from the monastery, past a group of Tibetans sitting on the pavement drinking tea and alcohol. Quite a few old characters were spinning prayer wheels as they were walking along. The monastery itself was architecturally interesting with many chapels, paintings and tombs. The bright drying sun was a contrast to the dark candlelit interiors (lit with a tray of candles) and the prayer circuit behind the main statues. It is impossible for such a large group to keep together. I stopped for refreshment at the shaded entrance and returned to the room. I have skipped lunch so should have a good appetite for dinner. Some feral children temporarily grabbed my plastic bag containing a soft drink. I was kept company at the restaurant and joked with a stranger at the other end of a mobile phone line.

Primitive Transport between Zhangmu and Lhatse, Tibet, China

Prayer Flags and Shigatse, Tibet, China

Shigatse Monastery, Tibet, China

Shigatse Monastery and Yak Butter Candles in Gyantse, Tibet, China

Shigatse to Gyantse, Tuesday 29th May

It was a short drive but a long wait at the barley grinding house. I had to negotiate my included breakfast in the morning. My dodgy toe meant I had a slight limp – it seems wearing sandals put a strain on my right toe. The air-conditioning overnight is not good for the throat. I rushed into the taxi and joined the rest on the bus. The flour making place was driven by water wheels. We soon arrived at a good standard hotel. They all seemed to have a large courtyard. I had a light lunch at the café next door, in front where I had dinner later and where I am writing this now. I wandered to the internet café and then walked with the large group to the monastery – interesting architecture but not as fascinating as the monks dancing performance at 5.00pm. The watching crowd was the spectacle and very interesting to photograph: old faces, prayer wheels, children and monks. Amazing! I spent about 2 hours taking photos. There was some kind of castle monastery high on the hill that I originally thought we were going to visit. I chatted to Steve returning to the UK from living in Australia and to others from this varied and large group.

Gyantse to Lhasa, Wednesday 30th May

Again I have neglected my diary duties and I now struggle to remember the details. Some random observations include: many of the dinner tables are round and have a central turntable to make items accessible; the government buildings (I assume they are government buildings) often have two soldiers standing at the front in green uniforms; many people near or in the monasteries make themselves continuously prostrate in an act of worship to Buddha. The room I stayed in was an annexe just off the entrance to the hotel. There was a stop at some small sand dunes and an unscheduled 2-hour stop rumoured to be due to speeding. The restaurant was overwhelmed by the sudden appearance of bus loads of tourists. The umbrella was moved to provide more shade against the strong sun and I was surrounded by Israelis eager to talk about travel. The old lady continuously refilled our paper cups with Chinese tea. There was a stop to look at a carved Buddha in the rock face before finally arriving in Lhasa. The widely circulated picture postcards of Potala give the wrong impression of the town. They suggest a small town dominated by a palace whereas the palace is actually a structure surrounded by modern tall buildings in a large city. Briefings turn out to communicate simply the time for breakfast and time for departure. Although the hotel restaurant with a view of Potala was reasonably priced I walked into town along the main shopping street to another restaurant. I enjoyed my food next to a French table. Francois and Narissa again discovered my restaurant location. I limped home and entering the Hotel met Paul and joined the group for some beers in a bar run by a Dutchman. The evening

Offerings in Gyantse Monastery, Tibet, China

Gyantse Monastery with Young Spectator, Tibet, China

Gyantse Monastery Band with Audience, Tibet, China

Gyantse Locals enjoying Dancing Monks, Tibet, China

ended with a cab back after midnight and everyone received a phone call offering a massage service.

Lhasa, Thursday 31st May

The Jokhang Monastery was amazing! Initially the inside was too crowded so we delayed entry with a circuit past incense smoke and walked in between practising pilgrims. The red-robed monks and other brightly dressed monks were seated in rows, receiving offerings and chanting in low voices. As this was happening there was a chain of people snaking through the small chapels, worshipping the statues and refilling the yak butter candles from thermos flasks they were carrying. It is amazing to be surrounded by such religiosity. Incidentally I am amazed that I have managed to keep up a journal for seven months. The view from the floor above the monks and towards the main town square was spectacular. Just when I wanted to take a few photos a large cloud appeared. It is a full moon. The hotel room along a very long corridor is of top quality, not really a backpackers but of a luxurious travel standard. In the afternoon we visited Potala Palace initially up many stairs. This was the chief residence of the Dalai Lama until the 14th Dalai Lama fled to Dharamsala, India after an invasion and failed uprising in 1959. I ended up following a Chinese tour group through all the gold and jewel encrusted altars and rooms – internal photography was prohibited. The exit was at the back of the palace and I walked past the prayer wheels and park back to a familiar area of town near the hotel on the corner. I walked to the internet place, a room full of hundreds of monitors with most people playing games. They were not really geared up for foreign surfers but after some persistence and patience I was shown to my seat. I rushed a yak burger in the Dutch bar and cycle rickshawed back. I can see moving neon signs through the hotel window.

Lhasa, Friday 1st June

The interesting thing about the Drepung monastery we visited was the kitchen: the size of the pots, the monk sitting at the desk in the corner and the shafts of sunlight visible in the smoky atmosphere. The other monasteries were the usual Buddhas, piles of money and yak butter candles. I wandered to the department store and stopped for posh lunch in a comfortable sofa. As is often the case when travelling in a large group, others from the group appear in the same restaurant. The afternoon trip was to the Sera monastery the highlight of which was the debating monks in the courtyard – very animated and noisy. I did my photo duties and stopped for Chinese food - one restaurant was completely full and referred me to another. I kept bumping into the Israeli bloke. I had

Captivated Audience, Gyantse, Tibet, China

Jumping Monk, Gyantse Monastery, Tibet, China

Gyantse Girl and Watching Monks, Tibet, China

Gyantse Crowd, Tibet, China

difficulty trying to find something to buy with the last of my Yuan currency. Some little observations I forgot to mention yesterday: the floors of the monastery are often slippery at the entrances due to spilled yak butter and there is a mat in the hotel lift with the name of the day of the week. I do not believe there are shopping bargains in Lhasa. Much of the traditional stuff is cheaper in Nepal.

Lhasa to Kathmandu, Saturday 2nd June

Paul left the room early to catch a bus and Julia was feeling a bit rough and tired and needed waking up to go on the bus. I believe the only international flight into Lhasa is the one to and from Kathmandu. There was a great view of the Himalayan range on the way. Visa re-entry was fine and the airport was just as chaotic as usual. I reconfirmed my onward Delhi flight in the adjacent building. I returned to the same Horizon Hotel with friendly receptionist but this time to a different room. The flight made me tired and I was forced to snooze. The postal place was closed and I spent the time in a virtual world. At dinner I sat near some young Indian tourists, some of whom tried to reposition the fan. I listened to the live jazz band with no piano and watched a movie in the smart and busy Kathmandu Guest House. My foot is still painful and quite annoying. The fan in the room requires a manual spin to start it up. I am feeling the effects of moving from an expensive to a budget hotel and the contrast between being immersed socially and suddenly being alone. I bought my singing bowl – it rings like a bell when a wooden mallet is rubbed around the rim. The sellers offering their brightly coloured zipped bags are persistent.

Kathmandu, Sunday 3rd June

My space pen has now broken as it could not cope with the strains of being in a pocket. I have bought some tiger balm for my toe so hopefully I will have a more restful night and a quicker healing process. I did not feel confident doing a lot of walking today so I ended up doing very little. In dark Helena's I had the set breakfast which has gone up in price since I was last here. There was vacuous wrestling on the TV. Internetting, bookshops, newspapers and coffee filled my day. The Lonely Planet site has recently become more sophisticated and the Delicious site is such a great idea, harnessing the world to enhance a familiar function. I was caught by the rain and there was another power cut. Luckily I bumped into Julia at the internet café and dinner was much more entertaining than sitting on my own – she told me the story of being robbed by her porter on the Everest trek. I believe I will experience more of the same

Prayer Wheels and Scenery, Gyantse, Tibet, China

Jokhang Monastery, Lhasa, Tibet, China

Jokhang Monks, Tibet, China

Offerings at Jokhang Monastery, Lhasa, Tibet, China

relaxation tomorrow, partly due to my dodgy foot. I have little desire to do more shopping and do not really need anything apart from a new pen.

Kathmandu, Monday 4th June

Again I am frustrated by my lack of full mobility. I just have to be patient. Basically the day was the same as yesterday. I booked my future Sharm el Sheikh air ticket. I discovered the aroma shop. I look like a Buddhist monk with my short and comfortable haircut. I had fun reading the LP website. There is no continuity in my sentences! More people are offering me marijuana in the street and some faces are becoming very familiar as I have been here a long time. It is so luxurious to have time to relax. I seem to have lost my $100 luggage address tag.

Kathmandu, Tuesday 5th June

I made an effort today to visit a tourist site: Pashupatinath, a Hindu temple about 5 km from Thamel. It just started to rain when I arrived and a stall keeper kindly offered a sheltered seat and a book to read. The monkeys were quite entertaining as they playfully jumped into the river. Sadhus or holy men seemed to be strategically positioned for good photos. There was some serious business with a funeral cremation happening on the other bank with much grief on show, finishing with plumes of smoke from the pyre. The initial asking price for coke was five times the normal restaurant price. I taxied back and acquired some US dollars from the bank. I also discovered a forgotten small stash of Nepalese currency which will make my final day a little more comfortable. I was entertained by a Mayan adventure film at the Kathmandu Guest House and rickshaw drivers on the way back asked if I was interested in girls. I avoided the puddles on the dirt road leading to the hotel. I feel I have "done" Kathmandu and if I were to return it would be for nostalgic reasons. I have really had generous time here to just live and spend time doing things I would do back home. I still spotted some familiar faces from recent trips and enjoyed just people watching from the bakery balcony. Food as always was excellent. The monsoon season is about to begin here.

Kathmandu (Nepal) to Delhi (India), Wednesday 6th June

Waiting at an airport is as good a writing opportunity as any. I am sitting at Delhi airport with 45°C heat outside – more bearable than I thought as it does not seem that humid. I had an easy morning buying a souvenir - a Thanka

Jokhang Monastery and Potala Palace, Lhasa, Tibet, China

Jokhang Monastery with Worshippers, Lhasa, Tibet, China

Jokhang Monastery and Potala Palace, Lhasa, Tibet, China

Drepung Monastery Kitchen, Tibet, China

mouse mat and perfume. I am quite privileged to have travelled so much and some airports appear just hopelessly inefficient, giving the impression that none of the staff really knows what to do. Perhaps both Kathmandu and Delhi fall into that category. There were multiple checks for everything at Kathmandu; even a hut was set up at the bottom of the aircraft stairs for a last minute passport and boarding card check, bag search and body search – the third bag check. The government must think that there is an imminent coup. The "delay is deeply regretted" announcement is heard often on the public address system at Delhi Airport. I found the Continental Airlines office but had to wait 90 minutes for the office to open – I need to change the date of the New York to London flight in July. I have had my ice-cream and coffee and there is only half an hour to go. I enquired about booking a train but there is no easy communication with a central point of contact. Another bag of sweet lassi might be appropriate. I sorted out my Continental flight and one American girl was happy being reunited with a lost camera. The roads into town from the airport seemed to have improved and were full of cars. There were less chaotic human beings populating the pavements. I was sold hard but rejected a Rajasthan trip, a man with car for about $40 a day which does not sound much by UK standards but is quite expensive by Indian standards. I am open to sharing but if nothing happens in the morning I will probably just do it myself and see what happens. Paharganj itself has not changed much and maybe the roof restaurant at the top of a hotel is more hygienic due to its greater distance from rats and mice. The little boy playing internet games did not want to go to bed.

Delhi to Jaipur, Thursday 7th June

The brothers still tried to persuade me to accept a car-driver tour in the morning. I chose the significantly cheaper government bus option which was super air-conditioned all the way. There was a short 20-minute stop for lunch a welcome break as I had skipped breakfast. The window of the bus was hot to touch. It is definitely off-season here in Rajasthan, mainly due to the high temperature. After a 6-hour bus journey I autorickshawed to the hotel and just had to rest. I booked a half-day city tour for tomorrow and frequented the restaurant on the top floor of the hotel. The room is decorated in a luxurious manner and I even have a TV for Indian news, now showing a feature about cinema multiplexes. I need to firm up my route soon but tomorrow I will just enjoy what Jaipur has to offer. I am hoping for some interesting photos. Normally when you open a car window there is a refreshing breeze. Here it is like switching on a convector heater. The ceiling fan is essential.

Drepung Kitchen, Tibet, China

Debating Sera monks, Tibet, China and Return to Kathmandu, Nepal

Pashupatinath Temple with Monkeys, Kathmandu, Nepal

Pashupatinath Temple with Sadhu, Kathmandu, Nepal

Jaipur, Friday 8th June

I rushed my French toast and joined the Austro-Finnish couple for the half-day tour of the city. The scale of the city is such that it would be impractical to walk, especially in the heat. All the sites were being renovated including the astronomical observatory – note to self: it has been a long time since I visited Greenwich. There were textiles and weapons in the palace and a dance class. There was a group of women dancing outside a temple with an accompanying brass band. Marble seems to be the building material of choice. I wandered around the Amber Fort in the heat, managing to drink five litres of water in total on the tour. I must admit I was not stunned by the style of the architecture – it is just nice and elaborate. All the buildings in town are pink, a lighter shade compared to the palace. I discovered the common room with internet access. The heat is a significant factor in my travels here, tending to reduce my activity and confine me to the hotel unless there is a strong reason to venture further. The cold showers seem hot here! I have half decided to miss out Jaisalmer as it is too similar to my recent desert experiences.

Jaipur to Pushkar, Saturday 9th June

A communal air-conditioning vent in the window suddenly switched on last night but it was too noisy so had to be switched off again. The rickshaw driver with the dwarf nose took me to the bus station and I boarded the ordinary bus. I was satisfied with only a cold bottle of water in my hand. It was a crowded bus and I do not know if it is racism but I felt people were invading my space and less aware of their immediate environment. There were friendly exchanges and chats and I soon arrived directly to Pushkar. The locals play a "game" with arriving tourists encouraging them to cast a flower in the lake in exchange for a donation. This happened later with a more traditional and legitimate guru. I walked to the hotel with a balcony view room at half the price I was expecting. Things were casual at check-in being ultra low season and I still have not signed in formally. I walked along the main road to a rooftop restaurant and along the Ghats (broad flight of steps used by bathers) by the lake. Monkeys, bathers, cows and people were to be observed. The marble steps are too hot to walk on in bare feet. I treated myself to a shave. I believe I have drunk about seven litres of water today.

Pushkar, Sunday 10th June

Well the water has stopped flowing in the bathroom - never mind. I had breakfast in a restaurant undergoing renovations. The temple nearby was

Pashupatinath Cremation and River, Kathmandu, Nepal

Sundial and Palace, Jaipur, India

Large Vessel Reflection and Dance Class, Jaipur, India

Amber Fort Architecture, Jaipur, India

engaging, people ringing a bell, making offerings, monkeys and a general curiosity towards me. I joined the other westerners for lunch in the restaurant. It is fun discovering a smaller town by foot. I am hoping that my body is adapting to the heat. Strangely a lower fan speed feels cooler. The internet café tried to charge me two hours instead of one so I had to spend quite some time looking indignant before receiving my change. I have decided to limit my travels to two further cities - Jodhpur and Udaipur as going up north would make the schedule too hectic. I felt a bit aimless about my future job in life and settled on surfing to try to provide the answers. So it was time to bury my head in a book and a scientific one about chaos should keep me occupied for some time.

Pushkar to Jodhpur, Monday 11th June

I had to wait a while for the boy to appear in the hotel so that I could pay for my room. Many Indians stare at me in a curious way and this may be partly due to my height (and of course my western features). The transfer at Ajmer was quick and I had enough mineral water so I was happy. I decided on a hotel near the "action", namely near restaurants rather than in an isolated place more than a kilometre walk away in this heat and increasing my dependency on hotel food. I do not mind lack of outer windows if it means a cooler room. I headed to the clock tower shopping area and the world famous Omelette Shop with friendly owner. The saffron creamy lassi with lots of curious locals was next. It was heaven to cool down in the air-conditioned internet café where locals were playing Counterstrike. I had a Thali (selection of different curry dishes) at the restaurant on the corner and walked back alongside traffic chaos to my green hotel room. I had only arrived in the afternoon around three and so managed quite a lot in that time. I flicked through the TV channels and kept the super dim light switched on.

Jodhpur, Tuesday 12th June

I switched on my neon light to signal morning light. Breakfast with super sweet jam on the roof of the hotel with some other hotel resident started my day. I autorickshawed to the palace fort and did not realise that the more direct route was only for pedestrians. The audio commentary tour was great – I have never used one of these before and was truly impressed. Some rooms were quite spectacular and there were great blue views of the old town. I walked down narrow streets past the bloke with a currency collection, back to the clock tower and usual touristic entertainments - a bit of a repeat of yesterday. The rickshaw bloke outside the hotel was really annoying, offering help to the post office which I did not need. The cooled restaurant opposite the station was pricey by

Pushkar Lake and Residents, India

Pushkar Temple and Café, India

Pushkar Side Street and Famous Jodhpur Omelette Shop, India

Saffron Lassis and Busy Street, Jodhpur, India

Indian standards but I appreciated the conventional restaurant atmosphere. I managed to update my site at the downstairs internet café at the hotel which in low season was opened especially for me.

Jodhpur to Udaipur, Wednesday 13th June

What can one say about a journey on local buses? I got on at 9.30am and got off about 6.00pm. It was often crowded so I had to put my bag on my lap. I am seriously considering flying back to Delhi to avoid a long bus journey or train journey retracing my steps which always seems less fun than the outward part. The room I am writing from in Udaipur has a marble floor and view of the lake. Again I feel comfortable in this place as it is pedestrian friendly. The rooftop restaurants are deservedly popular and have amazing views (and this one has a friendly well-fed dog). The ATM looked closed but it soon opened. Surprisingly I do not feel that tired from the all day bus journey. The hotel by the lake looks like an evolved backpacker place with everything a traveller might need in spacious surroundings. I am beginning to like courtyards and roof spaces but they may only be practical in hot countries. The people seem friendly and I have a feeling that I am going to enjoy a relaxing couple of days here. My reading book beckons. An eccentric Englishman with a beard dominated the café.

Udaipur, Thursday 14th June

Power failed a couple of times last night and in the morning. I had breakfast in the courtyard of the guest house next to the French couple. My only aim today was the City Palace Museum a short walk away. All casual conversations with people in the street are a means to tempt tourists to buy something. The palace was fine. I am trying to think of the most outstanding thing about it but it was just a palace! All the reputable restaurants seemed to be closed in the afternoon so my walk to the bridge was not fruitful. I swapped my chaos book for another and booked my Delhi Jet Airways flight for Saturday – Indian Airlines were apparently on strike. Some biting insects (not sure if they were mosquitoes) seemed to have bitten my feet five times in the space of a few minutes while I was surfing the net in the hotel – soothing balm was applied. Tomorrow is an extra day for exploring Udaipur because I have treated myself to a flight rather than a tiring overnight trip. There was no compromise with the dinner menu – I ordered everything I wanted.

Street Chaos, Jodhpur, India

Udaipur Temple Contemplation, India

City Palace Museum, Udaipur, India

City Palace and Temple at Night, Udaipur, India

Udaipur, Friday 15th June

I met a varied group at breakfast: a girl who grew up in Hong Kong, a tall English girl working for an NGO, an American who spoke many languages (!) and a French girl who swore a lot and talked a lot about rape. My only plan was a bit of shopping in town. I had wanted to visit the museum around the corner but was told it was better to come in the evening when there was traditional dance. I bought some Indian shirts and a silver ring. There was a gift shop full of ornaments but nothing appealed. I just read "The Inheritance of Loss" book in the afternoon. There was some public event happening in the museum so I delayed my entry. One dance involved balancing lots of pots on one's head. The group convened in a rooftop restaurant and the dominant conversation subject seemed to be Aids and sex. I did some late night surfing and felt quite satisfied.

Udaipur to Delhi, Saturday 16th June

I know all I had to do in the morning was have a relaxed breakfast and it would soon be time for my propeller aircraft flight back to Delhi. I must keep reminding myself how privileged I am to be able to travel so much. Delhi had cooled since I was there last and I soon installed myself in familiar surroundings. The small multiplex nearby was strangely not showing many films so I will have to think of something to do tomorrow. The chicken roll place around the corner was friendly and cheap. I experienced no real hassle while I was walking about. The internet is mostly a comfort but it can be useful to know when not to become further involved in discussion forums that lead nowhere. It is unfortunate but I will probably always associate Hinduism with shit on the streets. I cannot imagine the Paharganj area becoming a smart and tidy neighbourhood anytime soon. I foresee more of the same activity for tomorrow and Monday with research into my next destination of Malaysia. I need to find something to do in Delhi that I have not done before. I am going to lose myself in my book this evening.

Delhi, Sunday 17th June

As I was asking in reception for a recommended place for breakfast Yelena (studied anthropology, an Israeli Russian) asked if she could join me and ended up being a travel companion for the whole day. Yelena from New York had a Nikon SLR and enjoyed taking snaps of everything, posing locals – a great camera. Delhi was now in the rainy season so the National Museum seemed a sensible choice to wait for the weather to clear. Again the audio commentary was fun and the curry buffet at the top floor canteen was excellent. We

Udaipur Museum Dancing, India and Baby Orangutan, Kuching, Malaysia

wandered along the half-closed shopping street west of the Red Fort, swinging around to the mosque, climbing the minaret for great views with a rickshaw on the way back – the "driver" had to walk and push along the steep parts. Dinner was in the cheap café. There were stories of being over charged for visiting sites. She left early the following day to go up north. The pink walls with stark fluorescent lighting lack a homely touch. Even with supreme confidence you cannot persuade people to like you. I stayed up late finishing my book, contemplating the important things to contemplate. On balance everything is fine.

Delhi (India) to Kuala Lumpur or KL (Malaysia), Monday 18th June

I withdrew from the isolation of the hotel room. I could not find a suitable book to swap with in reception. I avoided the puddles and mud on the way to a high breakfast with many familiar Koreans appearing. There were intermittent downpours and I was just happy to sit. The bloke in the internet café asked where "Moscow" was, his label for the tourist from Russia. I looked at photos on the internet and had my daily dose of news and discussion. I had no trouble doing very little until my prearranged taxi arrived although there was a long walk to where it was parked due to the busy market day making the street inaccessible. I have had lots of experience of airports and Delhi is just not conducive to the free flow of people making them feel comfortable in going from one place to another. This is perhaps similar to an American visiting the UK and noticing lack of refinement in service or choice. I was happy to leave the chaos.

KL to Kuching (South Sarawak side of Borneo), Tuesday 19th June

I did not sleep on the Delhi to KL flight more than 20 minutes and ate all the food presented. I was kindly offered a seat with more legroom and the stewardess commented that I looked like I was going home. There was a Bollywood "Mission Impossible" film shown on the plane. The efficient process at KL including an airport terminal train quickly delivered me to the correct gate and on to Kuching. Malaysia is civilised and reminds me a bit of small town Australia. I rang the bell at the padlocked B&B door – cheap and fine. My body needed recovery sleep of 2 hours.

I walked to the river and was really glad to see modern infrastructure – simple things like just being able to cross the road in a controlled manner. I passed through many shopping centres and stopped for delicious seafood. The slight rain was cooling and not irritating. I am quite close to the equator here but

Orangutans Feeding, Sepilok, Malaysia

Sepilok Orangutan and Kinabatangan Scorpion, Malaysia

coming from stifling Delhi it feels comfortable, especially with the air-conditioned malls. I will explore the museum and sites in town tomorrow. There are more tourists here but I have not really talked to any yet. The B&B requires removal of footwear in the corridor area.

Kuching, Wednesday 20th June

My body needed rest. I discovered the bread and spreads in the breakfast room and promptly returned to my room, continuing to snooze until early afternoon. How had my perspective changed since yesterday? There was some rhythmic drumbeat knocking on the adjacent wall. I walked to the museums, across the footbridge but did not enter the children's dinosaur exhibition. Everyone was so incredibly friendly and flirty. The gift shop woman, the canteen staff, everyone wanted to have an extended conversation. I followed the narrow roof overhangs to shelter from the rain on the way to the tourist information centre to enquire about transport to sites and parks - they were so non-committal. I was curious about the place with lots of karaoke booths. The cinema was on the ninth floor. I had low quality food from a recognised chain and found the menu pricing as complicated as mobile phone charges – there was time dependency, an "a la carte" price, an add-on price, a blurring of quantities (a different pizza size for the offer) and diluting of food value with so much ice in the drink. I have been spoilt with so much fresh high quality food for my previous dinners that I must remind myself that factory food should be avoided. I was indecisive about when and what to watch at the cinema. The traditional cheap Malaysian restaurant ignored me. There is less noise and more apparent clarity in my general thoughts.

Kuching, Thursday 21st June

I responded to my alarm, walked along the wet, recently cleaned corridor and had an easy taxi ride to the orangutan rehabilitation centre. There was a short walk to the feeding area, near a shop and video presentation room. At the appointed time a large orangutan (I originally wrote gorilla!) started to feed on the fruit placed on a raised platform. More orangutans arrived near the open area after most of the crowd had left. The economical bus waited for me for the return journey. There was food, postcards, a trip across the river to the fort near a massive building site - a large concrete temple. After a Fantastic Four film it was soon time to return to my orange room. Today I was unfocused - less able to discern movement in a complex visual field spotting wildlife and slow at resolving or making sense of ambiguity. Green tea is great. The plan tomorrow is a coastal national park with large–nosed monkeys. I did not realise the place was so Muslim.

Kuching, Friday 22nd June

I walked to the bus station with a lack of signage and officials, found the No. 6 and sat down. The BAKO national park is a peninsular a further boat ride away and it made sense to wait for more people to share the cost of the boat. A school party arrived and departed, lead by an Irishman. The raised wooden walkway lead to the headquarters for registration. I took the Proboscis monkey trail, a short boat ride to a beach further along the coast and a walk back along the jungle trail. The school party were making slow progress along the first trail and swam in the sea at the second beach. I forgot to mention the basking crocodile which reminded me of Costa Rica. There was a strange circular rainbow effect around the sun and the heat was relentless. I did see a fleeting glance of a monkey as I tramped back towards headquarters. The small monkeys were causing havoc at the canteen stealing all the food inside and cans of drink from the tables outside. There were wild pigs in the grounds. I had to wait with German Anais as the others were an hour late. I wore my sunglasses to shield my eyes from the storm shower. A plastic sheet was provided for shelter on the boat. Back at the pier a wild cobra was caught and put in a cage. The blokes on a cheap package tour staying at the Hilton suggested a shared taxi back which was a good idea. It made a change to be entertained at the Chinese restaurant and the bar with black sofas with a beer of course.

Kuching, Saturday 23rd June

I broke my sandals yesterday and most shops did not have my size 11 (UK) 12 (US) – but I eventually found a replacement. I did my usual coffee with newspaper and magazines, felt relaxed and continued my shopping tour buying unnecessary novelties. The PC in the internet café seemed to delete the photos on my Sony memory stick and the session turned into a frustrating 5-hour marathon looking for free software to recover the lost data. Some were costly and only informed you that there was a cost when you were just about to save recovered data after a lengthy bit scan sequence. The software was slow and I eventually found something that seemed to recover most of the pictures. I had forgotten how frustrating computers can be and I needed to escape fast. Food helped and I returned to my room. At least one mosquito bugged me last night and the situation seems worse with the fan off. Some days you feel as if nothing goes right and nothing is easy. Simple things like changing batteries in a torch, a broken laser pointer, everything is frustrating and you feel clumsy, with a lack of concentration even though objectively with hindsight nothing really negative happens. I swapped my reading book again. Oh well, I have a change of scenery with my flight further north tomorrow morning. I phoned home on a phone with wall mounted digital display but felt uncomfortable talking in an internet café. I did not realise Singapore had a completely separate currency to Malaysia. The people continue to be friendly.

Kuching to Kota Kinabalu (KK), Sunday 24th June

Maybe it is the lazy tropical weather that is making me fill my journal every two days. Malaysia seems to have autonomous regions where it is necessary to pass through identity checks when travelling domestically by air. I was glad I was flying – it would have meant days on a bus otherwise. It is terrible that I cannot even remember any details about the airport so it must have been just normal, no quirks and no glaring inefficiencies. I was still in India mode questioning if the local taxi driver was sure he had reached the backpackers hostel - according to the map there was a one block navigational error but the identifying sign was clear.

I have wiped off the spicy prawn sauce so I can continue writing. I was installed as the only person in a four bed room. The owner was selling the tours in a way that felt he was really trying to accommodate your tastes and budget. I ended up deciding to visit a jungle lodge and the orangutans, rejecting an expensive excursion to turtle islands. I sought the coolness of the shopping centre on my initial stroll around town. There were some islands in view just off the coast. Walking around shopping malls is part of the culture here. I bumped into the hostel owner and almost did not recognise him. The Sunday stalls around the hotel had disappeared on my return. I walked past the food stalls at sunset and was attracted to the buzz of life in the enclosed cool areas – a cinema near the bowling alley on the eight floor of centre point. I enjoyed a culturally familiar humorous cartoon.

KK to Sepilok, Monday 25th June

Breakfast was early at 6.00am on the top floor with fried eggs hidden under the metal tray. Unusually I was surrounded by touts at the bus station: five blokes encouraging me to go to a particular tour bus. I chose the company associated with the least number of encouraging or intimidating touts. I felt detachment from the environment. I relaxed and half-snoozed in the reclined seat and it was soon time to disembark. The first choice hotel due to volunteer residents and cleaning could not accommodate me so I ended up at the Jungle Resort with wooden walkways. The 4-bed family room (a dorm with no bunk beds) was fine as I predicted no one else would arrive and I would have the room to myself. A noisy friendly cat was stationed near the door. I was just in time for feeding and this time I captured some playful orangutan action shots. On the way there I even managed to snap a pair of butterflies, unusual as they normally follow such a random path making them impossible to photograph. A group nearby in the darkened restaurant are playing with white dominoes. Some old bloke with grey hair wanted to show me some flowers to photograph. A group of girls from Denmark arrived in the adjacent room. The high humidity suppressed any energetic tendencies. The staff here speak Malaysian except for the English words "good night". The resort is fine as it is here to serve a specific purpose, namely observation of orangutans. I feel relaxed writing my diary with few concerns about knowing what I am doing over the next two days. I still have enthusiasm for travel after eight months, the key being that it is essentially organised so that within a few days there is always something interesting to see or look forward to. The fish in the tank have been fed and I am almost ready to say good night myself.

Sepilok to Kinabatangan, Tuesday 26th June

The roar of rain on the corrugated roof was deafening over night. I found out that organised scheduled transport to Kinabatangan would be too late. I rejected another look at the orangutans in the dim grey morning light and set off to the meeting point called Medan Selera by public transport. I did not have to wait long. I received conflicting advice at the junction but soon found a minibus going my way – the roof was a bit low. I was soon met by the wildlife lodge representative and continued through palm plantations on a bumpy road with a final transfer by small boat. The huts were primitive and there were two fighting cats. There used to be more but rumours were that a giant hungry lizard had paid a visit. A film crew from Discovery Australia happened to be staying there. Unfortunately the main generator was broken so there was no light or cooling fan during the night. On the safari boat trip (with Australians Dave and Emily) we spotted comical proboscis monkeys jumping among the trees, a shy crocodile, various birds and a large lizard (but not a komodo); On the night walk, sleeping birds, bugs and a gentle scorpion. I could sleep after the noisy generator had been switched off.

Kinabatangan to Kota Kinabalu, Wednesday 27th June

On the early morning 6.00am boat safari we saw very little. Spotting wildlife is a matter of luck. The light was perfect. I retraced my route back to KK with a twisting tiring route towards the end. The bus ticket man was hoping not to give back any change. I returned to my familiar bunk room surrounded by comfortable civilisation rather than noisy rainforest in a humid atmosphere where one's t-shirt never quite dries out. Apart from holiday chores (transport, hotel booking and photos) I can not see myself doing much tomorrow. A visit to the bar with Tasha (who helps to look after the hostel) and some late TV with the British Prime Minister changeover on the news finished the evening. Mobile phones are called hand phones here.

Kota Kinabalu (KK), Thursday 28th June

It was an admin day: update site, burn photos to CD, buy Singapore guide, investigate quicker flying options to Singapore (Malaysian Airlines only have a presence at the airport), see a Transformers film, walk around cool shops and relax with newspapers in a café. For people that do not need to work I can see how easy it is to fritter away a day. I bought some disk recovery software to try and retrieve my corrupt memory card. The fan is clattering and the temperature is bearable.

KK (Malaysia) via KL to Singapore (the city in the country of Singapore), Friday 29th June

Oops! I accidentally took my room key with me which is the first time this has happened so I hope to post it back while I am in still Malaysia. It was quiet in the morning. After an hour's delay the flight left for KL. I had missed the 15:40 shuttle to Singapore and had to haggle to get a place on the 17:30, passed between the ticket counter and the transfer counter. As soon as you enter a big city expect to have to reserve in advance for places and transport that may be fully booked. Even the airport shuttle was fully booked for an hour so I took the efficient train with RFID charge card. I was disoriented leaving the underground station and seemed to only ask help from people who claimed poor eyesight and an inability to read a map. I was too late with my reservation (with only one dorm bed left for the following day) and tried five more expensive hotels before finally securing the only room left in a hotel in the same road – a tiny room (one floor above lift level) with separate tiny bathroom. I ventured to a steamed dumpling place and hydrated often.

City Views, Singapore

Singapore, Saturday 30th June

Breakfast was just bread and coffee on a table next to reception. Someone tapping away on a personal organiser had to move out of the way. I targeted the shopping along Orchard Street. Singapore is the place to come for shopping. They really do excel at these cool oases: One after the other, different styles, upmarket and haphazard all along one street. My ATM card split (the well used plastic backing with magnetic stripe fell off) and was taped back together by the bank staff. I did not buy much just some underwear and spent my time wandering. The payment for goods involved writing on an LCD rather than on the receipt slip of paper. Most places had about six or seven floors to explore: travel shops, designer shops, Sony showrooms (like art galleries) and food malls. I switched from cool to humid and back again. It is all part of the culture here. I treated myself to a coffee and cake at the Hilton Hotel, something that would be ridiculously expensive back in London. The Asian Cultural Museum was cool with so many electronic display stations. I walked along the riverside to the hotel near Raffles for city views near the compound dome architecture. My dress code at the white Raffles lobby was not up to standard (no sandals!) and I was refused entry. I whizzed back to the shopping street and relinquished my travel card after completing my last train journey. The internet PC in the shop down the road was well protected but filtered out some legitimate sites. The dumplings fragmented as I picked them up with chop sticks, entertaining a family sitting opposite. There were friendly and efficient staff everywhere. I should be able to sleep in the dorm as it has air-conditioning.

Singapore (Singapore) to Kuala Lumpur (Malaysia), Sunday 1st July

I rushed to buy and send a postcard in the morning before the pickup but could not find a post box so left it with the staff. The coach was as luxurious as an aircraft with personal entertainment screens and the 5-hour journey with customs stops passed painlessly. Even my Green Hut Lodge was just a short walk from the drop off point. I reserved yesterday so had only managed to secure a dorm for the first night and a whole room for the second. If I had been a bit quicker I could have secured a room due to a cancellation – it is always worth asking. There is free internet in the sociable reception area. I walked to the famous Petronas twin towers (you have to queue early to obtain tickets to the walkway with views which I am planning for this Tuesday). Again the shops and food malls were impressive. I could not stop eating delicious food. On the sweaty walk back I visited the tall slender KL tower for night time revolving views – the audio commentary was unnecessary.

Kuala Lumpur, Malaysia

Kuala Lumpur Restaurant and View from Petronas Towers, Malaysia

Petronas Tower View, KL, Malaysia and Diving, Levuka, Fiji

KL, Monday 2nd July

After breakfast in the lean-to I set off walking in Chinatown and Little India – fragments of the real India; Colourful buildings and a toy remote control helicopter in a refrigerated mall. I posted the key I mistakenly took from the KK hostel. After a stop in a darkened Chinese café for "make your own snacks", I felt the need to buy a powerful green laser pointer (being a geek). The cool history museum overlooked the green square with 100m flag pole. Past the fountain under the monorail, I enjoyed the latest action film in an Indian style cinema with only one other person in the audience. I returned by monorail to my own room. Thai food is great! There is nothing left now but a bit of recreational internetting.

KL (Malaysia) to Sydney (Australia) in transit, Tuesday 3rd July

After little sleep and a jump of 4 hours in time zones I will try and recall what happened on Tuesday. With the lack of sleep even simple arithmetical currency conversion seems painful. I set off for the Petronas towers, just after a German bloke staying at the hostel. After queuing in the long snaking queue I was issued a ticket for the bridge for an 11.45am time slot. I had plenty of time for a wander – I bought myself a travel bag as the day pack was almost bursting. The view from the 150m bridge is impressive. There were some exhibits near the lift to pass the waiting time; one where your height was measured and used as a reference unit for famous towers around the world. I must sadly admit that it is quite a pleasure to walk around a smart shopping centre and look at things, stopping from time to time for a coffee rest. I taxied back and it was soon time to leave the friendly hostel and zip to the airport by monorail and fast train. They had to telex Australia because the recently introduced check-in system required a visa number even though I had only a long 5-hour transit. The KL airport with exhibition and competition space was impressive and spacious with a tent-like roof and cylindrical glass lifts. The plane left late due to passport problems with some passengers necessitating removal of luggage.

Sydney to Nadi (Fiji), Wednesday 4th July

The journey passed quickly with films and food and even an hour of sleep. Most international Fiji flights arrive in Nadi. I am writing from the Nadi Hotel near the disco that lasts until 1.00am. Sydney is a pleasant airport with free internet and plenty of shops and gadgets to look at. I cannot believe the size of the latest compact cameras with 5x optical zoom with a lens that does not expand outwards. I looked at the magazines for a while before boarding the plane full

Diving off Levuka, Fiji

of young Australians going on their holidays. The karabiner link disappeared from my luggage. My first choice of hotel no longer existed and I ended up close by. People seem friendly saying "bula" or hello but the higher prices relative to Malaysia make it seem less friendly. I am concentrating on a small part of Fiji called Levuka in my short time here and have booked the bus for tomorrow. It is a pleasantly cool (22°C). The more you travel, the more you can gauge accurately what is achievable and possible.

Nadi to Suva, Thursday 5th July

Fiji's main island is not that small as it takes about 4 hours by bus to arrive at the capital on the eastern side. A short walk to the hotel dragging my trolley bag and I was directed to a cheaper hotel just next door - an apartment style hotel. I was still suffering with jet lag so had to rest and had no energy to explore the capital. Apart from finding a food court opposite the cinema and internetting in comfortable chairs with headsets I did nothing. I retired to the reality of a John Irving book. Having a trace of food in my bag (chocolate) was enough to attract small insects. It was too cold with the air-conditioning switched on. I felt comfort from the urban environment.

Suva to Levuka (Island of Ovalau), Friday 6th July

I was rudely woken by people having a party on the balcony outside my room at 6.00am with loud music. I grumpily asked them to stop and phoned reception. I slept till late to recover and left the hotel at 11.00am. I needed to buy a ticket at an office in town and had time for breakfast in a friendly café, part of a brand new shopping mall. I still felt I was recovering from jet lag as I read the paper. I wandered around the bus station with little signage to the Levuka bus. The bus revved noisily in low gear during the climb and as the temperature rose the driver had to refill the cooling system with water under a flap. The ferry to the island took about an hour and they had run out of cake at the caged snack bar. Finally after many stops to drop off passengers I arrived at Levuka. The Royal Hotel was full so I secured a place next door. I immediately got chatting to a group doing voluntary marine research for wildlife conservation. The people at the lodge were friendly sitting on the mat having a Kava night: a drink that looks like muddy water and tastes like a mild earthy ginger, using half a coconut as a drinking vessel, taken from a wooden turtle-shaped main pot. Beer was also shared from a single communal glass ("low tide" is a half measure of drink).

Levuka Sky and Rugby Lineout, Fiji

Children and Royal Hotel, Levuka, Fiji

Levuka Restaurant and Main Street, Fiji

Levuka, Saturday 7th July

The town is small and friendly and important buildings seem to be made from stone rather than wood. I was too late for breakfast in the hotel so had some in town reading magazines including "The New Yorker". I reserved the diving for tomorrow but the airline shop was closed. I was just appreciating the small town atmosphere. There was rugby in the afternoon, three matches in different age bands with a visiting team from another island. The quality was excellent and the whole community appeared to cheer, shout and sing at significant action. Some of the referees had stayed in the lodge last night. I attempted some action shots and although a fancy SLR would have been very appropriate for fast sports action, I learned to press the button early when the ball was thrown in the lineout to allow for the variable delay of the "shutter". The kids were cheering on the teams and it was a great local cultural way to spend the afternoon. The clubhouse with bare walls, floors and loud music, like a sports pavilion was an appropriate place for some beers. I had good company for dinner, talking to the volunteers. They were watching the rugby on TV till late back at Mary's Guesthouse.

Levuka, Sunday 8th July

I refused breakfast because of the diving but the calm conditions meant that I probably could have eaten some. The laidback German dive instructor Nobi organised things well with zero stress, diving with an American living in Tasmania. The diving was relaxing, surprising for a first dive after a few months without diving. Visibility was excellent with reef sharks and also emphasis on very small marine life. The factory for canning tuna has a waste outlet pipe that attracts all the fish. There was great chocolate cake during the surface interval back at the shop – I do like cake! You always learn something at diving – removing your buoyancy vest is much easier if you undo all the clips including the shoulder clips, otherwise it is a bit awkward. Sunday means hearing occasional church choirs. The afternoon was a post dive snooze. It is not ridiculously hot and humid and I did not need the fan last night. I like the style of the hotel: vast wooden floors with wicker furniture – it suits the place and town. The transition to July heightens the sense that my travelling time is finite and I am approaching the final quarter of my year of travel.

Levuka, Monday 9th July

I have again neglected my journal duties. It was a dive-snooze-eat day. The visibility was so variable on the second dive, from snow storm to clear. I

Levuka Refreshments and Airport, Fiji

Levuka back to Main Island, Fiji

conserved air well. I stood up on the boat trip back from the dive site, drying myself and shorts in the breeze.

A dead mosquito squashed in the journal page -> *

The diving assistant in a multicoloured wetsuit was just learning and had difficulty controlling depth. The buffet at Kim's was excellent and I had to move because a large party with great inertia needed a long table.

Levuka, Tuesday 10th July

Activity was much the same as yesterday but the dive was enlivened because I had an underwater digital camera to take photographs. The first dive with Nobi's partner Andrea was a deep 40 metre dive and I seemed to use too much air, only enough for a 30-minute dive. Maybe the excessive use of air was partly the excitement of taking photos which I found enjoyable. I hope at least one or two good snaps come out of it. My USB memory had picked up a virus, which is not that surprising considering the number of different internet connections I have used. Logger Phil tried the frog-style swimming leg action during the dive but he did not feel comfortable with it. We were shown videos of shark feeding by hand with no cage. I booked my air ticket (instead of the ferry) for tomorrow back to Suva. The people in the restaurant knew that I had been diving because they had spotted me standing on the boat. The 6.00am ferry signals the horn many times. In a more conventional holiday style, a few beers and a slow dinner finished the day.

Levuka to Suva, Wednesday 11th July

Today seemed to be my only opportunity to have a small lie-in. I picked up the air ticket and took photos around town. I am actually writing my journal early in the Whale Tale restaurant after a full breakfast. I can see the lighthouse in the distance: more like a concrete tripod with a platform large enough for one person. I may wander around the shops but I have little motivation to buy anything. Shops close at lunchtime so I sorted out my photos after lunch. My sandwich at the restaurant near the tuna factory came in two stages – they forgot the avocado. I had to weigh myself (110 Kg) as part of airport procedures for the short 10-minute flight. The sunset during the flight between islands was amazing. The Harry Potter Phoenix premier was on at the cinema which ended the day in a scary manner.

Suva to Nadi (pronounced Nandi), Thursday 12th July

It rained heavily overnight but was fine during the day. I had my egg burger near the couple signing to each other. The handicraft markets were desperate for tourists. The museum with a potter making pots outside was fine. After an Indian curry (where the smell from the toilets was strong) it was soon time to board the bus back to Nadi. I rested my feet on the metal bar in front. I have only really seen Nadi high street in the dark. I have the dorm to myself at the hotel that seems deserted and I slept in my clothes last night mainly because of mosquitoes (which I hate). I double checked the 22:50 leaving time of the flight. Staying at dormitories for the last two nights means that my money has lasted with enough left for a day of normal frugality tomorrow. The fan is whipping, drivers are using their horns and the nightclub music can be heard faintly. With people hanging about on the streets some would find the place intimidating. I have a big jump to New York tomorrow evening via Hawaii and LA, with a marathon transit in Honolulu. There is a pool outside between the two dorm blocks. I have plenty of time for contemplation on the flight to New York. Accommodation is sorted out with a double email confirmation. I will make a special effort to sleep on the plane so that I am reasonably fresh for my two days in the city. My writing seems a little disjointed and staccato today.

Crossing the Date Line, Nadi (Fiji) to Honolulu (Hawaii, USA) to LA (USA), Friday 13th July Twice

If I was lucky on the first Friday 13th, I had another chance to be unlucky on the second Friday 13th given that I was crossing the International Date Line. I managed an insufficient one hour's sleep on the plane and this determined my grumpiness for my full day at Honolulu airport. There was an agricultural (organic) materials baggage scan but I had to do it again as two different airlines have different coloured stickers – I needed the pink sticker. Using the internet was a ridiculous $12 an hour so I limited my time on it. I had no trouble filling my day at the airport with plenty of food outlets and shops in a long corridor style with some sections open to the fresh air. You needed an international boarding pass to enter one shop. I spent time eating and reading a couple of science and computer magazines from cover to cover. I am actually sitting in the Chelsea Centre garden, a hostel near Penn Station, New York, trying to recall my journey. At Honolulu, Northwest still showed my previous unchanged booking with Continental which I had to double check.

Times Square, New York, USA

Brooklyn Bridge and View from The Empire State, New York, USA

Coney Island Buses and Seaside Souvenirs, NY, USA

Coney Island Amusements and Promenade, NY, USA

Central Park Busker NY, USA

LA to New York, Saturday 14th July

I had a quick transfer at LA which is becoming very familiar now. My dehydration meant drinking a bottle of water very quickly. The American crowd on the plane were very stationary not shuffling about, not facing different directions and just sitting there quietly in a civilised manner. The bus went through the Lincoln tunnel to reach Manhattan from where it was a short walk to the hostel near Penn Station, the one I had stayed in all those years ago and still just as friendly. I am sitting out in the garden writing this on the Sunday morning. Back to Saturday: I walked to Times Square along 7th Avenue that stretches north up to Central Park, past Madison Square Gardens, Macys and a toy shop with a full size Ferris wheel inside. I stopped at a café and continued to the Central Park summer stage but there was nothing showing. It seems at the weekends the stage is active only during the day and during the week just in the evenings. I took the subway to Brooklyn Bridge (vibrating due to the traffic) and walked across enjoying the night views of the city. After this I just had to zip up to the Empire State and look at the views I have seen before that are still just as spectacular. I did not get back to the hostel until past midnight. The basement dorm was lit with a night light and it was easy to sleep on the first top bunk.

NY, Sunday 14th July

In a dark basement dorm you are isolated from the morning light. I ventured to Borders to look at a detailed NYC guide and cool down. A pair of girls were evangelising in the café. I decided on a trip to Coney Island, about 40 minutes away by subway – an old-fashioned seaside resort where they have a hot dog eating contest every year. The general atmosphere was interesting and a worthy subject for photography. There was a Russian area near the subway station – Brighton Beach, home of the Russian mafia! I sat at a platform for a while and eventually realised that the B-line does not run at weekends. I whizzed back to Central Park, full of dancing confident rollerbladers and joggers and a rapper for kids at the summer stage. This was followed by Spamalot, a funny musical. I bought a cheap standby ticket which was not too bad as you could lean against a wide wooden barrier and support most of your weight. I enjoyed the Americanised version very much. The dorm is in civilised silence with a few people reading under their personal lights. As this trip is coming to an end I am reminded that my whole year's trip is coming to an end too – which is sad. The culturally rich experiences will eventually end and the inevitable and relative mundanity of a working life will begin again. NY deserves the description of a vibrant city. I took a few photos of Times Square balancing my camera on the plastic bollards. The bunks are extremely sturdy and well separated and the fan may help to mask sounds a little. I sometimes find people speaking French annoying - I do not know why. It has to be said that in summer NYC seems full of pretty girls.

Jump forward to the next trip.

Vrhnika, Slovenia

Pre-departure

I am off again on my final round-the-world trip, completing my full year travel break. After NY I had a conventional holiday in Slovenia visiting relatives. It was meant to be restful but ended up quite a busy time. I climbed the highest mountain Triglav and swam in lakes including one in Austria. I have another cousin in Milan, Italy but there was just no time to visit. I am privileged to be able to intimately experience two cultures and after the introduction of the euro at the beginning of the year, Slovenia is becoming more like Switzerland or Austria. I visit about every three years and can spot the changes. Of course all the children seem to grow up. Breda came back from Shanghai and there is more building going on in Vrhnika. Overall it was an exhausting but satisfying time

4. London (England) to Chicago (USA) to Ottawa (Canada), Thursday 2nd August 2007

Heathrow is as busy as ever with the minimum staff on duty to keep people moving without rioting. The old bloke next to me on the plane was really condescending to everybody and wondered why people were so negative towards him. I had to jump to the fast track security queue at Chicago to reach the Ottawa gate at the other terminal. The small jet was quite cramped and my bag did not fit in the overhead lockers. Unfortunately my cold blocked my Eustachian tube and I felt the painful changes in pressure and was slightly deaf in one ear as a result. I was a suspicious profile at Ottawa airport and was sent to immigration for questioning and bag search. Canadians are friendly people chatting to me during taxiing, queuing up for passport control and queuing up for my extra bag search. The 5-hour time shift meant a slight headache but I managed to get off at the correct bus stop and walk to the hostel. In place of someone attending reception there was a mobile phone on the chair with instructions to call someone. I chose the semi private option (bed behind a curtain) in the cool basement. The brightly coloured inn was full of young international backpackers. I am sitting here after consuming my chicken kebab sandwich. My ear has fully unblocked. I will have a chance to explore the city of Ottawa on my return.

Ottawa to Quebec City, Friday 3rd August

The dark cooler basement helped me sleep. I felt fulfilled just drinking coffee and reading the paper in the garden. A quick taxi to the bus station and I was on my way to Quebec City with stops for food at the bus stations. The fast smooth efficient service transported me to this little slice of Paris. There were no places left at any of the hostels. Cheap hotels were full. Even the reasonable hotels only had expensive rooms remaining – more than $200! I felt stressed for a while. Sometimes things are expensive because you are paying to avoid thought. An internet search also came up blank except for a vague suggestion to stay at the university halls of residence from where I am writing now. The receptionist at the hostel in town was helpful with specific advice about exactly where to buy bus tickets and where to wait for the bus. I am on the ninth floor in a typical student room minus the posters on the walls. I even joined the crowd watching a film downstairs. I am reminded of York and how great and free those days were. I bussed into town for cheap food, internetting and watching the evening restaurant crowd. Strangely I have not taken any photos yet. After nine months of travel I am quite fussy about what is significantly new compared to past photos. The bloke in the shop used the pronunciation "Bon Soy" for "Bonsoir".

Triglav National Park, Slovenia

Views from Triglav Peak, Slovenia

Idrija and a Srebrelje House, Slovenia

Srebrelje Barn and Guard Dog, Slovenia

Srebrelje Town, Slovenia

Quebec View and Promenade, Canada

Quebec Murals. Canada

Quebec Architecture and Crepes, Canada

Quebec City, Saturday 4th August

I had my exam panic dream, triggered perhaps by my educational surroundings. There were queues at the popular pancake place so I moved on. I explored: the wooden walkway in the humid heat, narrow shopping streets, music performance stages and people dressed in historical outfits - a pleasant stroll among sophisticated tourist trappings. By lunchtime I was exhausted and had to rest near the gold man street performer (robotic statue busker). The history museum was through a chapel, down a corridor and past another stage in the courtyard. Add a few cafes watching people go by, a Bourne film in dubbed French (which I enjoyed because it was an action film with more predictable and less essential vocabulary) and the day is at an end. The bus ride back now seems normal. This really is a popular town for tourists; crowds fill the streets, the type of place I could enjoy in my 70s. Having to stay out of the centre has probably enhanced my experience, making it more authentic.

Quebec City, Sunday 5th August

The spires silhouette the orange sky as I write my journal entry. I waited between the outer doors as requested before having my crepe at the counter "tout seul". I ate so much that she forgot to add my first crepe on to the bill. I intended to walk along the wall to the citadel but the first section was blocked but essentially continuous after that. I skirted the citadel and was content strolling along the walkways. I stopped at a small square where buskers performed some break dancing. I visited the civilisation museum which had sections about dragons and Tin Tin (!) and a Punch and Judy show. I walked back along the street lined with café tables and antique shops. The sun was still strong. I wandered in and out of shops and the English language magazines seemed to be very expensive. My ordinary observations included a trio of opera singers and a large dog – and perhaps some pretty girls too. I enjoyed eating comfort food (Chilli crisps) back in my room as I feel pleasantly tired. Voices at ground level are quite audible from the ninth floor. The city really is a miniature version of Paris.

Quebec, Monday 6th August

I spent the morning investigating the facilities on campus: book shops, pub and canteen. The morning downpour encouraged me to stay at the university. The cavernous canteen had space for me and my cake. I imagined how busy it would be during term time. I wandered to the library building for the fast free internet. A power failure across the campus ended my session. I zipped into town for a

Ottawa Centre and National Gallery, Canada

stroll, entering shops I had not visited and sat with my *Wired* magazine eating my usual crepe. The canteen seemed to close early so after another stroll I had dinner at the university pub. My tip for the meal seemed compulsory.

Quebec to Montreal to Ottawa, Tuesday 7th August

It was essentially a mentally unfocussed bus journey from Quebec back to Ottawa. I had no enthusiasm for picking up a Laval souvenir university item. The bus stopped at out-of-town stops and Montreal airport (so different in summer!). Again I had trouble with accommodation being full, both the Ottawa Backpackers Inn and the youth hostel so I arranged to stay in the local halls of residence. I wandered around the shopping mall, had three meals in the food hall, took some photos of the canal from the bridge and it was time to return to my new student room, modern with no sink.

Ottawa, Wednesday 8th August

I dropped off my rucksack at the Backpackers and headed to Parliament Hill, past the cattery and a Mountie on a horse to the National Gallery in an impressive building. I looked at the permanent exhibition including modern art (which I sometimes regard as misguided engineering). I find the audio commentary quite entertaining. I missed the rain shower and took a photo of the giant spider sculpture just outside the entrance. The market area was quite pleasant with an inviting bench in a secluded street. The heat made entering the cool air-conditioned shops refreshing. Ottawa is a friendly city. I did not see anything extraordinary, just general pleasantness. Even some of the edginess (for example beggars) seems sanitised – compared to a Rio favela! I had a burger at the place opposite the cinema where I offloaded my accumulated change. The hostel where I am writing now is friendly. Some bloke needs an ancient 3.5 inch floppy disk to resurrect a computer. There is an old bloke here who makes unfunny jokes and inappropriate remarks. I went for a walk, rehydrated and returned. There are maps on the walls and a TV behind the other sofa. A German couple have just walked in. My plan for tomorrow is just the Civilisation Museum across the bridge. An easy rest day as I have to get up ridiculously early for my 6.25am flight on Friday. The yellow and green walls and comfy varied furniture makes it feel homely. Have I really been travelling for over nine months? I have the bottom bed in the first room at the top of the stairs. There are cuddly toys to my left and racks of tourist information leaflets. I have been walking all day and feel satisfied. I do not feel it is good to go to bed early in a dormitory. It is 10.30pm and I do not expect much more to happen before I fall asleep tonight. I internetted at the reception desk.

Ottawa Civilisation Museum, Canada and Grid-like Flight Across the USA (to Seattle)

Ottawa, Thursday 9th August

I managed to fill the day easily. After breakfast at Nates with lots of "or" choices on the menu, the music store almost next door was interesting and I must seriously consider trading in my acoustic piano for something electronic (Yamaha?). The next stop was the university shop and as I walked to this underground shop I imagined walking about the campus during a snowy winter. The next target was the Civilisation Museum across the bridge and I almost walked too far. There were lots of reconstructions of environments and random paths through exhibits, all very entertaining. I did not fancy watching the IMAX. Across the river the area is more French. There was a cafeteria below the posh restaurant with many scavenging birds. I headed to the southern area of town for some recreational internetting, another pleasant urban environment. With some entertainment news and sport on TV I am now vegetating as I write this. I have a taxi ordered for 4.00am so expect little sleep tonight. Listening to the old man staying at the hostel I expect to be just as insensitive when I am in my seventies.

Ottawa (Canada) to Chicago to Seattle (USA), Friday 10th August

So should I listen to my own advice about making reservations in large cities at the height of the summer tourist season? I think yes. My alarm went off at 3.35am and the hostel is active at this time with conversations coming from the bathroom: "You're the best looking girl I have ever had sex with!". The taxi rolled up at 4.00am and I was soon on my way to the Chicago US hub with plenty of breakfast eateries. Customs was sorted out in Ottawa before entry to the USA. The flight from Chicago to Seattle is still a further full 4 hours. There was an entertaining Jewish group on the bus into town with the young daughter proposing gambling guessing games where if you agreed you quickly lost $100. The youth hostel was closed down and the popular backpacker place was totally full for the next three days but I was able to make a reservation for my return last two days. I was forced to stay for one night at an expensive motel style hotel (I did not get past the TV shopping channels) as even the cheap hotel in downtown was totally full. I was able to reserve a spacious room for the following two nights from where I am writing now. I walked to the fish market area with small trendy shops and found the cheap food mall. I would describe Seattle as an advanced urban environment that has seen decay and regeneration. All the young kids seem to be forced to adopt an identity, expressed clearly in their fashion attire. I notice the cliché obesity. Generally I am impressed.

Flora and Fauna, Seattle Centre, USA

Seattle Centre Butterflies, USA

Seattle Monorail and Market Produce, USA

Seattle, Saturday 11th August

There was some filming happening in the street as I transferred to the cheaper hotel. It was no longer sandal weather so I changed to my trainers – a significant event considering I have been wearing sandals for the last nine months. I hopped on the monorail to the Seattle Centre with Needle viewpoint and science centre. I gave the viewpoint a miss as I have done very comparable activities recently. The science place mainly catered for children and the central building had some Cambodian cultural event on the stage. I headed to the square full of underground fancy gallery boutique shops and near a toy shop crammed full of novelty items – a flying monkey! There were more mild tramps hanging about in this area. I enjoyed walking about and entering shops and buildings that looked interesting. The Americans seem to be more sophisticated marketeers. The Simpsons film was entertaining with great reactions to the humour from the Saturday night audience.

Seattle, Sunday 12th August

I bussed to the Fremont Sunday market, the usual flea market items in a suburb with a river and steam pleasure boats. I frittered away the day walking, stopping for coffee, food, novelty shops and just soaked in the comfortable urban atmosphere - again nothing extraordinary, just urban pleasantness. I wandered looking for the return to downtown bus stop and it was right in front of me. I explored the market area and stumbled upon a cinema in a smart shopping centre for a fantasy comedy with Robert de Niro. I do not know the origins of the pig statue mascots scattered around the city.

Seattle (USA) to Victoria (Canada), Monday 13th August

After the inefficient check-in queues I embarked on a smooth hydrofoil ride to Victoria, past some seals. I found the backpackers hostel quickly and was conscious of being much older than the others. Not in an awkward way just aware that there is just no point in me going down to the bar to socialise – oh that is sad! It is early, 9.40pm and unusually early for being in my bunk. The queues at the museum were constantly long throughout the day. The Titanic exhibition was so crowded I sped through the exhibits. Perhaps it is because I am winding down or perhaps it is the destination I have chosen but I seem to be doing things I would be doing normally back home. Nothing particularly associated with a small Canadian island town. I am just enjoying the atmosphere and the positive and hilarious film "Hairspray". The backpackers place is super friendly. I dumped my bag in the cupboard downstairs and the red dorm is

Seattle Docks, USA to Whistler, Canada

through a further security door with a combination lock. It is a fleeting visit and I feel the nature activities available are not exceptional enough compared to my past experiences. The hostel seems efficient with flexible and orchestrated assignment of bed spaces in the dorms.

Victoria to Vancouver to Whistler, Tuesday 14th August

In the morning I tried to capture the friendliness of the hostel on camera. I had incredibly filling "eggs benny" at the popular place on the next block where I had to put my name on a list and sit in a waiting area. The journey involved a ferry crossing, a large luxurious ferry with many facilities including a biologist giving a wireless microphone commentary on the surrounding sea life and geography. There were massage chairs distributed on the decks. I returned to the bus on "lower deck two" of the ferry to continue the journey to the terminal in Vancouver, as smart and civilised as always. Over the bridge through pure forests and sea views, I arrived at Creekside one stop short of the village. The hostel door was around the back with a doorbell (slow response) and telephone number. I can imagine the place being full of snowboarders during winter. There was a Mac computer in the kitchen. I was sharing with a Canadian mountain bike rider (with a $4500 bike with hydraulic disk brakes). The Creekside area is a holiday village with many hotels.

Whistler, Wednesday 15th August

I am actually writing this on the bus back to Seattle on the following day. After a comfortable sleep I got a lift into town and bought my bus ticket, postcards and breakfast. Relaxing with coffee, newspapers and soaking in the atmosphere was the theme of the day. The village is like a theme park, full of pedestrian areas, restaurants, hotels and tourist shops. I ventured to the Whistler peak by gondola and chair lift and enjoyed the views without having to endure a tiring hike. There were friendly tourist personnel to help guide you on your way. To pass the time and cool down from the bright sun I saw a pulp film. I am happy with some coffee and cakes. Is Canada a civilised and mellower version of the States?

Whistler to Vancouver (Canada) to Seattle (USA), Thursday 16th August

I waited patiently for my breakfast downstairs. The bus driver had a deformed hand. At the Canadian-US border there was an irritating wait of 2.5 hours to clear immigration formalities. At least two people on the bus missed flights as

Whistler View, Canada and Fake Bookcase Poster, Seattle, USA

Seattle Pavement Dance Instructions and Cuddly Toys, USA

Seattle Flower Stall, USA to Maracana Stadium, Rio de Janeiro, Brazil

a result. Passing through industrial areas under a cloudy sky we eventually reached Seattle at 6.00pm, beginning at 8.00am, an all day trip. I am actually writing from the centre of the common room: chatty guitar music, Japanese chatter, many people with laptops browsing wirelessly, free internet browsing - a hive of activity. There was even free food at 7.00pm but I could not wait that long! The dorm rooms have key card entry and bathrooms are luxurious. One of the most professional hostels I have ever stayed at. The internet room was too hot to hang about in. Writing in a diary with a pen seems so low tech compared with all the laptops around here.

Seattle, Friday 17th August

A good night's sleep in the sturdy bunks with a fan which masks ambient sound. After a free breakfast I walked up the road to the Capitol Hill area of town with more small shops, more tramps and a park with an Asian museum, reservoir and water tower with a view of the city. I had lunch at a Mexican takeaway where Spanish speaking builders also stopped to eat. I was nudged by a van whose driver just did not see me crossing, an event which reminds me to be extra careful crossing the roads. The market area was busy with buskers and fishmongers throwing fish around. The sun was still strong and bright during the late afternoon. The hostel seemed less chaotic than last night. I enjoyed a rat animation film and a takeaway luxury cheesecake from opposite the cinema.

Seattle (USA) to St Louis to Miami to Rio de Janeiro (Brazil), Saturday 18th August

I was reading the amendment reference on the bus stop timetable at 3.20am when some bloke said that at 3.30am the airport bus actually stops around the corner. I quickly rushed to the waiting 174 bus. There are more black people around town and on the buses at this hour. At the airport I was surprisingly alert at this time of the morning. I am writing from a connecting corridor at Miami airport as a group just ran past to catch their flight. I could have remained on the plane at St Louis but felt like stretching my legs. I read a computer magazine and looked at the pictures in a celebrity magazine – not the most productive activity. So really just a day of travel and perhaps I should write about my random thoughts on other things: You cannot really reason with racism or stupidity; black and Asian people will continue to be filtered out of senior positions; I must concentrate on the serious issues, not the ones equivalent to a small child losing a balloon. I am really conscious that my trip is coming to an end soon.

Maracana Stadium and Favela Wiring, Rio de Janeiro, Brazil

Rocinha Favela Art and Views, Rio de Janeiro, Brazil

Rocinha Favela (Shanty Town), Rio de Janeiro, Brazil

Rio de Janeiro, Sunday 19th August

At the airport I left the celebrity magazines on the chair opposite and within 5 minutes they were picked up. I managed to sleep most of the way so decision making at my destination was quite logical. I saved some cash by taking the bus to the domestic airport and then a taxi from there. Rio and the hostel seem so calm outside carnival season, particularly on a Sunday. Everything was familiar and I settled in my new environment in minutes. The atmosphere in the dorm was a bit sweaty due to the lack of fans. My only plan was to watch the football at the Maracana, with pickup at 4.30pm. I slept on the sofa for a short while with calming Brazilian guitar music. The tourist group was ushered to a section of the stadium with the home fans (Botafogo V Internacional 1:1). I was more entertained by the singing and samba of the fans and collective hand-clapping. I ordered a takeaway and relaxed in the pool area. If this was a private house it could be a place for a millionaire.

Rio de Janeiro, Monday 20th August

The favela man arrived early and I had to leave without breakfast and hydration. Motorbikes took our group to the top of the largest favela called Rocinha which initially reminded me of India but I suppose the point here is the close proximity of poverty and wealth. We walked through the narrow alleyways, through a small art gallery, bakery shop and nursery. When a young bloke was striding in the opposite direction with a large pistol in his hand the guide quickly instructed us not to take photos. I talked to an Irish couple. This puts fear of crime back home in perspective. At this point it is relevant for me to quote the security tips notice for the Rio Hostel as it is in a relatively unsafe area:

Avoid walking around with bags or small rucksack, better to use plastic bags.
Store money and credit cards in your bra (for girls) or in your shoes (for boys)
Avoid withdrawal of money at night, or at cash points without a security guard.
If you are coming back late at night and you've had a few drinks, take a cab.
If you are in a club, don't leave your drink unattended (a sleeping pill could be dropped in)
Avoid the city centre at weekend; it is empty and quite dangerous.

Mentioning such things may only emphasize the cliché image of Brazil, a view with a lack of detail, without any meaningful nuance. As a complete contrast I was dropped off in a large smart shopping mall. The taxi driver was a bit slow finding my hostel so I paid less than the meter amount. I tried buying a flight

Rocinha Favela, Rio de Janeiro, Brazil

Rocinha Favela Houses, Rio de Janeiro, Brazil

ticket from a cheap carrier but the website does not seem to accept an international credit card and requires some kind of Brazilian tax code, CTV or something like that. I weighed up the risk between having valuables with me when going to dinner at the local restaurant and keeping them in the locker. The pen attached to a string is swinging from the fridge door handle. The flight option to Salvador is looking like a more attractive option compared to a 24-hour bus journey and is only a little more expensive than the bus.

Rio de Janeiro to Salvador, Tuesday 21st August

A 1-hour-20-minute flight is preferable to a 24-hour bus ride. I arrived in Salvador (or Bahia) and braved the short walk along cobbled streets and squares to the hostel. Of course there was a man on the corner directing me to the wrong hostel but I soon settled in my single room with window to a narrow column courtyard. I walked to Jesus Square and sent off my photos. My normal chores encourage me to talk to locals. The Brazilians instil carnival skills at a young age with many schools practising samba processions in the evening. I tried to stay ahead of one such procession. The pudding I chose was disappointingly small so I swapped it for another. I was really just walking around determining how safe the streets were.

Salvador, Wednesday 22nd August

With free breakfast the single room rate (double a dorm rate) is good value. I reserved my Candomblé religious ceremony visit for tonight. The plan was just to walk the extent of the compact historical district. The guidebook advises not carrying a camera outside this area which has many patrolling tourist police. The view to the lower town and lift was fine. I was reminded a little of Valparaiso in Chile (a little lower in latitude) with all the funicular lifts. They weighed the lunch at the cafeteria to determine the cost of the meal. Even though my knowledge of Portuguese is not worth talking about, I feel comfortable just guessing the meaning of words, a confidence born from months of previous travel. I popped in the Basilica (I am not really that interested in all the other churches) and the Afro-Brazilian museum with ethnography section in the basement. With a few brief showers I had to shelter in doorways. The free caipirinha cocktail was very acceptable. Question: am I tired of travelling all this time? Answer: No, because it really is different all the time with different new experiences just around the corner. I have little to complain about. I suppose I knew that travelling would be more interesting than working.

Historic Salvador Street, Brazil

Salvador, Brazil

Salvador Lift and Traditional Dress, Brazil

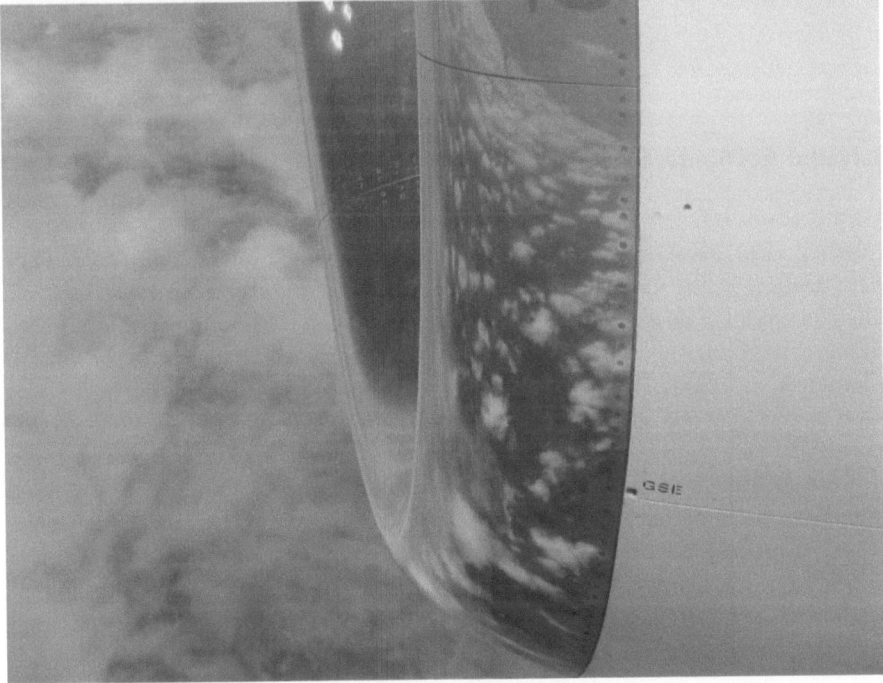
Salvador Views and Jet Engine Reflection, Brazil

The religious ceremony was like standing for a 2-hour mass with added features such as Latin rhythms, uncontrolled dancing, throwing of popcorn, placing hands on the head, palms on the forehead and even collective smoking of cigars. I can not recommend it as a tourist experience but it was authentic in that the local people would do this even if the tourists were not present.

Salvador, Thursday 23rd August

Without a plan, I walked on more cobblestones. I paid for one more night and wandered to tourist information to enquire about buses; all buying of tickets required a trip to the bus station. I opted for a flight instead. Comparison: one hour instead of 13 hours for double the price. The original plan was to travel around the coast by bus but the novelty of two-day long bus journeys has worn off a bit. The arrival of cheap airlines makes the choice easier. I talked to the friendly ex-Holland Park nanny at the corner restaurant. I managed some token sightseeing going down the funicular to the lower town with tourist market then and back up again. The famous lift had a long queue. I did not feel adventurous today. I was internetting (my website is down due to a migration fault) and restaurant sampling. The day was soon over. I am not sure I have done justice to Salvador though I imagine it is transformed during carnival. My facial hair is growing fast. The background noise consists of samba drumming. I almost forgot to mention seeing lots of music shops, mainly selling percussion.

Salvador to Olinda, Friday 24th August

I rushed after breakfast to catch the airport bus which left straightaway. They were dancing in the underwear shop at the airport. So many people had laptops. The sun sparkled in the reflective metallic rim of the jet engine. I persisted with taking a bus into the centre then a taxi after a friendly haggle for the final 6 kilometres to Olinda. The entrance gate was secured by a chain and bell. I was soon in my apartment room with bathroom and partly due to lack of sleep due to caffeine last night, I fell to rest for 2 hours. I walked around town on more cobbles before it got dark. Being a smaller town it immediately seemed friendlier. A couple of local girls thought I was German. They thought I knew more Portuguese because I looked so relaxed walking about town. My attitude to language has evolved: lack of understanding no longer elicits a feeling of confusion or dread but now I playfully try and guess what has been said, repeating things, suggesting things and then observing the reaction. Well, I felt that way today. The crepes were relatively expensive but necessary. My plan tomorrow is just a simple circuit of town hoping it is good photographic weather. It is more humid here further north and closer to the equator.

Recife Skyline (from Olinda) and Riverbank, Brazil

Olinda, Saturday 25th August

The mosquitoes that drink my blood may soon die. Sleep. I am not sure whether it was the humidity but I woke with no energy. After a quick breakfast I just continued sleeping until the afternoon. I cannot remember sleeping so long on this trip. Again I missed the angled road and had to reverse my walking route around town. The modern Recife city was visible in the misty distance. All you need is "obrigado" and "guarana". I walked along stalls and past churches. As I sheltered from the brief shower a handicapped boy reached for the guide book tucked under my arm, in an inquisitive way and was also curious about my watch. The buses sped by along the hostel road. I can cope with infrastructure from Mali to New York and felt the need for a greater level of comfort. I felt indecisive and left the choice whether to move on for tomorrow morning.

Olinda to Recife (a short journey), Sunday 26th August

I am sure the Tariff 2 setting on the taxi meter is the setting that overcharges tourists. The first choice of hotel near Independence Square was shut so I walked to the 1930s Central Hotel with old-fashioned lift. I asked the receptionist if he spoke English. In reply he said "no", do you speak Portuguese? So I just used some Spanish and a few Portuguese words I picked up to secure my "Quartos" (a room without bathroom). I crossed the bridge to the Sunday market area, a bit too early as only a few stalls had been set up. The streets were quite deserted for a quiet Sunday. The tourist information was helpful in finding out about bus times to Fortaleza. After coffee at the nearby mall I returned to the market area which was now lively and crowded with practising samba carnival groups which are so entertaining to listen to and watch. I walked back along the other bridge. I almost forgot to mention that this morning as I left the Central Hotel in Recife, three police on motorbikes pulled over another motorcyclist. One policeman was pointing a pistol towards the suspect. Some people in a car seeing my reaction advised me to "take care". The food mall was a pleasant oasis which I took advantage of twice. I will try the night bus tomorrow, a 12-hour journey leaving at 8:30pm.

Recife, Monday 27th August

The large black mosquito (fast and an expert in camouflage) stood watch by the head of the bed. The buffet breakfast was nothing nice. I dropped off my bag behind reception and started exploring. A church building with courtyard occupied some of my morning. The place is completely transformed on a weekday. Many shop assistants in branded t-shirts compete for your attention.

Fortaleza and Belem, Brazil

Belem Fish Market Area, Brazil

There are bicycles carrying PA systems spreading music and advertising. The market area sold lots of relatively low quality goods: many brightly coloured plastic things of little use to anyone. The White City fort museum was closed – with no closed sign of course you have to go in and attempt to buy a ticket to find out. I caught a bus to the monster air-conditioned mall for a walk and food. I am struggling to take photos because my rule in the past has been to essentially take photos of exceptional things. I have seen so much variation in the recent past that a normal street scene, cityscape or beach is no longer special enough. I walked along historical streets full of traffic to the metro station to reach the bus station. There was a cancellation from the next customer that allowed me to buy the last ticket for the overnight bus to Fortaleza. A Norwegian bloke who had lived and worked in Brazil for three years (building and renting apartments) approached me and talked about Brazilian girls.

Recife to Fortaleza, Tuesday 28th August

I managed to sleep for more than 2 or 3 hours on the bus, despite the cooling from the air-conditioning. After a night bus trip of 12 hours I tend to be overly cautious and suspicious, particularly with taxi drivers. The single room in the hostel was too expensive so I had enough energy to move to another just down the road. The room with a collapsing flowery bed was warm but I caught up on some lost sleep. There was a prostitute sitting at the entrance table to attract customers to the restaurant and perhaps clients. In Spanish "Js" seemed to be pronounced as "Hs" but Portuguese seems to replace "Rs" with "Hs" too, for example Hio do Haneiro. I walked to the tour shop (past a pavement in danger of being splashed by passing traffic) to buy my Fortaleza to Belem flight. I do not fancy the alternative of a 24-hour bus trip. I also rejected a trip to a small fishing village and beach. There just would not be enough time to enjoy the place. The town centre was nothing special. I relaxed with a fancy coffee in the arts complex on the way back to the hotel, actually and surprisingly called a hostel. The air-conditioning does not switch on until 22:00. I feel quite safe walking around. My plan to find a beach tomorrow should not take too long.

Fortaleza, Wednesday 29th August

I am not really a beach person. Beaches are for stressed out executives seeking calm from their work or for large groups of people to party – and children. They are probably not even for retired people. Today I felt there was just sand and it was too hot. There were adverts every 10 minutes during the film I was watching last night on local TV and the "Friends and Rivals" soap full of

Belem Zoo, Brazil

beautiful people. The website is back up again finally after the migration, although the internet café banned YouTube so I could not upload a video. I walked to the end of the pier made from rocks removed from some building works I imagine. As I was reading (looking at the pictures in) the magazines in the hotel entrance a prostitute offered her services. Here in the restaurant the complementary olives and meat are quite salty. Some of the tall skyscrapers seem so narrow and I am guessing so that each apartment can have a sea view.

Fortaleza to Belem, Thursday 30th August

Socially it is sparse at the moment. A combination of staying in almost empty accommodation not conducive to socialising, travelling at quite a pace and not choosing well known tourist hotspots. The plane does a milk run, stopping at each major city along the coast. I must remember the arrival taxis are a good place to hail a cheaper airport taxi. I noticed a downgrade in infrastructure – untidy buildings, pavements, more street stalls and people hanging about. The Central Hotel I arrived at had closed down, the disadvantage of using an older travel guidebook. There was another not that far away. The cheaper rooms had gone but I could change rooms on the second night. The tourist agency, a hot and humid walk away was expensive and did not really cater for the lone independent traveller. Again a mall comes to my rescue: cool, cheap food and cheap internet access. The large noisy fast moving buses dominate the roads.

Belem, Friday 31st August

I left my passport, tickets and cards in the hotel safe as I was to enter a high risk market area. The enclosed modernised wharf by the yellow cranes was shut for a function. The market again was not exceptional compared to Central America and African markets – I have high standards! I walked towards the fort past fish stalls and stall holders hosing down the pavement. There were many scavenging birds. I had to return to the hotel for 2.00pm to transfer rooms. I returned to the waterfront to eat my buffet lunch sold by weight (not something I have seen in England). I like my "pudim" (pronounced "pujim", a caramel flan). My t-shirt was soaking from sweat and I just reached the mall before the rain started. I engaged in some aimless surfing, just searching spontaneously for interesting things. The rooms are branded precisely. The cheaper room has normal TV with no remote (as oppose to cable with remote), fan (not air-conditioning), no fridge, one towel, no mirror in the wardrobe and is slightly smaller. I am not thinking much about my future. I only have my rucksack and refreshing water to drink. What else do I need?

Belem, Saturday 1st September

Let me remember this complete freedom to act, not constrained by an employer-employee relationship. The friendly taxi driver drove me to the botanic gardens. An interesting block of forest, museum and lots of educational ecological stalls run by school children. The pacing jaguar was quite sad but impressive. I walked back via the church, coffee and croissant place but the intellectuals café (mentioned in the guide) was not there anymore and past the cemetery. A super short haircut is very appropriate for this warm weather (about 34°C) with enthusiastic hair dresser. There is a rodeo programme on the TV with a number of badly tuned channels. I really have not got a clue what I am going to do tomorrow – maybe some forward planning? I was watching the young teenagers expressing themselves with diverse fashions. I must have been emanating a friendly aura as everyone seemed super friendly today and I had no trouble guessing the gist of what people were saying. I checked for cinema info on the internet and found there was one at the back of the mall near the furniture shop but it was showing films that I had seen already.

Belem, Sunday 2nd September

The morning turned out to be planning admin time: basically how I divide my time over the next two weeks. All the stalls had migrated to the green plaza for a Sunday version of the market with toy electric vehicles for the kids. There were thematic sculptures inside light bulbs made from single matchsticks and coconuts. I found that I did not have a map of Sucre in Bolivia so did some online research for accommodation and also for tour companies in the Pantanal wetland area. In summary there was nothing very interesting today – I was just surviving.

Belem to Brasilia to Campo Grande to Corumba, Monday 3rd September

After a 3.30am alarm, it was a day of travel – what else? Multiple flights, three sets of taking off and landing, the changes in pressure make the process more tiring. I arrived at Corumba airport and unusually I was persuaded by a bloke at the airport to join an imminent (within 30 minutes) tour to the Pantanal region. I made sure that I agreed at the agency in town (an identity check) and negotiated a little discount. I was straightaway put on a local bus which was forced to detour from the main road, a transfer to a small van and then a safari vehicle to the camp arriving just after dark. Dinner was served after the bell and sleeping was in hammocks. I arrived with a couple of Manchester girls Laura

Pantanal, Brazil

Cayman and Birds, Pantanal, Brazil

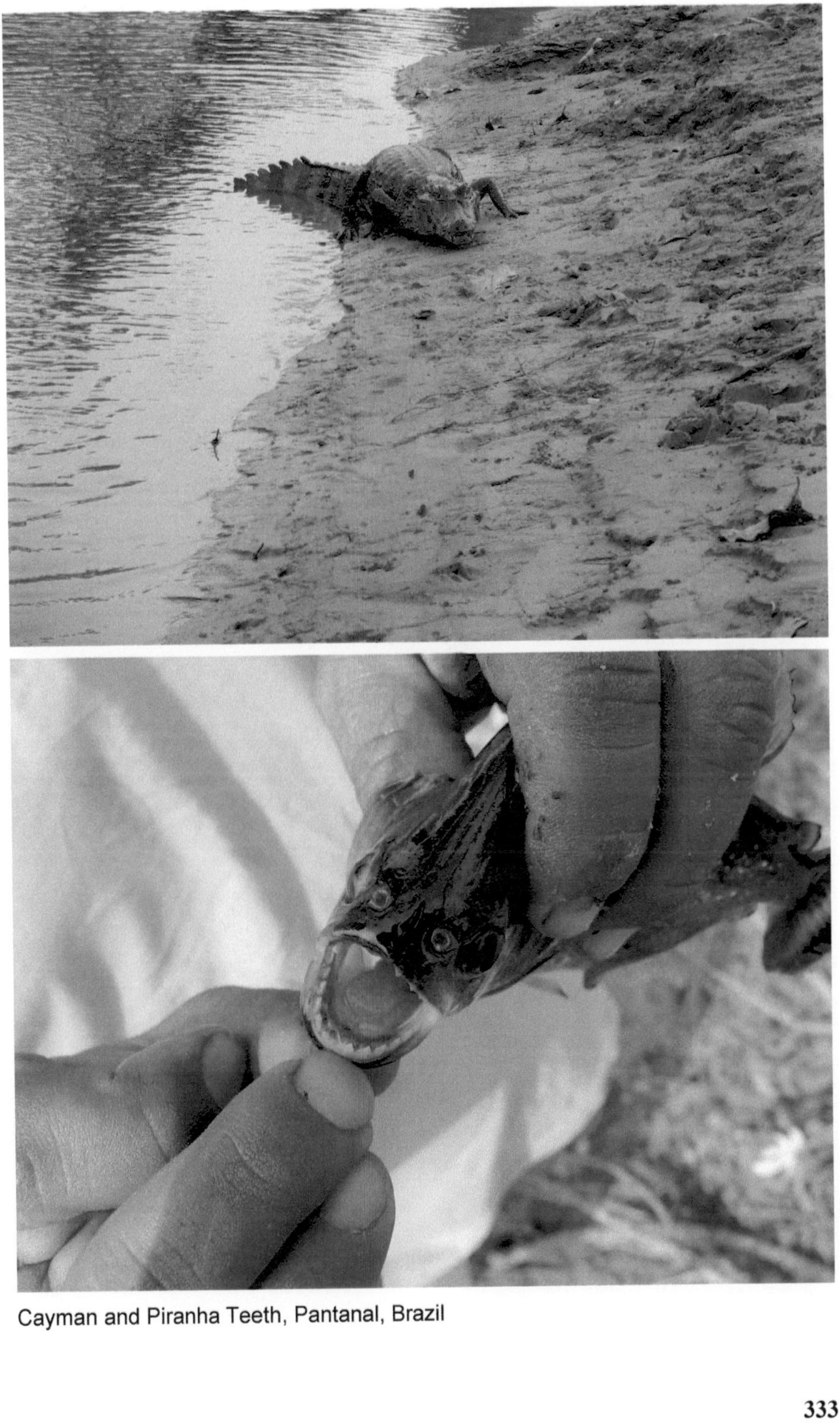

Cayman and Piranha Teeth, Pantanal, Brazil

Watchful Cayman and Local Cowboy, Pantanal, Brazil

and Andrea on a South American tour for ten weeks. They seem more trusting on their travels compared to me.

Pantanal Region, Tuesday 4th September

I slept well in the hammock as I was exhausted but a little cold just before morning light. One girl's hammock was not secured properly and she fell and bumped her head. The breakfast alarm call was a cacophony of squeaking parrots and birds. On the morning hike there were capybara (a very large rodent), alligators (more accurately cayman), an armadillo poking its head out of a hole, parrots, cranes and horses with cowboys. The flat plastic water container proved useful. Some went swimming in the river which was reasonably safe despite the small cayman and piranha! The dining room has suddenly cleared – I believe they have gone to a bar a short walk down the road. The dinner was filling and included polenta. The afternoon walk was through thicker vegetation.

Pantanal, Wednesday 5th September

Some stayed up till 5.00am. I did join the full safari truck to the bar shop just down the road. There was music, dancing, dogs, a spare rib barbeque and people chatting round the table - a group of French and German students studying in Sao Paolo for six months. Multiple languages were spoken. The morning activity was piranha fishing using a bamboo fishing rod. While fishing several small alligators gathered and were attracted to the water disturbances and very large crane. Later they were given the smallest of the catch. The process of fishing is quite absorbing and I managed to catch five fish (two medium piranhas, one trout, and two small piranhas). A small piece of red meat is placed on the hook and you wait a few seconds for the slack line to tighten. Too slow with the jerk action and you end up just feeding the fish. After a midday sleep there was horse riding in the afternoon. If I did not discourage the horse with the reins it would take every opportunity to stop and nibble grass. My second time on a horse and it felt far more comfortable than I remember. The path through forested areas, open ground, soft mud and under a setting sun was relaxing and enjoyable. There was piranha (the theme of the day) soup at dinner and a few of us went for a short walk to view the stars and fireflies, accompanied by a cat. Tall Richard jumped out from a bush and scared the girls. A beer over the camp fire and the day was over.

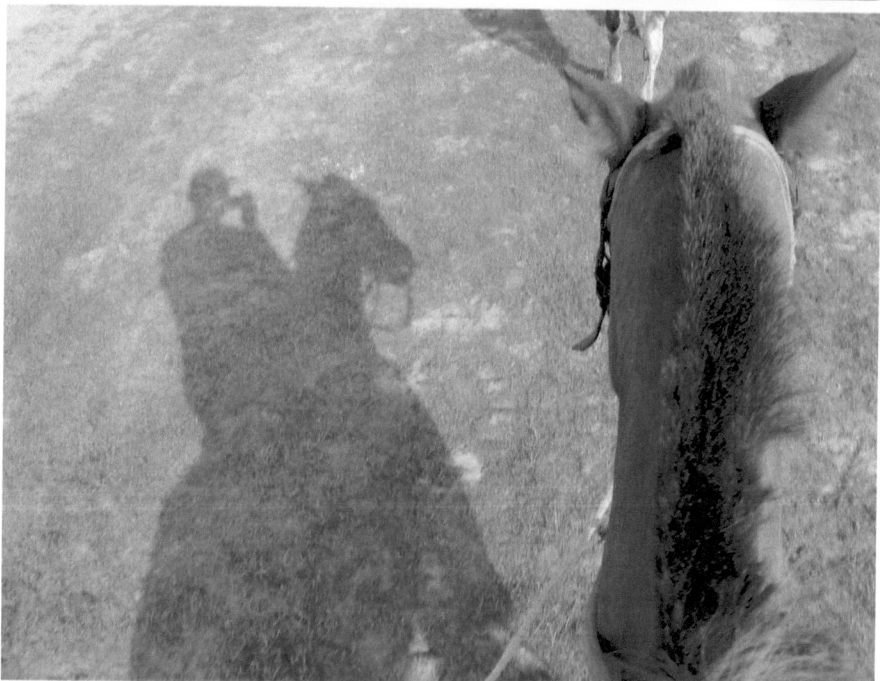

Horse Riding, Pantanal, Brazil

More Horse Riding, Pantanal, Brazil

Pantanal to Corumba, Thursday 6th September

The boat trip in the morning was at a later 8.30am start. There were two boats, one pulled along at the side. Little wildlife is generally seen from boats maybe due to the engine noise. After saying goodbye to fellow travellers and the friendly oasis of activity it was time to return to Corumba. In some countries roads can be blocked by sheep, cows and goats but here it was a group of baby cayman. At the main road some went to Bonito and others went to Campo Grande in the opposite direction. I bounced on the back seat of the coach with tinted windows. A little boy sat next to me. Diego the tour guide was waiting at the terminal. Any thoughts about flying out to Santa Cruz in Bolivia the following day were dashed as there was a national holiday meaning that the immigration office could not supply my exit stamps and I had arrived too late in the evening. I slept well in an air-conditioned dorm with red curtains with only me staying there. I feel like I am in the spare room of a large family house.

Corumba, Friday 7th September

I walked to the centre. I reassessed the map position of the hostel and I was one block in error. The town was sleepy and closed. There was some activity on the main square. All the international telephone places were closed and the best hotel only provided facilities for guests. I wanted to phone home and failed. There was a celebration parade mainly consisting of armed services, police, fire, medical personnel with rousing brass bands – entertaining for a while. Internet cafes are places of rest and coolness. A visit to the federal police station confirmed that an exit stamp was available at the bus station (unusually not at the border). I returned to the bus station and decided on an overnight train to Bolivia tomorrow in preference to the alternative of staying in a nothing town for a further two days and flying out on Monday morning. At the request of the tour guide I helped with explaining about the tour to a German couple. I wandered a little around town, bought snacks for tomorrow's Pullman class 20-hour train journey and failed to eat all my chocolate pizza – yes a pizza with a chocolate topping! I could have attended a barbeque but decided to rest instead. It really has been an amazing Pantanal visit, great wildlife and great company.

Corumba (Brazil) to Quijarro to Santa Cruz (Bolivia), Saturday 8th September

The train ticket was delivered with a departure time marked one hour later than the actual time. It is sensible to get to trains, buses and planes in good time. I

Corumba Government Parade, Brazil and View from Overnight Train to Bolivia

took a motorbike to the border and a taxi to the station. Normally it is not a good idea to change large amounts of currency at a border but I had lots of Brazilian Reais left so had little choice. Bolivia seems to have spruced up its image with a modern train station building. The train though was authentic Bolivian. I suppose trains are old style technology but I found it difficult to believe how much squeaking, banging, creaking, scraping of metal couplings and snare drum rhythms are involved with wheels moving along an iron track. Despite this I managed to sleep about 3 hours. Before departure I phoned home at a telephone booth place for my monthly check in.

Santa Cruz, Sunday 9th September

After a 20-hour journey I did not need the drama of a seized up combination lock attaching my bag to the luggage rack. There was no option but to borrow a knife and cut the loop on the bag. There was only room for one night at the favourite place which looked comfortable with a large courtyard. Eating lots of starchy food (pizza) and not moving for many hours may cause problems for your constitution! I needed sleep and had a little explore around the main square. I was expecting something less modern. The McD had disappeared perhaps due to lack of local patronage. The country is much cheaper. I am struggling to find something exceptional to photograph.

Santa Cruz, Monday 10th September

The breakfast area is quite compact which means you have to talk to the person next to you. The manageress said I could stay another night, as could someone else. Maybe she displays caution to most people to allow her to vet guests and reject undesirables. I walked to the Aerosur Company to book my return flight to Sucre. There was some inevitable misunderstanding and I sat outside an office for a while instead of the cashier window. The back pocket of my trousers seems to have been cut open (with a razor?) which I believe happened last night or on the overnight train; Again a reminder about the wealth differential. A bit like mosquitoes: take precautions and do not get too angry about being bitten. I enjoyed catching up with the news and updating my blog which I do now far more than at the beginning of my trip. Quite a few of my photos seem to be corrupted but they look ok directly from the camera so I believe the transfer process is just less reliable on some computers. I visited the Bolivian Irish bar for some great trout lunch – the place is quite modern. Coffee, cake and wandering! There was quite a concentration of computer game shops. There really is not much to do here. I watched dubbed Spanish TV in the breakfast area. The spherical fob is hanging from the key in the door and there is a dry unventilated odour in the room but I am still comfortable.

Santa Cruz to Sucre, Tuesday 11th September

I retreated into a virtual world full of non-Bolivian experiences, just relaxing and eating a Napoleon cake. Transactions for restaurants seem so slow. It was soon time to speed to the airport with a last minute gate announcement I began the 25-minute flight to Sucre. Exiting the plane was refreshingly cool. Although the receptionist was absent at the hostel, I was relaxed and waited patiently on the courtyard sofa. When she arrived everything was easy and super friendly. There were some political speeches happening in the square, followed by live music. Sucre has a friendly atmosphere. I walked around enough to find my bearings in relation to the main tropical square. The rain at night crescendoed to a roaring downpour on the metal roof.

Sucre, Wednesday 12th September

I visited the ethnography and colonial museum. The altitude has a deadening effect and I have little energy to generate imaginative phrases describing the place. I am struggling to remember how I filled my day apart from a very British experience of watching English football on TV in a pub where the commentator enjoyed pronouncing Gerrard with exaggerated rolling Rs. As I sat on a bench hawkers and beggars approached in a friendly way. While walking along the pavement older begging ladies thrust their hats in my path. Again I am struggling for photographic uniqueness – it is all quite similar in style to the rest of Latin America. This I suppose is an inevitable symptom of having travelled so much.

Sucre to Potosi, Thursday 13th September

I got off the micro minibus too late and had to walk back two blocks to the bus station. Potosi is simpler in style and more primitive compared to Sucre and certainly Santa Cruz. The taxi to the centre was about $0.50. I stayed at an old Carmelite monastery with rooms in all directions, my simple one only costing $5. I spent so much time wandering around looking for a good restaurant, some were closed, some had closed down and I eventually found a café on the corner of the main square full of westerners. The streets are only wide enough for one car and there was a policeman controlling the traffic. I booked the mine visit for tomorrow. In South America you do notice that many of the dogs have limps.

Potosi Central Square and Miner's Market, Bolivia

Miner's Market and Mine, Potosi, Bolivia

Potosi Mine, Bolivia

Potosi Mine Tunnel, Bolivia

My bed tilts to one side and I have about five blankets to keep warm. Not eating all day may have helped my acclimatisation although I still had that characteristic headache which disappeared after a couple of hours sleep.

Potosi, Friday 14th September

I almost overslept waking at 8.40am for the 9.00am visit to the mines (silver and tin). The group was French. After a short tour of the market to buy presents for the miners (coca leaves, drinks, milk, dynamite) we were supplied our mining outfit – orange jacket, trousers, boots, lamp and helmet. There was a demonstration of blowing up dynamite which I just caught on video. It was horrible crouching down, walking along the dark dusty muddy shafts, avoiding the occasional cart being pulled along the rails that often becomes derailed. The short tour guide (a useful characteristic for cramped mines) was sensitive and entertaining. We stopped at a phallic statue where miners were chewing coca leaves and drinking 96% alcohol. The atmosphere was dusty but bearable with fresh air being piped along the shafts. The mining conditions can be described as medieval and I was happy to see daylight. When a young man was injured we (the group of tourists) helped put him in a cart to be transported back to the top. My clothes were soaked in sweat. While writing this I am warming my feet under the bed covers. Potosi is the highest city in the world at 4090m!

Potosi, Saturday 15th September

It rained heavily in the early morning. Breakfast was up the stairs and I made my best guess for the Spanish spoken at me. I joined the large German group for the tour of the mint, an interesting mixture of old technology, art and architecture. Some machines were mule or slave powered. There was music in the main courtyard under the Bacchus face sculpture: the band was an interesting combination of mandolin and guitar. After my postcard tradition, it was time for lunch in the upstairs café past the dog on my own - the theme for the day. All the old computers from Europe and America probably end up sent down here in internet cafes. The church tower with view appeared closed. I flicked through all the magazines in the café and had a great dinner on the corner of the square with interested toddler saying "ola!" There was no water in the bath room so I had to ask for a bowl. The comedy drama on TV appears very slapstick and over-the-top. The dinner has warmed me up and I feel comfortable.

Potosi, Bolivia

Potosi Bus Station Sights, Bolivia

Potosi Bus Ticket Office and Santa Cruz Toucan, Bolivia

Potosi to Sucre, Sunday 16th September

Daylight barely registered through the translucent room door leading to the open courtyard. The "matron" of the hostel was at breakfast making sure everyone was ok. There was some bloke having breakfast sitting at the top of the stairs. My language discrimination and comprehension was operating at low capacity today. I had a little wait at the bus station and used the time to take some ordinary photos. There was competition between different bus companies on this popular route which meant that people arriving with luggage were mobbed like celebrities for their business. There was no discount back at the hostel for people with the name "Marko". I appreciated the better quality of restaurants and relaxed eating and thinking. The Simpsons film was enjoyable in dubbed Spanish as this second time I understood the gist and noticed different things about the clever animation. The hostel is comfortable but socialising with others here is not easy without a common area. I appreciate the higher temperature and extra oxygen in Sucre. I opted for the simple room without bathroom and feel good. I am retracing my steps back to Santa Cruz and I know there is little to do there before my giant leap into New Zealand. I do not know why I can not string sentences together and only start sentences with "I".

Sucre to Santa Cruz, Monday 17th September

I found out on the plane that the flight was going via Cochabamba. The familiar "Residencial" had tame toucans in the courtyard who love to grapple with your hand. I checked the cinema and it seems to be closed down. The streets around the square became more familiar and I stumbled upon a super market and barbers. I enjoyed a filet mignon overlooking the square and am becoming more familiar with the names of cakes. I dropped off my washing. I did not do anything specifically Bolivian. My breakfast was 100g of posh chocolate and my dinner dessert was the other half.

Santa Cruz, Tuesday 18th September

Activities: Barber, pick up washing, lots of surfing, pizza, beer, "tarte de frutilla", coffee, stroll, games shops (no cheaper), the other cinema had become a church, playing with the toucan with clipped wings, relaxation, changing $20 into Bolivianos, giving nothing to beggars, ordinary things and so it went on. I do not expect anything amazing to happen or to have great cultural experiences here. I discovered that I have no travel info about New Zealand so quickly booked an Auckland hostel over the internet.

Hostel Toucan and Courtyard, Santa Cruz, Bolivia

Santa Cruz, Wednesday 19th September

Perhaps there is a class of wildlife or animal that everyone likes and toucans can be added to the group. I spent the morning writing a potential article for Trailfinders and we will see what happens. I treated myself to exactly the lunch I wanted with no thought about the expense just the quality. This does not happen very often. I even had an Irish coffee from the posh coffee shop and three different cakes for dessert. An English couple were doing a year's travel too. I retreated to a global cultural standard – the modern suburban cinema multiplex building. It appeared that most of the films were in English with Spanish subtitles. I enjoyed the escapism of the "Perfect Crime" known as "Fracture" in English. The room fan seems to only work with a timer and cannot be put into continuous mode.

Santa Cruz (Bolivia) to Santiago (Chile) to Auckland (New Zealand), Thursday 20th September

The Santiago leg was via Iquique where we had to disembark and clear Chilean customs. I had a "Colossal" burger at Santiago airport and easily entertained myself there before the final leg to Auckland. I managed to sleep on the long smooth 12-hour flight that flies close to Antarctica at the bottom of the world. Maybe with long haul flights the pilot makes a special effort with landing as it really was super smooth.

Auckland (missing Friday crossing the Date Line), Saturday 22nd September

4.30am was too early for the airport bus. I had to wait a while for the other shuttle passengers. I bought a New Zealand guide and immediately felt at home. The larger central hostel in town was professionally run. I could not check in until 1.00pm and spent my time surfing and booking my Stray Bus tour of the North Island. An eggs benedict and bacon breakfast in a posh café was great. Auckland felt cold. I walked to the harbour and bought inexpensive impulse buys, things that may be useful. I hopped on the ferry to Rangitoto for a volcano summit walk. At the top some German students were having a picnic and I was asked to fill in an environmental survey. There was a Serbian group. A large dinner consisting of sushi starter, seafood main, custard dessert and coffee was needed after the hike. In the evening at a cinema (near the area I celebrated New Year on a previous visit) I finished with a film. An amazingly full day!

Auckland Breakfast and Docks, New Zealand

Auckland to Paihia (Bay of Islands), Sunday 23rd September

I got up at about 5.30am, slightly early which gave me enough time to clean myself up before the 7.15am hop-on hop-off bus to the Bay of Islands. I was with an Italian, Brazilian and German group of boys. We stopped off on the way for breakfast to look at a landmark tree and a shopping area with cafes and souvenir shops. The rainy cloudy weather soon cleared to give an enjoyable and free boat trip among the islands. Dolphins were spotted quickly on the way to the lighthouse and a rock formation with a hole. I chickened out of the brief swim with dolphins in 15°C water, less than 10 metre visibility with agitated water (the Kaikoura area near Christchurch seems to be the ideal place in the world to do this). There were some fancy houses built on the islands. Passengers included an elderly western gentleman with very young Vietnamese girl. I had the free beer on an empty stomach and I am waiting for the barbeque. Another "Base" trademark hostel with very small pool and a hot tub. They were watching world cup rugby in the living room behind the reception area. I feel tired after a long day and am still adjusting to the time zone.

Paihia to Cape Reinga (day trip), Monday 24th September

An alarm went off at 6.15am actually announcing "It is six-fifteen and time to get up!" I got up at 6.30, walked to the beach and took some early morning misty photos. There was a large yellow bus also doing the route up to the northern tip of the North Island. Our bus was a smaller truck, a modified army vehicle. I managed to slip and cut my foot on the back seat. The bus was completely full and I sat at the back. Due to mechanical problems the bus was exchanged (in fact there was a fan belt problem with the new bus at the end of the day). After a stop for breakfast it was a long drive along the "90 mile beach" (Actually 55 miles long). Sounds simple but it really is spectacular driving along a beach between the surf and the dry sand - a smooth journey. There was a lighthouse to see at the northern tip. After the beach the bus actually drove up a stream with a sandy bed and there was sand boarding. I did two runs and it was great fun and I managed to record my second downhill run on video. A stop at a woodcarving souvenir shop, a fish and chip shop and a farmer's fruit stall before finally returning to Paihia after dark. The girls in the room were very sociable while I was writing this entry. I have chosen an extra day here rather than in Auckland which means a quiet relaxing day tomorrow with maybe a 5-minute ferry ride and that is all. No long bus journeys. Tour guide catch phrase: "Love your work brother!"

Rangitoto View and Paihia (Bay of Islands), New Zealand

Bay of Islands and Paihia Morning Mist, New Zealand

Paihia and 90 Mile Beach, New Zealand

Paihia, Tuesday 25th September

Staying here is my alternative to spending another day in Auckland. I did my usual chores: burn photo CD, send it off, coffee, seafood and a fast ferry over to Russell, although the speed of all boats is limited to five knots close to the shore. The weather alternated between one minute of rain then sunshine. I did not take photographs of anything, suggesting a very ordinary day. There was a pub quiz at the hostel which towards the end deteriorated into an 18-to-30 atmosphere, rather than the multicultural international character I enjoy. While I was surfing there was a loud film on TV and a loud Geordie telephone conversation. I enjoyed just reading a magazine and drinking coffee - a simple pleasure. At times I feel comfortable not being particularly sociable. There are so many estate agents in town. NZ is a very pleasant place to live with beautiful nature. I can perhaps realise for the New Zealanders who decide to live elsewhere, they crave a less isolated country with a richer history and the richness a large diverse population generates - the use of the term more sophisticated may be too condescending. The area does not seem to have mosquitoes but other small black flies that bite. The atmosphere in a dorm varies from day-to-day as people come and go.

Paihia to Auckland, Wednesday 26th September

There was a couple in the top bunk above me. A generous breakfast at the place almost next door and I was ready for the day. I walked along the beach across the bridge to the place where the original treaty between the British and Maori was signed. There was a walkway among the trees, a café, audio-visual presentation, war canoe, flagpole and a restored nineteenth century house. Lazing about in town feeding myself it was soon time to return to Auckland. Most people boarded the other large adventure coach. With a friendly receptionist I was soon installed back in the city: Food, internet, swipe key fob to get to the sixth floor and bed. I slept well. I was disappointed I missed the one night gig with Randy Crawford and Joe Sample a few days ago. I should have done a quick review of upcoming entertainment events.

Auckland to Hahei, Thursday 27th September

Off I go again on the Stray Bus to a view point and shopping centre before a beach and cove at Hahei. I still feel the refreshing glow of an afternoon's kayaking. It is chilly now. People on the bus seem sociable: Paula and Clare the Irish girls, Anna the Swiss exchange student and the others. I decided on the spur of the moment to go kayaking and it was fun: Stable with good back

View from Northern Most Point and 90 Mile Beach, New Zealand

Tracks on 90 Mile Beach and Wood Carving, New Zealand

support, going close to the cave and rocks, having fancy coffees on the beach, making sure you are facing the waves head on, steering with pedals and synchronising your action with the person in front - a hot shower and barbeque to follow.

Hahei to Raglan, Friday 28th September

In the morning the bus atmosphere was quiet while everyone was waking. The usual short stops and we were soon at the surf school in Raglan. The dorms were behind the main building with kitchen, pool, dinner table and TV room. After a lesson in how to mount the board from a young Czech woman we were off to the beach. One of the guests drove the minibus. I managed to stay on the board standing up for a couple of seconds: a reasonable achievement for one lesson. It was genuinely a lot of fun. A good excuse to mess about in the sea and the time went really quickly. My muscles did not ache too much. The dorm is pleasantly heated and comfortable. I played a game of pool, internetted and enjoyed two platefuls of Mexican food with a can of 10% lager. There was even a sauna. The surfers' life is not a bad one. Young Amanda has a great Alanis Morisette smile – her mouth's natural shape has a permanent smile shape so that she always seems on the verge of smiling. Just as many animals tend not to breed in captivity, in my normal life I feel economically captive by employment.

Raglan to Rotorua, Saturday 29th September

The heater worked well in the dorm. After leaving the surfers' paradise the next stop was the Waitomo caves. I decided in the morning to visit the Haggas Cave, a combination of abseiling, walking, crawling and climbing. Really so much fun! I feel so comfortable in comparison with the Potosi mines - the cave was refreshing and airy. Even the crawling through narrow gaps was fun. I enjoyed every minute. They took some photos of us and in one I look very evil. Again due to all the travelling I have done I feel fit and have no aches after the activities. I watched the Zorbing (riding in a wet plastic sphere) where some chose the zigzag path. The hostel is quite busy. I was desperate for food so went to a café restaurant and treated myself to great food at this late stage on my trip charged on a credit card. A German school teacher on exchange is sketching items in her journal. I feel I am winding down my trip and know that NZ and Australia are easy countries to travel in. I am also conscious that my freedom is only going to last another month. It is sad! The people on the Stray Bus are a nice sensible friendly group. There is a bar next to the hostel which is deserted

Hahei Kayaking and Rocks, New Zealand

Hahei Coast and Whaka Geothermal Cooker, Rotorua, New Zealand

Bubbling Mud, Rotorua, New Zealand to Melbourne Main Square, Australia

at the moment. Although organised tours are pleasant for a day or two, I imagine they can appear horrifically limiting for longer periods.

Rotorua to Taupo, Sunday 30th September

It was pleasant sitting at the barrel table with NZ easily beating Romania in the background rugby. There was a trip in the morning to the Whaka (the full name has many syllables), a Maori village with hot springs, baths, geysers, corn cooked in geothermal ovens, a culture show and lots of steam and sulphurous smells. The guide used lots of sarcasm. We stopped at the Huka waterfall in the rain (I have high standards for waterfalls) before entering sleepy Taupo, near a lake on an early Sunday evening. I wandered around the grid of shops and treated myself to an Indian curry. I was happy for some peace and quiet. I managed to snooze very easily on my bunk.

Taupo to Auckland, Monday 1st October

I had some posh toast and coffee and wandered the grid of shops, more interesting as they were open. It was soon time to get on the 1.00pm service back to Auckland, a 6-hour journey due to heavy traffic entering Auckland, sitting next to the small Swedish girl. The mp3 player to FM modulator was working well, with lots of mid-eighties music. The guide driver Noddy was brash and sexist. I returned to the large ACB hostel and secured a dorm bed on the sixth floor. It is difficult to meet people in these large institutional hostels. I suppose it is my choice. The Asian food court nearby was an oasis of pleasure. I am not feeling very sociable at the moment and have an easy and relaxing remaining few days in Auckland City. I am just going to go shopping and eating tomorrow and am not sure there are many authentic experiences for me to have here. I emailed the hostel in Melbourne.

Auckland, Tuesday 2nd October

It was an ordinary day full of ordinary activities: Breakfast, wandering around gadget shops and musical instrument shops (Roland HP-207 piano). I was drooling over the iMac 24 inch screen which could run an audio sequencer. Stops at CD and DVD shops with very long queues of teenage girls outside waiting to meet a band and buy tickets, haircut, cheap and tasty sushi, burger, fired off a speculative email, the film "Perfume" at the cinema – nothing authentically from NZ. I may have to try harder tomorrow. So many people were surfing including me, updating my site. I have certainly done more updates as the trip progressed. The dorm is quieter tonight with only a few beds occupied. Although I spent most of my time walking around shops, I did not actually buy anything. My return date to work is looming ever closer.

Auckland, Wednesday 3rd October

I had more of the same: walking, eating well, bookshops, magazines, coffee, walk to the Sky Tower (but not interested in going up) and shelter from rain - normal leisure activities. I bought a little electronic Connect-4 game for my father. Green tea really seems to help my brain think. After a lethargic day of rest I will probably go to the cinema tomorrow. I have seen most of the films currently showing. Not many travel thoughts are going through my mind as the urban environment seems familiar. I have no complaints. I feel satisfied that I have managed to keep this journal up for almost a year. How can the rest of my life compare to the last year! I suppose it is my fault for doing amazing, inspiring and extraordinary things.

Auckland, Thursday 4th October

Big events of the day: I bought some socks and watched a terrorist action film. It was obviously a day not worth writing about. Everyone seemed super friendly for some reason.

Auckland (NZ) to Melbourne (Australia), Friday 5th October

I enjoyed my last breakfast with the friendly waitress. Departure tax was inefficient and the bloke at the gate asked about the origin of my name. I was tired after the 4-hour flight with no window at my seat row. The hostel, a short walk from the station is smaller than the large impersonal mega hostels. There are some friendly sociable people in the room. I managed a short evening walk to the supermarket.

Melbourne, Saturday 6th October

As my life returns to a style I am accustomed to there is little to write about. This is partly because Australia is easy and familiar to travel in, planned as a winding down stage of my year without the need to voraciously consume touristic interests. The modern architecture at Federation Square was

Central Melbourne, Australia

Pixar™ Exhibition and Shopping Mall, Melbourne, Australia

Melbourne Aquarium, Australia

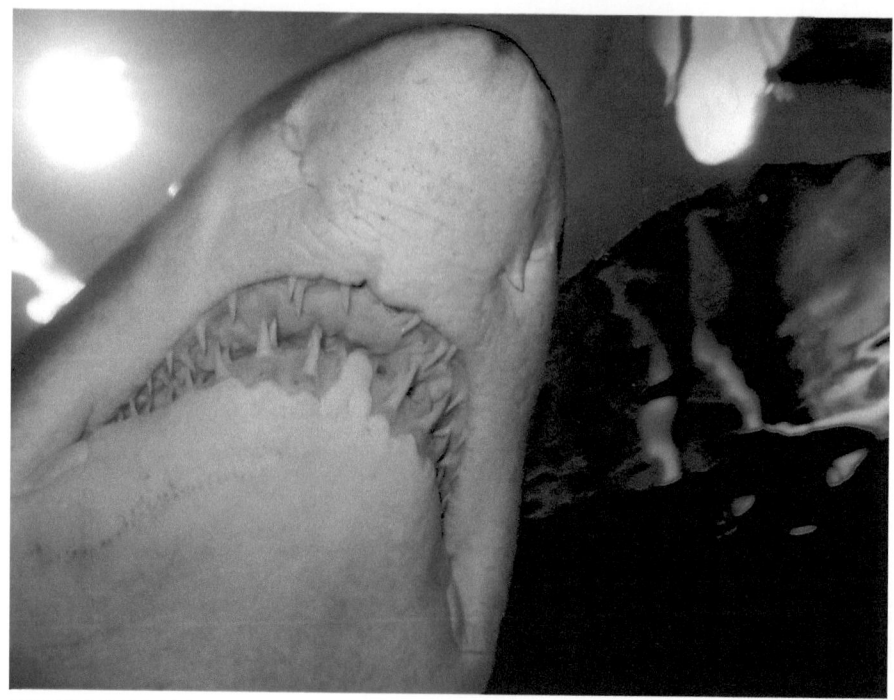

Melbourne Aquarium Shark and Southern Coast, Australia

interesting, near the river and fairground wheel. I looked at the Pixar™ animation exhibition and was attracted to the Mac store opposite. Coffee shops, TVs and computers (very geeky but I like looking at them), a walking circuit and the day was soon over. I was reminded of Seattle but the people here seem more relaxed. It was warm in the sunshine. I rejected the cinema because I have seen all the films. All I need to do is book the trip to Adelaide by bus. The hostel is quieter this evening. An older woman was getting stressed out using a blogger site and needed some technical support. I believe there is a rugby world cup match on tonight at 10.00pm between England and Australia so I may search out a local pub to watch the game (England won). Obviously staying in hostels and dorms I meet lots of younger people and I should not forget their more positive, refreshingly less political approach to life. There is very little headroom from my bottom bunk. Previous people have left food and items in the lockers.

Melbourne, Sunday 7th October

Slow relaxing breakfast, newspaper, watch exhausted people complete the Melbourne marathon, read magazines in Borders, drink coffee, internet, eat, wander around shops, hardly items that should be included in a travel journal. I listened to the Surrey couple organize their luggage. One of the German girls is hoping to train as an actress and likes to dance around. I am enjoying myself relaxing in my bunk watching the activity. I had to grab an extra chair as a couple were Skyping together at one computer. There is graffiti on the planks of the bed above. There was a busker dressed as a spaceman playing a theremin (electronic musical instrument with antennae) in town. Yesterday there was a vocalist supplying the rhythm, bass line and synthesizer bleeps all with his single voice. I booked the three-day bus trip down to Adelaide with a ridiculously early 6.15am start. I might visit the aquarium tomorrow but it is definitely going to be a leisurely and relaxing day. I can not be bothered with the Neighbours tour.

Melbourne, Monday 8th October

One of the German girls transferred to the hostel opposite which has better facilities. My plan today was just the aquarium. The receptionist was actually from Reading. I enjoyed the jellyfish, seahorse and shark swimming over the Perspex archway. I continued along the south bank observing business people have their one hour lunch of freedom. Small birds scavenged inside the food malls. I frittered away the rest of the day. Melbourne looks great in the sun. I flicked through channels in the TV room as I could not sleep so early. The light has been switched off but I will try and continue to write with the distant

Tame Bird and Forest Walkway near Johnston, Australia

Forest Walk and Adelaide Vineyards, Southern Australia

Twelve Apostles Sunset, Australia

ambient light (writing from the Australian Grampians). I have to prepare everything for an early 5.30am start.

Melbourne to Johnston (on the way to Adelaide), Tuesday 9th October

Luckily there was a breakfast place open at 5.45am. The adventure bus tour companies seem to share their work load. We stopped at a surfing shop, lunch and various beaches on the way. The forest walk on raised walkways was great, followed by a spectacular view of the Twelve Apostles rocks jutting out of the sea. There was a sperm whale washed up on the beach. Everyone had to introduce themselves using the microphone on the bus. There was a stop for lunch and also time to buy some alcohol for the evening. I shared with the Japanese couple who were just friends. The barbeque eaten indoors was fine. There were many Germans in the group. I feel very much unfocussed. Brian originally from England is a capable and entertaining driver and guide. Unfortunately a cold disturbed my sleep. The slim heater kept the room warm. The cold temperature really reduced the strength of my camera batteries.

Hall's Gap, Wednesday 10th October

My brain is no longer working. I cannot remember the name of the small town we are staying in (the above added later). More beaches, coves, cliff top walks and many cakes from a bakery including a Cheesemite roll. The English bloke accidentally dropped his camera in the stream. There was a walk for about 45 minutes to the Pinnacle viewpoint, a lush green valley. There was a pasta dinner at an L-shaped table with Winnie the Pooh playing cards. The wooden dorm is very comfortable. Brian skilfully reversed the bus and trailer into the narrow entrance of the hostel.

Hall's Gap to Adelaide, Thursday 11th October

I ate a cereal breakfast, something I have not had for a year. It was a short walk down to a waterfall and a longer walk along rocks, through a cave to the top of a peak near Zero Point. There were grass trees on the way – they look like small trees of grass! A stop at a tiny town for a horrible sandwich near a duck that was keen on eating crisps. I sat at the front of the bus relaxing. People took turns with their mp3 players. With stops to break up the journey, we soon arrived at "My Place". There were friendly hellos from the receptionist (reading from a prepared list of reminders) and the people in the kitchen. I can hear chatting from the balcony outside from my top bunk. I walked to the internet café at the

Vineyards near Adelaide and Looping to Sydney Airport, Australia

other end of town through the pedestrian mall. I have lost my enthusiasm for Kangaroo Island as I have seen seals before and it has no penguins. I have four full days here and I can not see myself doing more than walking around town and shopping. Maybe I will choose a day wine tour. The group suddenly splits up and I am on my own. There was a bloke on the balcony saying I looked like a bloke I had not heard of. I have to think about accommodation for Bangkok and Bahrain.

Adelaide, Friday 12th October

Writing in a kitchen with French conversation in the background makes a change. The girl from Reunion is wearing a Madagascar t-shirt – I have been there! A bloke in a light coloured suit was going to an interview. I walked through the covered market, an impressive range of goods, smells and people. I detoured into a music shop and checked out the keyboards – a hobby of mine it seems when I have no external pressures. Past the green square near the post office where the tram goes to the coast, I completed my chores in the internet café. I will sort out the hotel in Bahrain when I arrive as I could not find any web presence. Fancy chocolate buttons are nice to eat. One day I will buy a watch with compass, temperature and altitude measurement. I walked along the road north of the pedestrianised shopping street, looping through the university and bridge crossing the river. There appear to be lots of sex shops in Adelaide or maybe they are just spread out rather than concentrated in a particular area of the city. Breakfast at the hostel is just cereal so I need to supplement it with something more substantial outside. I received an enquiring email from work which reminds me of my return to the real world. Coming from Melbourne everything here seems normal. I suppose the difference between London and Adelaide is that everything here is more spaced out, less ethnically diverse, fewer old buildings, more architectural uniformity, cleaner streets and no crowds. I will try and think of a few more things. There is an odd half-an-hour time difference between Victoria and South Australia.

Adelaide, Saturday 13th October

I exercised my latent vigilante emotions at a Jodie Foster movie. Breakfast at the covered market set me up for the day. The Glenelg beach was a short tram ride away – neat, clean, a random jet fountain, one main shopping street and a pier. The Australian taste event did not start until 4.00pm so I walked through the park across the river, stopping at a café next to a pond where kids were feeding the birds with cake. I rejoined the main shopping street. The Taste of Australia event was wine tasting with lots of food stalls. I treated myself to cake and coffee and the cinema afterwards. I booked the wine trip for tomorrow, Sunday, a good day to fill with an organised trip as many places are closed. The kitchen is a good socialising room. I will probably go and wind down in the TV room. It is Saturday night and the clubs are active.

Adelaide, Sunday 14th October

I am feeling the effect of a day of wine tasting. Here I sit on the balcony of the hostel with my free tea and a northern conversation in the background about "tsunamis…spiked drinks…Facebook and knob heads". There were only two other people on the wine tour: Three vineyards before a barbeque lunch and a giant rocking horse. With such a small group we could taste a wider range of wines including Jacob's Creek. Passing a sign for cheap helicopter flights (US $20) we stopped for a flight of a few minutes. An ice-cream and the day was over. It was a gloriously sunny day. I snoozed on my top bunk by the balcony windows. The TV room seems such a boring place to be. England managed to defeat France in the rugby union world cup – someone set their alarm for 4.00am this morning to watch the match. I walked into town for a cheap pizza and to get the blood circulating. I have one more day before I fly out on Tuesday. Again I can not see myself doing much. I could have organised a visit to Kangaroo Island but I feel no compulsion to view tourist sites. There is an eccentric bloke wandering around on the terrace and listening to his iPod.

Adelaide, Monday 15th October

Lazy breakfast, lazy bookshop, lazy lunch and lazy gadget window shopping. I watched an arthouse Argentinean film – normally you had to be a member but it was ok just to make a donation for a ticket. The paper reported a local shooting over the weekend.

Adelaide (Australia) to Bangkok (Thailand), Tuesday 16th October

The first airport shuttle was 30 minutes late. Friendly hostellers talked to me as I waited outside the main door. I am becoming familiar with airports, particularly Sydney and the national to international shuttle bus service. Films occupied the 9-hour flight. As it was late I just took a taxi from Bangkok airport to the relatively posh hotel near Khaosan Road. I needed the shower.

Pantip Plaza and Tuk-Tuk, Bangkok, Thailand

Khaosan Road Delights, Bangkok, Thailand

Khaosan Road, Bangkok, Thailand

Bangkok, Wednesday 17th October

The short entries indicate that my adventure travel has turned into conventional holiday travel. A buffet breakfast is included. The famous backpacker street does not really come alive until after dark. I still did my systematic loop. Coins were necessary for the internet café. I decided to head for Pantip Plaza, the IT shopping complex, the location of which I found on the internet. There are large active maps on the pedestrian bridges showing drivers which roads are clear and uncongested. I felt information overload looking at all the goods on display. I looped to the other main shopping complex which used to be called the World Trade Centre. Heavenly Thai food went down well. Streets are full of food stalls. I moped-taxied back and my helmet was dangerously loose – a conventional taxi would have been stuck in traffic. Writing fatigue is setting in. I was bored so decided to take photos of the backpacker street reminding me a little of Phuket. Having experienced a warm climate for the past year the Bangkok air does not seem oppressive. Did I see anything surprising and extraordinary today? No! This was an answer partly due to experience. The locals are very clued up on how to trade and socialise with foreigners. There was an England international football match on TV that was popular with Thais. There was a petrol station that turns into a bar at night. I did not do as much shopping as I had expected. Maybe Bahrain will reveal some hidden bargains.

Bangkok (Thailand) to Manama (Bahrain), Thursday 18th October

The taxi driver (significantly cheaper outside the hotel) originally from China wanted to try out his English. There is so much traffic in Bangkok. For efficiency at the airport they declare the "Final Call" about 40 minutes early. Baggage had been checked through to Cairo so I was essentially without my tooth brush – the issued boarding pass should have given me a clue. I secured my hotel reservation at the airport booth and with free transfer arrived at the hotel. The city reminded me of Dubai - relatively sterile, hot, Arabic and mainly blokes on the streets. The room was air-conditioned to a cold temperature. The internet café had booths with curtains. I filled up late at the pizza chain. There was a late night call offering services.

Manama (Bahrain) to Sharm el Sheikh (Egypt) via Cairo, Friday 19th October

I did not wake up after my alarm but after a telephone call to let me know that my transport to the airport was ready. I felt tired after 6 hours sleep and the time zone shifts during the past few days. I had a rushed coffee. The flight was

Flying South from Cairo and Café, Egypt

delayed by 2 hours and everything on board felt chaotic. The airport at Cairo was as chaotic as I remember: Taxi drivers offering to drive to the other terminal, instead of the alternative airport bus; Blokes without uniform informing everyone that the bus to the other terminal would come in 5 minutes, every 5 minutes! There was actually a change of buses to arrive at the correct terminal. The driver of the second bus vacated the bus after I had entered. I had a generous allocation of 4 hours for the transfer; include the flight delay, waiting for luggage and customs and it was almost a rush. Will Egypt always be like this? I blame the heat. The small blue plane soon sped across the desert down to Sharm el Sheikh. I know how to react when a taxi driver asks for three times the expected amount. I checked out two dive places and settled on Camel Dive because they offered cheap dormitory accommodation. The receptionist did not seem super friendly but I was tired. The receptionist at the Red Sea College greeted me in Russian, indicating the large proportion of Russians that holiday here. I felt like I was in Benidorm, everything compared to my past year felt so culturally false in this expensive touristy enclave. There was an Egyptian diver in the dorm. I had doubts about whether I had chosen a good place for the final few days of my trip. I booked a three day diving package for Sunday.

Sharm el Sheikh, Saturday 20th October

The morning brightness and high temperature hit me as I walked to breakfast. The entrance to the hotel has a beeping metal detector. I walked to the bookshop but the travel guide was a few years out-of-date. There is no shade during the day until about 4.00pm. I wanted to relax and not launch straightaway into the diving. I hate paying over the odds for food and drink compared to the rest of the country. England is in the final for the rugby union world cup later this evening so I will probably sit at a TV bar. There is a swimming pool at the hotel but I feel too lazy to make use of it. The bottle of insect repellent spilled over into my bag during its rough journey so I had to spend time cleaning up.

Sharm el Sheikh to Cairo to London, Sunday, Monday, Tuesday, Wednesday and Thursday 21st-25th October

I basically had a normal holiday time in Na'ama Bay with three days of dives at the Camel Diving Club. The days just passed by. I tried this alternative to the Red Sea Diving College and everything seems to be so relaxed with no rush for anything. The first day diving is always an easy local site to test equipment and level of proficiency. The people on board seemed ordinary having an ordinary holiday of diving. The buffet breakfast each day was excellent with karkady (hibiscus) juice. This place is very popular with Russians, a quick hop down to warm weather from Moscow. I was lazy with fast food for a few days and managed a short trip to the old market and a grade zero haircut. My dorm traveller seemed quite sociable and was learning to teach diving in English, quite a challenge for this Egyptian. Nothing of any significance happened in Sharm. I enjoyed watching the beginners group learn the basics of diving in the swimming pool. Posting comments on the BBC blogs seemed to timeout. I am writing from the Ismailia hotel in Cairo, the third time in thirteen years I have stayed here – the place with the rickety old lift. After travelling for a year the chaos in Cairo is no longer overwhelming, compared to my first visit on the first stop of my very first global trip. I suppose I feel a little sadness that my trip is finally at an end. It feels right though to end now, otherwise I would definitely continue to feel unfocussed in my attitude. It is time to stay in one place for a while and earn some cash. A year's travel is a once in a life time experience. I have to get up at 4.00am for my early flight. There was enough time in the afternoon to explore an old café and stalls near the Hussein Hotel. Distant traffic beeping is incessant. It has been a spectacular year.

Jump forward to the next trip.

What no philosophical preamble?

5. London to Entebbe (Uganda) to Kampala, Tuesday 27th January 2009

I am sitting in the new Terminal Five at Heathrow Airport very early for my 21:00 flight with an echoing BBC News TV channel in the background. London is finally catching up with the impressive airports of the world. There are the usual contrary feelings of excitement and mild unease (which is diminishing). The row about BBC impartiality and the Gaza conflict charity appeal is continuing. After a hot chicken ramen soup I feel comfortable. I switched everything off at the flat and emptied the fridge. It was a cool but bright sunny day in Highgate. My last trip seems so long ago but I only returned 14 months ago. After the poor infrastructure challenges of Uganda most of this short and quick two month trip is comfortable, concentrating more on smaller laidback places where there is little to do apart from dive and eat fresh seafood. I am sure time is going to pass very quickly. My boots are warming up. There was more news about cut-backs and recession. The pound is at a shockingly low value compared to the exchange rate I enjoyed during my last trip. The check-in process was new: the first stage, a self-service machine to verify the flight details, printout a boarding pass, choose a seat and a second stage checked the passport. Flight staff stroll by. It is the first time I am flying with all electronic rather than paper airline tickets.

Kampala. Wednesday 28th January

With a Hellboy action film and a young boy doing word puzzles close by the journey soon passed. Before takeoff there was a delay of over an hour due to a temperature fault in the middle cabin area. On arrival a canopy sheltered the aircraft steps from rain. I had to remind the immigration official about the £10 change for my £30 visa and strangely none of my cards worked at the airport ATM so I was forced to exchange my US dollars. The cabbie soon found me the backpackers, driving past building work, a pickup truck full of goats and primitive structures painted in bright colours advertising products. I had to rest for a couple of hours before negotiating the gorilla trek in the office. Yes! There is a permit available for this on Monday. I now have a full ten day itinerary in Uganda. I was trying to copy the relaxed cat sleeping on the chair.

Kampala to Jinja to Kampala, Thursday 29th January

I have now rearranged the mosquito net above my bed which had made last night's sleep feel restricted and uncomfortable. Any mosquitoes that penetrate the net will have a short life. I woke up early to join the rafting group going to Jinja – but not for the rafting, just to relax at the "source of the Nile" town. My excuse was that I had done rafting before and that my money was better spent on the gorilla trek. There were Australians on board representing a church charity group helping children. Being large I was offered the front passenger seat. I was dropped off near town and "boda-boda-ed" (back of a motorcycle taxi, literally "border border") to the centre to a café for strong coffee and breakfast. I relaxed at the shaded outside table watching people go by and then was offered another boda-boda but this time as a bicycle passenger. I warned the rider about my weight and was forced to walk the last part, past a golf course (women ride side saddle on the back of cycles). I just relaxed with a beer by the river before walking back. After lunch I was ready for the return by shared public taxi. The centre of Kampala was so congested that I had to take another motorcycle taxi through the dusty streets back to the hostel, this time hosting atmospheric live guitar music. A ginger beer on the settee near the side entrance feels right. It is only day two and I am not expecting it to be a non-stop party socially. The staff always seem attentive to my needs. Hopefully I will sleep better tonight. Today was a gentle introduction to my trip.

Kampala, Friday 30th January

There was sudden noise and loud voices when a school party arrived at about 1.30am. People shouted out "shut it!". I woke up at a lazy 9.30am and had simple fried eggs on dry toast breakfast. Riding on the back-of–a-motorcycle is a very effective point-to-point transport for less than US $2.25 a hop. The commentary at the Kabusi Tombs was detailed and the drumming at the museum was repetitive. Sunglasses were essential for all the dust while on the back of the motorbike. The museum also seemed to have a secondary role as a florist for the locals. The buffet restaurant in the busy centre of town was varied and I stopped at the café on the corner nearby. The roads are full of taxi vans with blokes shouting out the names of destinations from them. It was a short walk past the national theatre to the Garden City shopping centre. The internet was slow and virtually unusable. I watched and played pool in the evening with lots of taped up tears in the green cloth covering the table. Walking around Kampala feels so much friendlier than walking around Nairobi in Kenya.

Kampala to Bohoma (Gorilla National Park), Saturday 31st January

(Written in the dark)

As I left the hostel some people were just returning after a night on the town. It was a long tiring bus journey – apparently a baby was sick all over the front of a fellow tourist. I noticed some prominent posters warning about intergenerational sex. There were long waits at villages and the roads gradually became worse, deteriorating to a dirt track. For the last part of the journey there was still a negotiable pickup taxi ride to the Community Rest Camp. The reception was in darkness but for a few oil lamps. The Chimpanzee Dorm was down the rocky path lit by a trail of more oil lamps. A set meal was served in a circular sheltered area with the Danish couple and a Canadian girl on a short trip, both going gorilla trekking tomorrow. If I was sensible I would move closer to the oil lamp when writing this. Groups of young kids shout out and wave when tourists drive past. I lie here on the top bunk comfortable under the octagonal roof. The temperature is cooler so mosquitoes are less of a problem. Some strangers just walked in. I will add anything I have forgotten tomorrow morning. Newspaper headlines declare that O-level results are out with photos of top performing students.

Bohoma Community Rest Camp, Sunday 1st February

Daylight only entered through the ventilation brick above the door. About four staff were staying in the six-bed dorm. They chatted in the early morning and made sure that I had not forgotten to wake up for gorilla trekking (which I have tomorrow). The plan was a lazy day. After a patient 5 minute wait the shower water became hot, heated by a wooden stove. I walked down the road under the hot bright sun. The village is just a collection of simple wooden houses on either side of the road. There was a short self-guided walk along the river passing people swimming in the fast moving water and a clump of several hundred butterflies perched on decaying leaves. I assembled a lunch of chapatti, banana, pineapple and soda and sat eating in a shaded area in the village. The circular restaurant hut was a base for drinking coffee and looking at what was happening around the camp. The German traveller was an experienced driver and expert on Africa in general – his jeep formed the base for a small tent mounted on top. Drums attracted everyone to the orphanage where there was dancing and selling of handicrafts, such as miniature gorillas. The dorm was quieter with only Kristen from Canada.

Gorilla Trekking and Lunch Stop, Bwindi, Uganda

Gorilla Trekking, Bohoma, Monday 2nd February

After a civilised breakfast at 7.00am and registration procedures it was time for gorilla trekking, the main reason for coming to Uganda. The sky soon darkened and optimism for good photography faded. We sheltered from the rain and felt wet and damp for about 6 hours. Information about the location of gorillas, tracked from yesterday's camp was relayed by walkie-talkie. Our chosen family of gorillas was going round in circles and zigzagging. There were rumours of inter-group fighting causing them to progress through the Bwindi forest in a haphazard manner. Sheltering under the trees we were trying to be optimistic by emphasizing only potentially good news. The rain stopped. We walked back down the path and waited. There was a sudden late rush along a rising "waterfall" path with some urgency under the dimming daylight. Our group did not reach the gorillas until 5.30pm leaving only about 40 minutes of available observation time. I wedged my camera into the v-branch of a tree to take a steadier shot as the low light meant blurry hand-held shots. The gorillas were active, feeding, playing, walking about and were less than four metres away. Some followed at the back and temporarily came even closer to us. The gorillas were luckily in a small clearing lying on a soft bed of vegetation. To reach where they had gathered I struggled through narrow spaces and sharp thorns along a steep slippery path. I remembered to stop taking pictures and just to enjoy the moment for a while. We reached base at dusk to receive our certificate of achievement. I was dehydrated and a little tired. The reception had closed quite early and I paid the waiter for my accommodation expenses. The place is much quieter tonight and I am actually alone now at the dining table by the paraffin lamp with noisy insects in the background. Another early start tomorrow and I hope to go most of the way back to Kampala before dropping south for the ferry to the Sese Islands. I just need to review my gorilla photos and hope there are one or two good ones. There were some environmental researchers at dinner. I am feeling quite satisfied. The small international community disassembled as quickly as it temporarily assembled never to be formed again.

Bohoma to Masaka, Tuesday 3rd February

I seemed to slip and slide in the cold dark morning and fell off the back of the motorbike setting off on the steep upward slope with my backpack unhelpfully pulling me backwards. It was just a little tumble but the incident made me super careful on the journey keeping my weight forward on the uphill sections. During the hour long dawn journey to the bus I passed young kids walking to school. One observation: young kids less than ten years old seem to play in the dark in the cities, particularly here in Masaka. After the rubbish was cleaned from the bus I got on for another tiring 10-hour run. The guesthouse was the

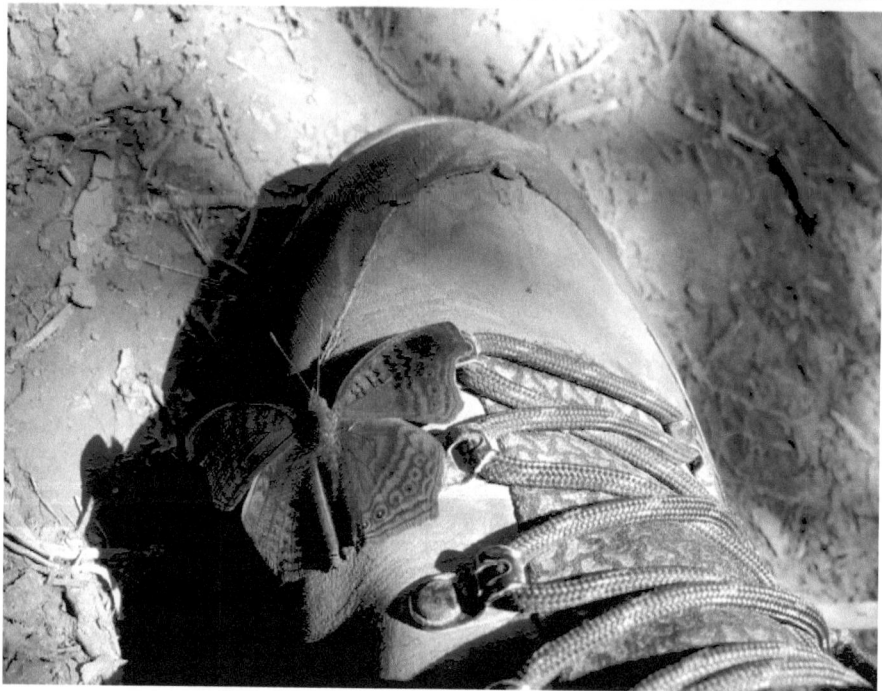

Dusty Kampala Streets and Butterfly on My Boot, Uganda

cheapest so far: a room with bathroom and TV for US $9. I immediately headed out for chicken fast food and cake. One bloke shook hands and followed me but I felt this was more curiosity than weirdness. They forgot to charge for one drink on my order and quickly followed me into the internet café to recover the cash. I am trying to weaken my internet addiction to one hour a week. I have run out of US dollars and need to make sure I have some with me at all times for things like visas and departure tax. This guesthouse is full of Ugandans. I am looking forward to waking at a reasonable hour tomorrow.

Masaka to Kalangala (Sese Islands), Wednesday 4th February

The key feature of Ugandan transport is that it must be completely packed to begin to function. I was overly optimistic to expect to be able to make it all the way to the Sese Islands yesterday. It takes a ritual 2 hours before the taxi-bus begins its journey and prior to that the boda-boda motorcyclist was a little unstable with my weight. There were two vans both trying to attract my custom. Tossing a coin seemed to be a fair way to decide, which they all found hilarious. I met Canadian Dan who was spending a couple of months in Uganda, interested in primates and just recovering from malaria – apparently hospital costs for three days in a private room with IV treatment came to about $40! Progress was slow along the poor roads with many stops. During a very steep part a number of passengers exited to walk allowing the bus to progress up the steep slope. The ferry was primitive and packed full of vehicles and people. Boiled corn-on-the-cob was available. The exposed propellers were driven by what seemed like converted tractor motors. We did not arrive in Kalangala until about 4.45pm. A dog sprinted alongside the motorcycle and suddenly darted into the trees to chase monkeys. The camp was relaxed with its own area of lakeside beach, open air pool table, bar, hammock and dorm. Dorms tend to be empty and cheap as most people feel they are not worth considering as the single rooms are so cheap. The large and bounding friendly Great Dane dog had a scar on his back due to a car fire. Dinner was vegetarian and the empty plate attracted insects - an ant persistently holding onto a mosquito leg. There were distant music beats from the neighbours. A tall Dutch couple stayed in a large tent. A stranded boat on the beach made a great plant pot and photographic subject. To be safe I could only stay one night to ensure stress free arrival in Entebbe in case of transport break downs.

Kalangala to Entebbe, Thursday 5th February

It rained heavily at night. I walked along the beachside path to the ferry, accompanied by the small dog. It was still raining. After a scan with the metal

Kalangala Hostel on the Sese Islands, Uganda

detector I sat down in second class by the porthole window full of mosquitoes trapped in a web. My brain was barely working as I ordered a boiled egg breakfast at the canteen window where I had to stoop down. I soon made it to the renamed Backpackers Hostel to a large empty dorm for a snooze. I seem to have picked up a sore throat and slight cold. The TV was dominating the atmosphere in the reception area. I had enough energy for a walk into town, a more relaxed, greener town compared with Kampala with the lake in the distance. A supermarket stop and food at a bar completed my day. The mosquito net drops neatly down over the bottom bunk. My general impression of Uganda is that it is a super friendly country. I do not expect much activity tomorrow. The normal weather pattern appears to be rain in the morning with the afternoon clearing up. I always seem to have an interesting time when I go travelling!

Entebbe, Friday 6th February

I forced myself to look away from the rubbish on the TV for breakfast. I walked to the Ugandan Wildlife Education Centre. The bloke who walked with me for part of the way chatting expected a tip for some reason. I enjoyed watching the chimps being fed: food was thrown to them on their own little island. I relaxed with a soda at the restaurant with a view and accompanying loud radio music. A school party of very young kids could not take their curious eyes off me as I exited the park entrance. I am writing unusually early from the yard of the backpackers where a worker was just burying a pipe under the grass. I am sitting in a chair made from branches under shade. Every so often a jeep starts up and disappears or arrives. I have just enough Ugandan Schillings left for my dinner – everything else was prepaid. Light aircraft taxiing can sometimes be heard in the distance. The tropical birds are noisy. I am ready to jump to a new continent.

Entebbe (Uganda) to Johannesburg to Hong Kong to Denpasar, Bali (Indonesia) to Padangbai, Saturday 7th to Sunday 8th February

Not much can be written about a 32-hour journey from Uganda to Bali, three flights with 20 hours of flying time including about 10 hours waiting in total and a final motorbike and bus journey. The airports were familiar. I ordered some US dollars on my debit card at Johannesburg airport. There is no need to eat at airports when you are being fed on all three flights. By the third flight down from Hong Kong I got to the exhaustion stage where you know you can immediately fall asleep just by briefly resting on the head rest. To secure cheap transport from the airport I had to wander quite far towards the exit gate. The black helmet from the motorcycle taxi actually fitted my head. With the crowds of mopeds on the road and warm temperature it felt very much like Thailand. The bus station looked inactive (on the Sunday) but with local help I found the right bus further up the road. The driver was happy to receive the generous extra tourist custom. There was a last motorcycle leg following the downhill trail of parked lorries waiting for the next ferry. I entered the nearest place I recognized where the moped dropped me off and lay in my room just off the reception area – only US $6 a night with bathroom including breakfast, great value in Padangbai. Sleeping was a higher priority than having a shower.

Padangbai, Monday 9th February

There are trays of offerings (a ritual to appease spirits and bring good health) placed everywhere containing leaves, rice, flowers and incense sticks including one on the pavement outside the entrance to the Kelmar Guesthouse. This tiny port village is a great place to relax. The memory card for my camera somehow corrupted and at the moment I am not in the mood to persevere for a few hours in an internet café – I do hope my valuable photos are recoverable. Most of the money belts are too small to go around my waist and I later decided to get the zips on the old one repaired. After a Bali coffee in the dark café next door there was a short burst of rain. The success of this port village is all because people are passing through to the ferry. This first floor restaurant looks out onto the beach. My next week will be full of opportunities to eat more seafood.

Padangbai, Tuesday 10th February

It does not take long to get used to the humidity and feeling sticky and not quite dry all the time. The plan was to go for a walk to both north and south of the main bay. A stop for coffee on a bench with magazines was essential. The high temperature and humidity while walking meant constant rehydration. There was a major building project just south – it looks like some kind of luxury development. I stopped at the roadside where a bloke was looking after his pet cockerel – fighting cockerels is a hobby around here. A short haircut in the beauty salon helped me feel more comfortable and look smarter. I am writing from the corner seafood place near the group of moped riders sheltering under a tree. I managed to recover the pictures and update my site – luckily, but retrieving the video files needs more work which I will probably tackle when I return home. The water pressure failed at the hostel in the afternoon. I booked my 6-hour Gilli islands trip for tomorrow (ferry to bus to boat) which will take up most of the day – specifically to Trawangan, the third tiny island off the coast of Lombok. A crowd of surfing backpackers walked past. In countries like Indonesia people live in outdoor houses. Banana pancake and ice-cream finished off the day.

Padangbai to Trawangan (a small island off Lombok), Wednesday 11th February

There were English lessons in Indonesian outside my room last night. I quickly sat on the back of a moped and was dropped off on the ferry to Lombok. Sitting at the stern the sea looked calm but the ferry seemed to sway a lot more than expected. I transferred from the Hindu island of Bali to the Muslim island of Lombok. I entered the small minibus. There was a brief stop at the office where a mangy dog was shooed out into the rain. There were voracious sellers at the small port to the little Gilli islands off the coast, a tiresome but bearable experience. I was soaked more by the sea crossing than by the falling rain. It was a scam zone wandering about looking for a room avoiding puddles and passing donkey carts. I eventually settled on one in the village away from the main strip, past the place where they seemed high on drugs. The hotel was very clean with a scrawny cat and welcome from next door. I was glad to sit out of the wet for a while. I secured the diving with the two instructors sitting at the bar and quickly searched for restaurant food. Even during the low season many recommended hotels were full. I am here for the diving rather than the atmosphere which I am sure is much livelier during the peak August high season. There are too many local restaurants competing for too little business. It reminded me of the tourist-local relationship in Vietnam. The living room is open to this restaurant. I have booked diving for 9.00am and 2.00pm. Even though I am doing a lot of travelling it does seem more like a holiday. There is very little stress associated with the journeys although sometimes they are frustratingly long because of too much waiting time. My shorts are still damp.

Trawangan, Thursday 12th February

I caught the sun on my face and legs from the ferry crossing even though it was cloudy. I rushed my breakfast for the first dive of the day. The shower water in the room is slightly salty. The turtle and manta ray were gigantic and the others saw a dolphin, a rare diving event. When entering the water you had to be careful to avoid the stabilisers on either side of the boat. There was a long break of a couple of hours between the two dives. The rain faded and the sky brightened up. The dive site was changed to a less choppy one. There was not much to see on the second dive apart from mesmerising cuttle fish. Water temperature was 26°C. I watched keep-it-up foot-volleyball for a while and had

Volleyball on Trawangan Island, off Lombok, Indonesia

food at a bar. The photographic light near the pier was excellent at the end of the day. The cinema is free if you buy food or a drink. People seem friendlier today than yesterday – perhaps it is just the drier weather. I must reserve a day to walk around the island. There is a swimming pool at the diving place to wash away the sea water after a dive. I could effectively lock my bag of valuables and put it in the locker at the dive shop. Activities such as these should repeat for the next three days.

Trawangan, Friday 13th February

I have no energy – a combination of diving, large beer and sunburn means sleep is the only option now. The final dive was with a larger group including some open water divers and a trainee divemaster on the larger boat. This time I actually saw sharks at Shark Point. I rested on the roof of the boat. They were doing some painting at the dive school and everyone seemed to help out a little. I saw a reef shark very close up on the second dive, more shoals of fish, better coral and a few turtles and at the end there was a snorkel boat chase for manta ray. I had the same meal at the bar listening to a conversation about working at a nudist camp in Sicily – after a month you just forget about the nudity.

Trawangan, Saturday 14th February

I barely lasted 35 minutes on my dive and followed the float line to finish early. I thought I was relaxed enough during the dive so it is probably down to tiredness or lack of fitness. I enjoyed escaping reality with the Slumdog Millionaire film but the following film's atmosphere was disturbed by dance music next door. It is so not worth writing about normal holiday activities. Nothing uniquely memorable happened.

Trawangan, Sunday 15th February

After a relaxed breakfast I walked around the island in one-and-a-half hours. Stinging sweat dripped into my eyes as I walked past discarded flip-flops along the sandy path. I drank water sitting outside the air-conditioned ATM booth. More luxury hotels are being built. Tomorrow I have an all day trip to Kuta on the main island of Bali. I expect another non-entry in the diary, indicating ordinary holiday activities and perhaps a healthy sign.

Dive boat and coastal view, Trawangan Island, Indonesia

Trawangan (Lombok) to Kuta (Bali), Monday 16th February

I was expecting a long day of travel and it was a long day. Adding the single fare back from this island was more expensive compared to originally purchasing a full return. A fast boat was available for many times the cost. I sheltered under the hut with the other tourists. I was stubborn at the other end and refused the horse-and-cart ride between the boat and bus terminal, an artificial one kilometre margin designed to generate revenue from passing tourists. In the port full of stray dogs and hawkers, I haggled the price of bananas down from 5000 to 3000 rupiah. There was loud techno karaoke and a simplistic slapstick comedy DVD shown on the rusty ferry. Eventually I had to retreat to the upper deck with all the other backpackers. There was a delay outside the port as a previous ferry was occupying the single space. I saw a dead dog floating in the sea. The Irish surfers were chatting to the Finnish girls and we were in Kuta after dark. I found my cheap hotel with balcony terrace from where I am writing now. The room was not quite ready and so I had dinner first and walked in the thick of touristy Kuta looking at all the goods and services a backpacker could desire.

Kuta, Tuesday 17th February

I walked south along Kuta beach to the large cool shopping mall. The hawkers seemed less in-your-face than I had expected. Just walking, stopping for coffee and reading the local paper was fun. I then walked north to the other end of the beach past the flags marking the supervised swimming area and stopped for lunch. Inevitably the expensive luxury places by the beach are full of old people. I was dropped off at the Bali bomb memorial. The pool below the balcony was little used. My card reader seemed to stop working so I had to download photos directly from my camera. I could not resist buying a Blu-ray disc for the future player I intend to buy. My wandering included the two almost parallel Poppies One and Poppies Two alleyways. At one end it is dark with people begging from dark doorways and at the other there are bright lights and music. Most of the shops did not re-open after the heavy rain. Large puddles remain on the paths. I must admit that I do not recognise the place from 15 years ago. It has changed so much with many more hostels and restaurants.

Kuta in Bali (Indonesia) to Hong Kong to Manila (Philippines), Wednesday 18th February

Writing on the Thursday: what did I do only a day ago? I walked to the German breakfast place after having a little fruit breakfast at the hotel. There were many

Kuta Beach, Bali, Indonesia

people beckoning for massages. I was looking to use up the last of my Indonesian currency (which was eventually spent on departure tax!) I dumped my travel guide asking the owner to give it to someone who looked lost. The air-conditioned taxi arrived and whisked me to the airport. The orange sunset light reflected from the jet engine. I recognised the flight approach to Hong Kong airport. The transfer route was the same as my previous recent transfer. Filipinos sat next to me were curious about my trip. The taxi procedure was quick, painless and not too expensive. I entered the hotel past the coffee place at about 1.00am, paying in advance as requested. The "economical room" with a noisy fan was adequate and the bathroom was designed for a much smaller person.

Manila, Thursday 19th February

I was woken by urban noises: traffic, beeping, construction, hammering and playing children's voices. I am sitting on a bench next to the coffee place now with the security guard standing at the front. I did not walk far enough to find his recommendation for breakfast. I walked to the Intramuros or "Walled Town", past the fancy decorated buses, motorcycle-powered carriages, walking along the busy main road going further than I had intended to the fort, past a photography exhibition housed under the damp archways. The river view with excited school children was gloomy. I briefly chatted with the drinks vendor before wandering around the old church and museum with a courtyard. I fantasised over the fancy Protrek watches (compass, solar powered, pressure and temperature measurement and with world time zones) but could not justify a purchase – I already have a robust working travellers watch. After eating at many food places and a quick derivative film there were many prostitute "hellos" as I left the cool mall. I imagine the same happens in London but I do not frequent those areas. The mall culture is understandable. There are few international travellers staying at my hotel. The touristy area with the old walls is quite run down. There does not seem to be a unique global feature that the Philippines offers to attract tourists. Children play in the busy urban streets. This does seem to be a happening area: saxophone jazz, a few Korean restaurants nearby and it is still busy at 11.15pm. I am not sure how much advice I will receive here about the best way to travel down to Donsol. Finding out how is my only planned task for tomorrow.

Manila. Friday 20th February

This morning I was woken by a loud droning generator of some kind. After enquiring about the price of a tricycle (five times what I was expecting) I walked

Fancy Jeepneys, Manila, Philippines

south instead. The large cultural centre with a musical instrument museum was described as "bombastic" in the guide – grand, out-of-place, underused and decaying. There are foot-high pavements, poor almost shanty housing, particularly along the banks of the canal and blokes playing a board game with bottle tops on a playing surface chalked on the pavement. At one point there was noisy chaos: lorries, cars, buses, people streaming out of the train station and vendors. I stopped for sugary drink energy. Near the financial district there were glass and aluminium modern structures almost like Singapore City, passing five same brand coffee shops in the space of a kilometre. The art museum was fine, starting on the third floor and working down with numbered dioramas or scenes of important points in history. There were preparations for some kind of Oscar party. The museum merged into multiple connected shopping centres with an open air chapel in the gardens. I had such low energy that I had to sit, cool down and surf in an internet café. An air-conditioned cab sped me back to base with a begging child filling the car door window at a junction. There are occasional smells of sewage. It is difficult to gauge whether there is more begging in London where it is more difficult to differentiate between tourists and locals and specifically target tourists.

Manila to Donsol (overnight bus), Saturday 21st February

Knowing that I had a late afternoon overnight bus to catch I had a slow morning. There was a rare tourist from Lithuanian in the cafe. I braved the underground train system which was packed with people but air-conditioned super cool. Bags were searched before entry to the platform. It was again urban chaos at the other end, perhaps more chaotic and noisy because I had experienced calmer places recently. It took five minutes to cross the road via the shopping mall and raised walkway. I found the bus depot and secured my air-conditioned bus at 5.00pm. I left my rucksack with the guard and killed a few hours with food and wandering about but not too far. The waiting in the pre-departure lounge with a doughnut seller was casual. The coach did not appear and depart until 6.00pm. Passengers all hated the overly strong air-conditioning and tried to block and divert the air vents in some way. I was lucky the seat next to me was empty. A t-shirt worn as a head scarf kept me warm.

Donsol, Sunday 22nd February

The journey is the equivalent of a long-haul flight with constant turbulence but amazingly I slept for about 4 hours. The successful outcome of sleep on a coach requires a real determination to sleep, tiredness, warmth and finding the least uncomfortable position. I was surprised waking up a few kilometres from

Boat and delivery, Donsol, Philippines

the final destination where local sellers had flooded the bus. More palm trees and a drop in infrastructure appropriate for a remote place reminded me a little of India with added American franchises. The last leg was a motorcycle sidecar to the resort arriving at 6.30am. There was however some activity at this hour as boat trips start early and people were preparing for breakfast. I found out there was a diving opportunity (about one-and-a-half hours away by boat) which seemed a better way to see the butanding or whale sharks, at some kind of aquatic cleaning station dive site. If I do not see any whale sharks (which is unlikely) I will join one of the snorkel boats where they might find and swim with typically eight individual sharks on one trip. Anyway, I need to have another chat with Carlo the diving organiser. I walked up and down the beach, the road past the other resorts, registration centre and paddy fields. There is an American family here with babies and young children keeping isolated as a group. People are friendly and I have a cheaper and perfectly adequate room off the reception. The "normal" accommodation is a self-contained cottage. It would be nice to take a photo of the shark which may only be possible using one of the disposable "down to five metres depth" cameras during a snorkelling trip.

Donsol, Monday 23rd February

With too few people there was no diving available so I joined a group for the snorkelling for whale sharks - a great activity. Every 20 minutes or so after spotting a fin the guide shouts "ready" and we all jump in and try to keep up with these graceful eight metre long creatures. I lost the bottom part of my snorkel (outlet valve) while attempting to wash the mask. The group: German, Swiss, Canadian and Dutch. Heiki (born and lived in the Philippines for her first three years) was quite enthusiastic. I looked around other diving places and all seem short of people. I watched a DVD about whale sharks from the dive instructor who lives in the loft above the hut. I met the group again and made up the numbers for the fireflies excursion with a quick beer at the end of a surprisingly sociable day. There were three people on the back of the bike and two in the sidecar on the way to the river trip. Building styles observation: my bed is made of bamboo and the concrete pillars are made to look like bamboo.

Donsol to Manila (overnight bus), Tuesday 24th February

I had a painful chesty cough and flu symptoms overnight and I am not sure it was wise to decide to take the bus back to Manila rather than rest. It is not clear whether the flu symptoms distracted me from or worsened the pain of the journey. Even at the last minute the resort receptionist was pretending that the

Whale Sharks, Donsol, Philippines

cost to the bus station by motorbike sidecar was 240 Pesos instead of 40 Pesos. None of the model souvenir whale sharks appealed. It turned into an epic 16-hour journey beginning at noon. During the first half of the journey the bus never went above 40 miles an hour and stops for food were every 15 or 20 minutes where vendors would walk up and down the bus. There was an hour stop where the driver played cards and 5 minutes later another stop for food. The driver even stopped to buy a bag of noodles. Although the system gives freedom and lack of discipline to be so inefficient, it forces many people to give up their freedom in submitting to such an inefficient system. Soon after I made some earplugs from tissues the loud 60s to 80s pop music stopped. The chord progressions were bland. The bus is no better than an Indian bus: the drone of the engine, the rhythmic metallic creaking and the bouncing of the windows and persistent sewage smells approaching Manila. Philippine bus journeys excel in the loudness of the traffic, horns and rasping exhausts. In summary the overnight trip was agony. I do not know why I subject myself to such pain; the seats are quite small and there seemed to be only two positions that provided any support in both of which I felt much heavier than normal. The roads outside Manila are bleak with little light and much concrete. The 2-hour delay extended the agony.

Manila to Alabang to Batangas to Anilao, Wednesday 25th February

There is no specific or compelling reason to visit the Philippines. It is a bit like Sri Lanka in that respect – there are better examples of what is on offer elsewhere. Without any sleep it was difficult to cope with the gaggle of taxi drivers on arrival. I managed a short tricycle ride to the bus station where the security guard allowed me to sleep on the chairs for two hours until it became light. In my non-alert sleepy state I managed a breakfast at the fast food Jollibee place and a train ride but the directions in the book were wrong as there is a local Mabini in Manila as well as a regional Mabini in Batangas. Anyway I had a ride in a jeepney for the first time and as predicted you never end up where you intend to go. A policeman on a motorcycle kindly gave me a lift to the correct regional bus stop. There was a final hour-long leg of the journey from a port to Anilao by motorcycle sidecar – fumy and hot and I had to crouch down to see through the windscreen. I had no difficulty in closing my eyes to sleep at the diving resort with a plan to do very little tomorrow and just recover.

I suppose with this trip I am tying up loose ends visiting places or parts of countries I was still curious about but never quite got round to visiting. I am writing from the diving resort with wooden floors and Japanese style window screens. The place seems deserted. I should be able to afford to go diving even if it is just me going out on the boat.

Scuba diving (me!), Anilao, Philippines

Anilao, Thursday 26th February

I was not expecting much from the day, just recovering and reading of magazines. I had no difficulty snoozing. My body demanded inaction. I committed to diving tomorrow just for me and perhaps with more divers on Saturday. The climate is hot and humid enough to make most European faces appear greasy or shiny. I seemed to have regained enough energy to write and hopefully enjoy the dive tomorrow. Internet access was free and the staff gave me a laptop. Taking a camera on the dive also appears to be free. Hooray! I am beginning to warm to this place. I expected there to be more divers and to be able to join a group every day. My fluey cough seems to be manageable. I caught up with the Oscar results and was glad that Slumdog Millionaire had won.

Anilao, Friday 27th February

Basically it was just me and the crew on the boat. I kept passing the digital camera (with an underwater housing adaptor) between the divemaster and myself. There was a spectacular shoal of jack fish moving slowly and completely filling my field of vision. A mad feeding frenzy of small fish at the Cathedral dive site (there is a concrete cross and the site resembles a roofless cavern) gobbling a piece of bread in a plastic bag. Visibility was excellent and I was back at base by 10.30am because of the early start. I examined the photos and videos on the laptop in the afternoon. Activities: drinking coffee, taking photos of the sunset, eating tasty pork with rice and enquiring about making a phone call (apparently there is a mobile phone available somewhere). I will be diving alone again tomorrow. I am not sure if they intentionally keep people separate as normally part of the fun of diving is joining an interesting group. There is some kind of bird in the thatched roof that announces the dawn light.

Anilao, Saturday 28th February

There was a high current and poorer visibility. Again I can sustain only about 35 minutes rather than the expected 45 minutes. The place is much busier today with weekenders coming in from Manila requiring a buffet and a few more staff. It was more expensive than I had expected but still acceptable. I spent the rest of the day internet surfing. It is so addictive catching up with news and blogs and surfing for fancy gadgets. I cannot wait to develop my disposable underwater camera film. Time has passed here quite quickly despite doing very little. I am back to crowds tomorrow. Health is more or less back to normal after a blip.

Anilao Sunset and Manila Cock-fighting, Philippines

Anilao to Manila, Sunday 1st March

After standing in the bus shelter for a few seconds I was offered a quicker lift to catch the bus back to Manila. I probably could have got off the bus closer to my hotel rather than waiting until the terminal stop. I developed my disposable camera and there was at least one recognisable whale shot with a few inexplicable red streaks – a success. I hopped to investigate the cock-fighting arena with a mad shouting betting build-up before each contest. Each cock has a blade attached to one leg so that a scratching blow becomes a potentially fatal blow. It is primitive and incredible. There are blokes that annoy the birds in preparation to encourage them to fight producing a cloud of feathers. What on earth is the human race up to? I had a short cooling haircut on the way. The rest of the day I spent in the mall. If I remain in the Philippines I am destined to live in a mall for the rest of my life with its controlled atmosphere and large chicken dinners – an empty but comfortable life.

Manila, Monday 2nd March

People stare at laptops in coffee shops. I do not have to be at the airport until 16:30 so expect more of the same tomorrow - no great adventures in a mall. My motivation and justification to buy goods is small. The heat is making it more difficult to get to sleep. This hotel with wooden floors and staircase is popular and central. With energy saving light bulbs the room appears dim.

Manila (Philippines) to Sydney (Australia), Tuesday 3rd March

I managed to sleep in my stuffy warm room – the fan did not seem to make that much difference. I did nothing of any significance apart from feed myself. I was happy to jump to a new country but watching the films seemed more interesting but less sensible than choosing to sleep on the plane.

Sydney to Nelson Bay, Wednesday 4th March

Customs did the usual cleaning of my boots. The route to Central Station by train was so painless. I walked north to the Victorian shopping mall for a posh breakfast with the early morning commuters. I struggled to keep my eyes open but enjoyed it just the same. Visiting the IMAX theatre felt stale so I decided against it. The Darling harbour area was quiet on a weekday but I still managed to attract a weirdo while sitting on the wooden steps next to the group of

Harbour and bird, Nelson Bay, Australia

school girls. I think meeting people is like online discussion forums: a certain percentage will be sensible, unrelated, funny, weird or mad. I managed to return to the bus station under the arches. Sydney seems a little subdued without bright sunshine. There was an elderly Italian traveller going to the same place who seemed to show little initiative and needed too much guidance. Maybe I am the same if speaking a second language but I like to think I am more relaxed and less demanding of all the exact details. It took some time to clear the suburbs and join the freeway. There was a lift available directly to the hostel from the coach station. It rained heavily and I was glad to be in the dry. The large living room and kitchen hut was quite busy with the dorm situated at the back with the other wooden huts. The owner was going to the supermarket and kindly gave us a lift. I was out of practice buying food. An early night was appropriate considering I had no sleep last night. I squashed a mosquito on the armrest in the comfortable communal area of this hostel. A possum popped in to the room to say hello and there was a tame kangaroo and a tame exotic bird that landed on my shoulder.

Nelson Bay, Thursday 5th March

The Italian came in and out of the dorm about four times before eventually leaving (we bumped into each other in the town later). Hiring a hostel bicycle was free (no gears, no oil on the chain and a compulsory helmet). It was hard work cycling. I lazed on the local "One Mile Beach" before cycling to Nelson Bay. I had to revert to walking on the steep sections. My original plan was to swim with dolphins but I felt unmotivated. It just felt unnecessary – how can it compare with whale sharks? So I sat on the bench in the partial shade outside the post shop talking to the apparently senile bloke who thought I was someone else. I treated myself to fancy breakfasts and coffee I would not normally have back home. I booked my bus journey for tomorrow, a night bus up to Byron Bay which looks more compact and walkable. There was a partial train option but I picked the simplest journey. I talked to an American bloke who had lived in San Francisco for a few years and had done some kind of paragliding course. The atmosphere in the hostel is friendly and laidback. There were so many large gas barbecues being used last night on the wooden walkways outside the living room. I was envious of the sizzling food. It just does not feel right doing anything very active at the moment although I did expend some energy with the cycling which is good for me! I enjoy places where I can explore by walking everywhere. The morning was cool enough to need a blanket.

Byron Bay, Australia

Nelson Bay to Newcastle to Byron Bay, Friday 6th March

I finished my juice from the hyper–cold fridge with the glass door. The guests enjoyed watching the comedy "Yes Man" last night. The DVD built into the TV was more reliable than the separate. In the evening the hostel pet kangaroo kept coming up to the glass doors to see what was going on. I decided on an earlier bus so that I could relax in Newcastle for lunch. There was broken glass at the bus shelter and the other two got a lift before the bus arrived. I found the café near the train station and ordered whatever the staff recommended or was popular. There was no swimming and no dogs at the beach (a few minutes walk from the centre) so I just watched the sea under shading slats. I picked up my rucksack from station storage and the overnight Greyhound Bus to Byron Bay soon arrived, everything so ordered, logical and smooth.

Byron Bay, Saturday 7th March

I arrived in Byron Bay at 4.15am and attempted to sleep on the bus stop bench. There were other tourists there with noise from cars and locals at this time in the morning. I found the main hostel and managed to sleep on the sofa near reception. As often with popular hostels only those who take the care to reserve in advance manage to stay there. Even my second choice was full (but I reserved the following two days) so a short walk to the YHA was necessary. A shower was essential and although the fan was on full the room seemed extremely warm. A posh breakfast was essential. I had to snooze a little in the afternoon. I walked along the beach and swam in the pool nearby with the broken lockers. The spicy Mexican food was great and my unusually large ice-cream dripped all over the place. I enjoyed the two buskers (guitar and ukulele) while drinking a "flat white" coffee at a table outside reserved for someone else for 7.30pm. The place had self-service pin number lockers in the TV room. Often the TV room seems like a dead area and complete waste of time when on holiday.

Byron Bay, Sunday 8th March

I transferred to the other Aquarius Hostel and decided to book the diving – it was next door and I needed a sociable activity. I dumped my valuables so was beach ready and enjoyed just jumping up and down as the waves came crashing in and sitting under the shade of the tree. The diving involved launching the inflatable boats from the beach and speeding to the rocky dive site. An enormous turtle was trying to sleep under a rock. Amazingly I was not the first one to use up my air. The dorm is larger and better ventilated, found up the stairs at the end with a balcony and dedicated bathroom. I hydrated and had a Vegemite and cheese scroll. The place does cheap $5 meals if you buy a drink so I may try that next. Pool was free tonight. I wandered into town and sat on a bench watching the funky buskers where I met some Croatians.

Byron Bay, Monday 9th March

The Norwegian guests in the dorm are noisy with disco music, euro pop and constant gossip. There were birthday celebrations in the morning with sparklers on a cake and some swapping of beds last night but I managed to sleep in the cooler temperatures with the central fan. I just ordered exactly what I wanted for breakfast. It does not happen often enough. Activities: Cash from the ATM, buying a bus ticket for tomorrow, cake, coffee, replacement t-shirt, reading a newspaper about a cyclone further north up the coast and relaxing in a cushioned bench in the covered area of the hostel (where they are renovating and moving things about). With perfume smells in the air they look as if they are all going out to a club as a group. I had a tea in the Balcony Restaurant with more magazines and newspapers and walked to the eastern end of the beach and back. There is a wooden walkway where you can watch the many surfers. There is something therapeutic about walking barefoot along the wet sand with occasional surprising shallow waves of sea water. I do not think I could keep up with the Norwegians. The bathroom was full of all different types of shampoos and clothes drying everywhere. The cheap and tasty backpacker goulash meal is worth mentioning. My rucksack is packed ready for my short bus journey and surprisingly Queensland is one hour behind. You would not get this lively activity in an isolated expensive hotel room. I do not think they are bothered by my presence. I feel ultra relaxed and feel happy doing nothing really. I have a single room reserved for Brisbane. There was a party on the balcony with more birthday sparklers.

Byron Bay to Brisbane, Tuesday 10th March

I believe if you grow up in Byron Bay however nice a place it is you are destined to leave later in life to follow your ambitions. The minibus journey was a quick two-and-a-half hours and a short walk to the corner Palace Hostel, now renamed to a chain I remember from Auckland. I felt I had enough energy to do the Brisbane walk through malls and past important buildings. Australia is a civilised country and I am still surprised by the lack of people in the big cities - some would say the right amount. I bathed in the enthusiastic conversations of the university campus. It was quicker to cross the river by the bridge than wait for the next ferry. There was an artificial beach and there was no real point in looking at the Nepalese pagoda. I did the walk today partly because I do not know how long the dry weather will hold out. The downstairs bar offered a "steak and drink 10 AUS$ deal" but the atmosphere was not that inviting. Everyone is in the same boat and I am not sure how to encourage more sociability. A large sweet pie and coffee in the mall café and a comic book film ended the evening. The ceiling in the room is just big enough to accommodate the fan but it does feel good to have my own space, however small. I need to do something more sociable tomorrow.

Brisbane, Wednesday 11th March

It lightly sprinkled with rain on and off all day. I had my usual lazy breakfast next door to contemplate the day's activities. The koala sanctuary would not be so good on a wet cloudy day. I looked at some weather sensing gadgets then walked towards the other prominent area of town, around China Town with adventure shops. I almost bought a poncho for the wet weather but it was too flimsy. I drooled over the small netbook but could not really justify buying this gadget. I wandered quite far to the ordinary suburban streets full of traffic. After a quick Thai meal in China Town by the time I returned it was 4.00pm. My key card needed re-enabling before it allowed me back into my room. I bought another cinema ticket (escapism but not very sociable) and the usual backpacker meal and did some internetting. Strangely the bigger cities are less sociable or alternatively you have to be more targeted in your social interactions and cannot just easily talk directly to strangers. Walking all day means it is easy to sleep. The office opposite my fourth floor window reminds me of work.

Brisbane, Thursday 12th March

It looked a bit brighter today so I went to the top of the City Hall clock tower with a Croatian lift steward. I tried to follow a private group in to listen to council deliberations but was turned back. The state library had a large internet room. I engaged the interactive science exhibits and multi-reflection triangular mirror and I am 118 Kg in weight and 1.90m in height, obese according to the simplistic body mass index measure! I made an effort to visit the modern art museum and most of the normal art gallery was closed for renovation and preparation for upcoming exhibitions. There was graduation day at the Cultural Centre – mine was many years ago! I was on my feet most of the day. The window to my room was open. The trip to the airport seems straight forward with trains running every 30 minutes or so from the station next door. I have made the cultural inroads into Brisbane life that I expected. It all seems very neutral and predictable. A PA system just made an announcement attracting people to the downstairs bar. It is only my tenth trip around the world! I must have learnt something in that time. On this trip I feel like I am just passing through.

Brisbane to Fiji (Nadi), Friday 13th March

I have never been driven in an electric cart from hotel reception to my room before. Just as I do not quite fit into the getting drunk backpacker scene, I do not always feel quite comfortable in the opulent everything is done for you luxury resort, although the backpacker scene does seem more human and sociable! The strong sun appeared for the first time in Brisbane. Again the trip to the airport was just so civilised – a train from Central Station one minute walk away with lots of busy commuters arriving in the city. There was a supervised trainee in the currency changing booth who was painfully slow at counting out money. I noticed increased humidity in low season Fiji. Even though it is a luxury resort I still had to wait 10 minutes before checking in – disgraceful! The luxury is a real shock after backpacking these past six weeks - although in a nice comfortable way. At least eight active staff are always in view at the restaurant. Obviously it was an excellent dinner with a bit of coconut nibbling at the end. Prices are normal western restaurant prices but I was shocked at the £15 an hour for internet access which I obviously did not use. The luxurious room comes with a flat screen TV and sumptuous beds. Even I am going to have more than one shower here, this comfortable stepping stone to my next destination of Tonga (a stop was necessary because of incompatible connecting flight times).

Fiji to Tongatapu (Tonga), Saturday 14th March

The hotel room alarm clock beeped unexpectedly at 6.00am. After lifting myself from the soft bed I chose from the buffet and enjoyed. The whole breakfast process is guided. It was easy. The flight was only 1-hour-10-minutes to Tongatapu. I had to hang around a little before I secured a shared van to the capital, sharing with someone working for a tour company that organises round-the-world trips in a private jet, preparing for an expected group. The driver mentioned that he had been deported from Hawaii for dealing in crystal meth! There is again a reverse shock from the luxury of last night to normal budget accommodation; 15 minutes walk from the wooden palace in the centre of town - all very informal, a friendly owner and a kava (traditional drink) session in the evening. There was enough time to walk into town and sit in the "Friends Café" and pay for a day trip for tomorrow to fill a lazy Sunday where everything shuts down. I stopped at the restaurant for grilled fish on the way back. The Italian place looks expensive (normal European prices!). These past three days the room size has varied from 1 to 10 to 3 in relative terms. The place reminds me of Western Samoa with not too much concrete, very sociable, the same types of curved roofs, more traditional dress and less isolated. I love travelling! There used to be a sandy beach outside but to protect the houses from the sea an artificial reef was constructed. There are other people staying here but I have not talked to them yet. Hopefully the fan will discourage mosquitoes.

Tonga (Nuku Alofa), Sunday 15th March

The tour company had trouble finding my accommodation which has no identifying sign so instead of a 10.00am tour of the island it became a 1.00pm tour. In the mean time I read magazines sitting in the long veranda area and the owner kindly offered me a delicious curried chicken lunch. There was no point in being angry about the lateness of the tour. The blow holes were interesting and the other sites were historically significant but not that amazing in the present day (Cook's landing point and a few graves). My small torch was hopelessly dim in the second cave. I chatted with a retired traveller in the café for a while before walking back just before dark stopping at the same restaurant as yesterday with a large lively table of Australians and playing children. There is an opportunity for more kava tonight. This drink is a slightly pungent emulsion tasting like dirty water, giving a sensation of clear-thinking and calmness, similar to alcohol consumption. The owner is having difficulty deciding whether to go to his son's graduation (the first in the family) because of the expensive airfare to Fiji. The ceiling fan is creaking.

Nuku Alofa, Monday 16th March

There is much more life in this sleepy town on weekdays. I walked and sat in the main café, arranged diving for tomorrow over the phone and wandered around town. I may have to do some shopping here because at home I am over normal size but here I am average so trousers are cheaper and even though there are only two main clothes shops, they have a wide selection that fit me. I drank from a bottle of water as I walked and found the places more locals use. I may have to buy some kava powder as a souvenir. The Italian place did not have enough filling in the pizza but the tiramisu was fine – the restaurant was almost full. Again more discussions on the veranda over a kava drink. My third night and I feel comfortable and settled.

Nuku Alofa, Tuesday 17th March

I was picked up on time, traversed the large boat to reach the smaller boat for two dives. I saw a small turtle but the visibility was poor on both dives (later found out that this was probably due to the eruption of an undersea volcano 6 miles away). If I was serious about diving I would need more time and a visit to the islands of Vava'u and Eua, meant to be world renowned. I put on my Buoyancy Control Device in the water for the second dive. A post-dive snooze was necessary and I lazily taxied into town for food and relaxation. A school is next door and you often hear classroom recitation and repetition from 7.00am till late, as the school hours are arranged to avoid the warmer midday and afternoon temperatures. The kava seems to have a relaxing effect, making one seem more eloquent and awake. The only other activity that I might do is a quick day trip to one of the closer small islands. My trip is almost at an end. As I have been to San Francisco before I feel little pressure to rush to see sights.

Nuku Alofa, Wednesday 18th March

The key to an enjoyable visit to a country does not necessarily depend on the adventure activities that you choose. Just feeling and experiencing a part of the culture can be sufficient. I could not find the barbers nearby and took a taxi into town for my usual style of relaxation. I eventually found a barber for a close clipper shave. I replenished my wardrobe with many trousers (casual and smart) and bought a token turtle carving made from coconut – less like an epic trip and sounding more like a conventional holiday. There was talk of volcanic activity explaining the unusual cloud plume in the distance which could also explain the poor visibility of yesterday's diving. The owner was burning rubbish in a metal drum. I can only see myself doing more of the same over the next few days.

Nuku Alofa, Thursday 19th March

I lazed all day. I had an interesting long cultural conversation with the bloke who owned the café, originally from Germany and lived in New Zealand most of his life and now working many leisurely hours in the café. Discussion covered identifying cross-cultural values, transformative perspectives of living in a new place, quickly perceiving the essence of a particular culture allowing recognition of good and poor aspects and so on.

Nuku Alofa, Friday 20th March

I am now an expert at coaxing the fan in my room to work with the faulty rotary switch. The fault is not an annoyance but an acceptable situation requiring flexible thinking. People here on Tonga spontaneously offer you a lift, part of a low population island culture and a chance to talk to someone from the other side of the world in exchange. In addition to the recent geological volcanic event, there was an earthquake early this morning! There was about a minute of gentle shaking. Afterwards locals just got on with things. The person behind the tourist desk said that they had received a phone call from overseas relatives before hearing the official tsunami warning. There are cannons in the garden – a British influence on garden decoration? I phoned home. I still find the time difference amazing: London was 13 hours behind on a Thursday night and it was already early Friday morning here; And the technological achievement of phoning from a small island in the South Pacific and selecting one of millions of phones in London. The power failed in the Friends Café. I sent some volcanic plume photos to the BBC News website. The day disappeared with coffees, a toasted sandwich and internetting. I reserved my taxi for tomorrow's departure. I was a bit short of Tongan money but managed to change a few US dollars at the Italian place. I was offered raw fish when I returned to the guesthouse after my usual dinner in the restaurant down the road. By staying put for my week in Tongatapu I feel I have experienced more than I would by rushing around. A week is almost enough to develop a routine.

Nuku Alofa to Fiji to LA to San Francisco (USA), both Saturday 21st of March after crossing the International Date Line

I walked to the taxi booth. They accepted Fijian money at the Tongan airport. I felt a strong need for a drink. One end section of my bag split, maybe because the boot inside levered and tore the material. There was no point in complaining too much. I only had enough Fijian money for some energy giving fizzy drinks at the gate. The walkways were a favourite place for the flocks of birds sheltering from the rain. It felt great not having any hand luggage and dumping the 18 kilogram bag. LAX airport is now familiar. There were lots of standby announcements for flights. The shuttle van quickly left and sped me directly to the Green Tortoise Hostel. I am writing from the International Room of the hostel, a grand place full of character (an old ballroom), piano, music, kitchen, location of free breakfasts and a high brown ceiling. Although I was here 15 years ago I did not recognise anything inside the building. It has totally transformed and if I am able to judge objectively with my experience of hostels around the world, it is one of the most characterful. Sometimes this rating is so difficult to assess and dependent on where you are on your

Veranda and Blow Holes, Tongatapu

Coastal View with Volcanic Eruption, Tongatapu

Hostel and Architecture, San Francisco, USA

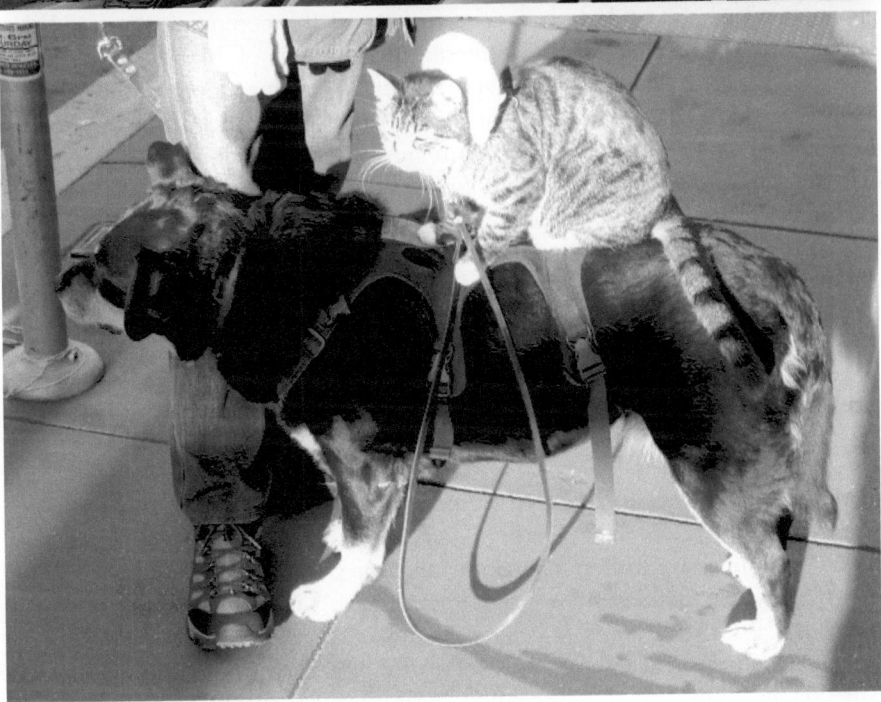

City with Rat on a Cat on a Dog, San Francisco, USA

journey – for example one might be more emotional at the finish. I was in the room at the bottom of the stairs on the same level as reception, past the free internet computers. Again all very well suited to the backpacker: sturdy bed, individual lights and a wooden locker under the bed. The queue was too long outside one Chinese restaurant so I went next door and just about finished the generous portions. A paper journal although less efficient than a computer seems preferable on adventurous trips because it is worth little to thieves. When I asked about good restaurants I was handed a thin strip of paper with all the recommended ones listed.

San Francisco, Sunday 22nd March

Sleep was intermittent but sufficient. The green sign of the hostel remained illuminated until about 4.30am. The Saturday night noise subsided by about 2.00am. The bagel guillotine was useful and efficient at breakfast. I like free breakfasts. The hoody I bought last night in the souvenir shop was useful and luckily it was not too cold. This is the first time I have seen San Francisco in the sun. I walked to the Market Street area but it was too early for some of the shops to be open on a Sunday. The mall was just designed to look good rather than be a place to regularly buy things. I found the computer shop and the Jollibee fast food place nearby reminding me briefly of Manila. I bought a netbook (small laptop) at the same time as another couple, an almost synchronised purchase and tested it in the organic café nearby with friendly customers just past the convention centre having a computer games conference. The Museum of Modern Art was an opportunity for a nice walk inside a building with gardens and waterfall. After a quick Disney sci-fi film and coffee back at the MOMA outside in the sun I walked to the Ferry Building housing lots of specialist food shops and back to base. I have found a nice spot here in the ballroom. I believe they are rearranging the furniture for a band later.

San Francisco, Monday 23rd March

I only had the vague intention of walking to the Market Street area of town. Everything was much busier. The Ferry Building shops were all open and tramps were pushing trolleys containing all their possessions. It was a cold but bright sunny day, making the reflecting skyscraper windows look spectacular. I took a trip on a trolley bus (a cable car with rails and wheels making a lot of noise) back from the electronic musical instrument shop where nothing seemed to be set up ready for demonstration, near the bank that had turned into a coffee shop. I was distracted by a beauty products demo and a sci-fi film in the shopping mall. I ate a massive and excellent scallop and sizzling seafood meal in the restaurant next door to the restaurant where they always queue outside for a long time, near the Chinese novelty shops. Americans perfect their communication skills while eating out at restaurants regularly. There was also a man with a rat on a cat on a dog walking around the streets collecting money. The views down the rolling hills of San Francisco are great.

San Francisco to London (England). Tuesday 24th March

I was buzzed in to deposit my luggage at the hostel. After a walk through China Town, past the pet shop I found a travel shop with lots of practical things like walking shoes and a warmer hoody (so practical). There seemed to be a strong smell of marijuana in many ordinary shops. My boots were too hot as I walked about so I wore my new shoes straightaway. I could not find a watch shop that sold a fancy three sensor watch that I liked – no matter. I bought a larger bag to contain my cheapie torn bag – now 20 kilograms in weight. This seaside city of San Francisco has a lot of character and variation in architecture. I am writing from the airport waiting for my final flight home to London with very few duty free shops at this terminal. There was a fancy scanner at security where you stand sideways with hands raised and a glass cylinder sweeps around you. All my world trips have been amazing, including this one.

THE END

Country Checklist

- ☐ Afghanistan
- ☐ Albania
- ☐ Algeria
- ☐ Andorra
- ☐ Angola
- ☐ Anguilla
- ☐ Antarctica*
- ☐ Antigua and Barbuda
- ☐ Argentina*
- ☐ Armenia
- ☐ Aruba and Netherlands Antilles
- ☐ Australia*   366, 413
- ☐ Austria*
- ☐ Azerbaijan
- ☐ Bahamas
- ☐ Bahrain* 382
- ☐ Bangladesh
- ☐ Barbados
- ☐ Belarus
- ☐ Belgium*
- ☐ Belize* 25
- ☐ Benin
- ☐ Bermuda
- ☐ Bhutan
- ☐ Bolivia* 338
- ☐ Bosnia and Hercegovina
- ☐ Botswana
- ☐ Brazil* 310
- ☐ Brunei
- ☐ Bulgaria
- ☐ Burkina Faso
- ☐ Burundi
- ☐ Cambodia* 60
- ☐ Cameroon
- ☐ Canada* 287
- ☐ Cape Verde
- ☐ Cayman Islands
- ☐ Central African Republic

- Chad
- Chile and Easter Island*
- China* 48, 205
- Colombia
- Comoros and Mayotte
- Congo, Democratic republic of (Zaire)
- Congo, Republic of
- Cook Islands*
- Costa Rica*
- Cote D'Ivoire
- Croatia*
- Cuba*
- Cyprus
- Czech Republic*
- Denmark
- Djibouti
- Dominica
- Dominican Republic
- East Timor
- Ecuador and the Galapagos Islands
- Egypt* 382
- El Salvador
- England*
- Equatorial Guinea
- Eritrea
- Estonia*
- Ethiopia
- Falkland Islands
- Fiji* 267, 420
- Finland*
- France* 89
- French Guiana
- Gabon
- Gambia
- Georgia
- Germany*
- Ghana* 124
- Greece
- Greenland
- Grenada

- ☐ Guadeloupe
- ☐ Guam and Northern Marianas
- ☐ Guatemala* 9
- ☐ Guinea
- ☐ Guinea-Bissau
- ☐ Guyana
- ☐ Haiti
- ☐ Honduras* 36
- ☐ Hong Kong*
- ☐ Hungary*
- ☐ Iceland*
- ☐ India* 227
- ☐ Indonesia* 395
- ☐ Iran
- ☐ Iraq
- ☐ Ireland*
- ☐ Israel*
- ☐ Italy*
- ☐ Jamaica
- ☐ Japan*
- ☐ Jordan* 163
- ☐ Kazakhstan
- ☐ Kenya* 136
- ☐ Kiribati
- ☐ Korea, North
- ☐ Korea, South*
- ☐ Kuwait
- ☐ Kyrgyzstan
- ☐ Laos* 71
- ☐ Latvia
- ☐ Lebanon
- ☐ Lesotho
- ☐ Liberia
- ☐ Libya
- ☐ Liechtenstein
- ☐ Lithuania
- ☐ Luxembourg*
- ☐ Macau
- ☐ Macedonia
- ☐ Madagascar* 147

- ☐ Malawi
- ☐ Malaysia* 254
- ☐ Maldives
- ☐ Mali* 89
- ☐ Malta
- ☐ Marshall Islands
- ☐ Martinique
- ☐ Mauritania
- ☐ Mauritius
- ☐ Mexico* 16
- ☐ Micronesia, Federated States of
- ☐ Moldova
- ☐ Monaco
- ☐ Mongolia*
- ☐ Morocco
- ☐ Mozambique
- ☐ Myanmar
- ☐ Namibia*
- ☐ Nauru
- ☐ Nepal* 174
- ☐ Netherlands*
- ☐ New Caledonia
- ☐ New Zealand* 352
- ☐ Nicaragua
- ☐ Niger
- ☐ Nigeria
- ☐ Norway
- ☐ Oman
- ☐ Pakistan
- ☐ Palau
- ☐ Palestine
- ☐ Panama*
- ☐ Papua New Guinea
- ☐ Paraguay
- ☐ Peru*
- ☐ Philippines* 401
- ☐ Pitcairn Islands
- ☐ Poland
- ☐ Portugal
- ☐ Puerto Rico

- ☐ Qatar
- ☐ Reunion
- ☐ Romania
- ☐ Russian Federation (FSU)*
- ☐ Rwanda
- ☐ Saint Kitts and Nevis
- ☐ Saint Lucia
- ☐ Saint Vincent and the Grenadines
- ☐ Samoa*
- ☐ San Marino
- ☐ Sao Tome and Principe
- ☐ Saudi Arabia
- ☐ Scotland*
- ☐ Senegal
- ☐ Serbia and Montenegro
- ☐ Seychelles
- ☐ Sierra Leone
- ☐ Singapore* 261
- ☐ Slovakia
- ☐ Slovenia* 285
- ☐ Solomon Islands
- ☐ Somalia
- ☐ South Africa*
- ☐ Spain*
- ☐ Sri Lanka
- ☐ Sudan
- ☐ Suriname
- ☐ Swaziland
- ☐ Sweden
- ☐ Switzerland*
- ☐ Syria
- ☐ Tahiti and French Polynesia*
- ☐ Taiwan
- ☐ Tajikistan
- ☐ Tanzania* 137
- ☐ Thailand* 51, 378
- ☐ Tibet* 205
- ☐ Togo
- ☐ Tonga* 420
- ☐ Trinidad and Tobago

- Tunisia
- Turkey
- Turkmenistan
- Turks and Caicos
- Tuvalu
- Uganda* 387
- Ukraine
- United Arab Emirates* 172
- United States of America* 278, 300, 306, 423
- Uruguay
- Uzbekistan
- Vanuatu
- Vatican City*
- Venezuela
- Vietnam* 76
- Virgin Islands
- Wales*
- Yemen
- Zambia
- Zimbabwe

* visited or recommended

www.TheTravelMap.com